Universal Principles of Living Life Fully

tom walsh

Living Life Fully Publications

Published by Living Life Fully™ Publications
United States of America
http://www.livinglifefully.com

Universal Principles of Living Life Fully

ISBN:

Contents

Introduction	4		
Awareness	8	Appreciation/Gratitude	12
Attitude	16	Giving	20
Love	24	Character	29
Principle	33	The Present Moment (Now)	37
Letting Go	41	Action	45
Peace	49	Nature	54
Oneness/Unity	59	Perspective	63
Failure	67	Work	71
Success	76	Self-Love	81
Motivation	85	Learning	89
Hope	94	Prayer	99
Beauty	104	Today	109
Friendship	113	Balance	118
Responsibility	123	Compassion	128
Kindness	132	Community	136
Self	141	Change	145
Adversity	150	Play	154
Acceptance	158	Forgiveness	163
Gratitude	168	Humility	172
Mindfulness	177	Patience	182
Rest	186	Solitude	191
Awe and Wonder	196	Simplicity	201
Thanksgiving	206	Sadness	211
Perseverance	215	Moderation	219
Feelings	224	Diversity	229
Creativity	234	Common Sense	239
Authenticity	243	Education	248
Life	253	Recreation	258
Competence	262	Motivation 2	266
Now 2	270	Now 3	275

Introduction

Welcome to a book that has been several decades in the making, one that I've been researching rather deeply for a very long time. This is the book that covers the material that has been most important for me over the years, for it includes concepts and ideas that have helped me to make it through years of severe depression, significantly difficult life changes, a number of huge setbacks, and a vast number of self-sabotaging behaviors that I wasn't even aware of until I started paying attention to my life and what I was doing with it.

I wouldn't classify it as a self-help book. That market has produced some very important material, but one of the realities of it is that most of the people writing for it are rather affluent, and they simply don't have to deal with the same issues that many of us deal with—they don't worry about not having enough money by the end of the month, or about getting sick and missing work and getting no paycheck, about their car breaking down and not having the means to fix it, and other things that many of us face regularly. I'm always rather astonished when I read about their brand-new BMW's and their vacation homes, especially since so many of them write so many words about not becoming materialistic.

This isn't that kind of book. This is a book that I've wanted to write because so many other people have helped me through their writing, and what they've told me has been instrumental in helping me to see the blessings in the life I'm living even without that vacation home in Maui or the brand-new car. I grew up in a military family without much money, so I've been working since I was thirteen, but that never limited me in the ways that I could enjoy life. While my two siblings turned to drugs and crime to try to deal with life, I turned to reading and studying. Having an alcoholic parent was another challenge that we faced, especially later in life—it's fascinating just how many emotional issues Adult Children of Alcoholics face when we grow up. Much of what's in this book helped me to work through those issues when I needed to.

As an adult, I chose to teach, which meant from the start that I was not to become a rich person. But that's okay with me—I've loved teaching, and I've loved the relationships that I've been able to develop with my students. And the one thing that I can guarantee you is that the principles in this book do not demand a large paycheck as a part of living your life fully. I always think of the Asian monks who often don't even know where their next meal is coming from, and how satisfied they are with their lives—if they can be happy with limited resources, so can I.

But that doesn't mean that money isn't necessary. It is. I look for ways to earn money, but I never make it my highest priority. And on days or in weeks when I don't have much to spend, all I have to do is look around a bit to realize just how blessed I am to have all that I have, whether I can go on an expensive shopping spree or not (which, by the way, is something I've never done—I've been lucky that shopping hasn't become one of my coping strategies).

Instead of money, I've placed my highest value on other people, education, and work. These are the things that I focus on more than anything else, for they're the things I most love. I've spent literally tens of thousands of hours on livinglifefully.com over the last 17 years, and I've focused most of my other efforts on my teaching, for my students are extremely important to me, no matter where or what I'm teaching. I've worked my way through a bachelor's degree, three master's degrees, and a doctorate, for I really want to be extremely good at what I do.

A huge part of my education was reading books that helped me to learn about life and living rather than simply about academic subjects or information. I really didn't care about the socioeconomic aspects of Charles Dickens' life when I was studying English—I cared about what Dickens could teach us about living and being happy (read *A Christmas Carol* for a great example of how he did that). I wasn't nearly as interested in statistics about test scores as I was about strategies to help my students really learn the material we were studying. And having a broad field of interest helped me a great deal, for the Western cultures greatly value testing and using testing as a way to form instruction, while the Eastern cultures understand strongly that we can't always have artificially high expectations, and that sometimes the best thing we can do is let go of expectations and allow students to find their own paths in their own ways—and when I've been able to combine the two approaches in my classrooms, the students have benefited a great deal and learned a lot that they might not have learned otherwise.

One of my most important learning experiences was when I read a book that explored different aspects of who we are—our emotions, our anger, our ability to live in the present—rather than our selves as a whole. That was a major turning point in my life, for I realized then that while I had a lot of gratitude, I wasn't very mindful. While my intellect had been exercised and developed, emotionally I was probably ten years younger than I was chronologically. So I could work on my emotions and not worry much about my intellect; I could develop my mindfulness and not have to develop my gratitude at the same time. This book and the website both follow this approach to life, as I believe that we all are a combination of many different aspects, and not just individuals. We are like precious diamonds that have been cut beautifully—individuals with a large number of facets that we present to the world.

So I offer you this book as a coming together of my studies of the last few decades. It is not meant to be completely comprehensive. I know that there are other topics that could have made their ways in here, and I'll admit that there are some that probably should have been in here. But I also know that it is what it is—I relied on a higher power for guidance, and I trust that it's what it's supposed to be.

Speaking of a higher power, you'll find very little about religion or spiritual matters in here. There are two reasons for that: first, there are no "universal" religions, so it would be impossible to discuss religion in a universal way. And second, that's going to be the topic of my next book for Living Life Fully, which I'm going to start working on tomorrow.

I sincerely hope that there's something in here that speaks to you, that helps you to grow in some important ways in your life. You'll find some repetition and a few redundancies, I'm sure, but we find those in life all the time, don't we? There are three pages on "Now" because I made a mistake while writing them, but even though it was a mistake, I've left numbers two and three in because I cannot know whom they'll benefit or in which ways.

Use the journal ideas as you wish, or not at all. Some of them have suggestions about what to write, but most don't. If you look at a topic a week, you have five days worth of journal entries to work with. If you look at a topic a day, use just one or two of the ideas. After all, it really is up to you.

Please enjoy the book, and thank you for being here!

A Note on What "Living Life Fully" Means to Me

These aren't just words to me. Because of all the years that I fought loneliness and depression, living a full life means something very important to me. It means that I'm paying attention to the gifts and blessings that I have, and it means that I'm actually taking advantage of them when I have them.

It doesn't mean being rich, and it doesn't mean having lots of material goods. It means appreciating what I do have, as well as appreciating all of the things that life brings to me—both the bad and the good. It means taking life for what it is and not wishing that it were something else.

It doesn't mean giving up, and it doesn't mean not trying to earn more money or not trying to improve my lot in life. But it does mean not losing heart when things don't work out, or blaming life because I fail to accomplish something that I set out to do.

It means being kind and compassionate to others, and it means spreading love whenever I can, which is in reality all day, every day. It means not judging who might deserve my love and who doesn't, but realizing that the person who may not seem to deserve good things may be that person who needs more love than others do.

It means accepting life and living. It means being mindful of my blessings and the needs and wants of others. It means being a part of a community and doing my best to help others as much as I can, even in the smallest of ways.

And what does it mean for you to live your life fully? That, of course, is for you to determine and decide. The principles here in this book hopefully will help you to define for yourself what it means for you to live your life fully. There are many, many aspects of who you are, and if you address them one by one and make them what you want them to be, then I firmly believe that you'll start to see things coming together like a puzzle that's being worked on and that will give you great satisfaction once it's done.

So use these principles that are here for all that they're worth, and heed the words of the wise men and women of our world who have taught us so much. I take none of the credit for what's in these pages, for I've simply been fortunate enough to be able to read and learn a great deal from others. My goal is simply to pass it on to you in a form that may be easy for you to apply to your life. It is your life, and you can do great things with it—it's up to you to do so!

One

Awareness

If I were to choose one category that seems to be the most important of all for this book, I would have to start with awareness—which, of course, is strongly related to mindfulness. This is where living life fully all begins—with being aware of the beauty and wonder of the world, being aware of the amazing qualities of the people in our lives, being aware of our own value, and being aware of the things within ourselves that need to be changed if we're to live happier, more fascinating, fuller lives while we're here.

I've spent much of my life being so focused on certain negative things that I've not even noticed some of the most amazing blessings that have been there for me. I used to get so depressed that I would lose sight of all good things in my life, choosing instead to put all my attention on what I saw as the bad. Much of my problem had to do with issues that started in my childhood and followed me into adulthood, but it wasn't until I became aware of those issues that I was ever able to deal with them effectively, first through accepting them and second through making changes in the ways that I saw the world and saw myself fitting into it. The process of accepting something, though, is not even possible until we're aware of that something that must be accepted.

So to a great extent, awareness has much to do with staying alert and keeping our eyes open so that we can recognize the problems in our lives, the things that hold us back and hold us down. If I don't see the things that are going right in my life and if I'm unaware of the mistakes that I'm making, then it's difficult for me to live a full life at all.

But awareness is also about slowing down, taking stock, and looking around. Sometimes the best thing that we can do to be fully aware of our blessings is simply to stop where we are and look around ourselves. We're surrounded by blessings all the time, and many of them we've gotten so used to that we don't even count them among our blessings any more. From the television set to the stove and refrigerator to the comfortable mattresses to the dining room table, our lives are full of things and people that make our lives easier, more comfortable, and more enjoyable.

A greater poverty than that caused by lack of money
is the poverty of unawareness. Men and women go
about the world unaware of the beauty, the goodness,
and the glories in it. Their souls are poor. It is better

to have a poor pocketbook than to suffer from a poor soul.

Jerry Fleishman

One thing that I do to continue to remind myself of things I need to be aware of is to write things down. Sometimes I make lists, sometimes I simply write a word or two or three. If I write down "cookies," I remind myself of just how fortunate I am that cookies are a part of my life (especially when I have them with a cup of coffee or a glass of milk). It also gets me to be aware that if things were a bit different in my life, I might be in a situation in which cookies and milk weren't a part of my life—but extreme poverty is something that I fortunately do not have to experience right now.

This world is full of beauty and mystery and marvelous things. But they will enrich our lives only if we're aware of them as blessings. When we get so caught up in our daily grind—the problems and the stress and the challenges and the difficulties—we often lose our ability to be aware of many of the positive things in life. Jerry's words above make this very clear: even if we're well off, we live in poverty when we're unaware. We are spiritual beings, and the many things that nurture our spirits are here already—but it's up to us to keep them in our awareness.

I have walked with people whose eyes are full of light but who see nothing in sea or sky, nothing in city streets, nothing in books. It were far better to sail forever in the night of blindness with sense, and feeling, and mind, than to be content with the mere act of seeing. The only lightless dark is the night of darkness in ignorance and insensibility.

Helen Keller

Let us not be ignorant of those things that enrich our world. Let us make sure that we continually strive to be aware of just how amazing it is that we're even alive in the first place, sharing in the experience of being human, of struggling and celebrating, of doing our best to help others and ourselves grow into being the best people we possibly can be.

We can become aware by listening to others, and learning about who they are and what they need and want. We can become more aware by reading books and articles and poetry that helps to open our eyes to new things and new ideas. We can improve our level of awareness by slowing down and looking around ourselves and seeing things on a very conscious level. We can become more aware simply by making an effort to do so.

I am here, now. You are there, now.

Are you and I aware of all that we should be aware of, me here and you there?

Questions to Consider

Do you ever stop and look around yourself to take stock of all the good things that are present in your life?

What do we risk if we allow ourselves to continue to go through life unaware of the good things that affect us regularly?

How do we reach a point at which we lose awareness? Who teaches us to limit our awareness? How do they teach us? How do we learn?

An Awareness List

Here are a few things that you can be aware of right here and right now:

Hold your hand up in front of you, and bend a finger or three. Are you aware of the muscles and tendons and bones and skin that all work together to give you this marvelous capability? The design of our hands is a scientific marvel, yet most of us never think of the blood flowing out to our fingers and then back to our heart in order to keep the whole thing alive and functioning well.

Do you have heat in your home in the winter? Be aware of the temperature difference between the outdoors and the indoors—heat is there when we need it, on demand.

Have you looked at a tree recently? Have you noticed how the leaves provide us with shade and beauty, and have you thought about how they provide us with the oxygen that's in the air that we breathe? Without them, we'd no longer be here at all.

Think of another person whom you know. Think about that person's history—his or her childhood, the trials and joys that they've experienced, the fears and dreams that they have. Think about their behaviors, and consider all that's gone into that person behaving the way that he or she behaves. Sometimes, the things we don't like in another person may be the results of situations in their past that would result in us feeling a great deal of compassion for that person rather than the annoyance or aggravation that we currently feel.

Food. It's amazing. Especially chocolate.
Electricity.
Light.

The work that other people do to make our lives better (road workers, supermarket employees, car manufacturers, police officers and firefighters, teachers, etc.).
Clothing, from the planting and harvesting of the cotton or polyester all the way to the designers who turn cloth into clothing. (That's a joke about the polyester, by the way.)

Journal Entries

Day One: In sixty seconds, make a list of all the things that you see around you. Then take sixty seconds to look around and see the things that aren't on your list. Write them down. Why didn't you notice them at first?

Day Two: Why do we tend not to notice many things that surround us in our lives? List five reasons why you may be too preoccupied to notice things, and then write how you might deal with those reasons.

Day Three: Think of someone you know who seems to be very aware of life and living. Why is this person aware? What benefits does this person experience because of the awareness.

Day Four: A young person you know doesn't value awareness at all. Write him or her a letter telling why it's important to be aware of your surroundings and your needs and such.

Day Five: List ten things that you can do each day to make sure that you're more aware of your life.

Two

Appreciation and Gratitude

For the most part, of course, the order of the topics in this book is fairly arbitrary. But it seems quite obvious to me that thankfulness should be one of the most important elements of our lives if we're to be living full and fulfilling lives. After all, it's one thing to be aware of this miracle that is our body, for example, but if in our awareness we simply take it for granted, then it contributes very little towards making us happy, contented human beings.

These two words, "appreciation" and "gratitude," are almost synonyms. Both of them remind us of just how important our own perspective is in life—if we accept all of the gifts that we have in life without appreciation and gratitude, then we take those things for granted, and they bring no richness, no brightness to our lives. When we allow ourselves to feel thankful for the things we have, though, then we know that they are blessings, and that they make our lives into richer experiences.

I have these concepts as the second part of the series because they seem to follow awareness as the most fundamental elements of living life fully. When we're aware, we see and feel and recognize all of our blessings. But that simply isn't enough—unless we also appreciate those blessings, then they really don't have much of an effect on our lives at all, do they?

There cannot be a sense of abundance or the experience of prosperity without appreciation. You cannot find beauty unless you appreciate beauty. You cannot find friendship unless you appreciate others. You cannot find love unless you appreciate loving and being loved. If you wish abundance, appreciate life.

William R. Miller

Appreciation unlocks doors and windows, quite simply. When we appreciate things, we allow those things to have positive effects on us, and we let more of those things (as well as similar ones) into our lives. We're also much more likely to take those things seriously and try to maintain them and keep them as positive parts of our lives when we feel and show our appreciation for them. This goes for people, things, pets, and even concepts such as freedom and friendship—their worth increases in our lives in proportion to the appreciation we show for them.

If we don't feel appreciation, then our lives can seem very drab and dull and uninspiring. Yes, we have friends, but so does everyone else. Yes, I have shelter and clothing and food, but so does everyone else. These things aren't all that special; they're just there, and they're no big deal.

How do you feel when you give a gift to someone and that person shows no appreciation for it at all? It's an empty feeling. No, we're not supposed to give with an expectation of getting anything in return—even appreciation—but when we do see that appreciation, then there's something special about the thing we've given. It's helped to create or deepen a bond between us, and the recipient's appreciation has been the acknowledgement of that bond, of that specialness that we share. A lack of appreciation seems to show a lack of caring, and that's a problem that can lead to so many other problems.

In the same way, if we don't appreciate something in our lives, we show a lack of caring for it. One of my constant battles is to feel a sense of appreciation for the classes I teach. They tend to be somewhat stressful at times, but I know that I'm very fortunate to have those students as a part of my life. It's important to me to keep my appreciation for them on a conscious level, to remind myself of how fortunate I am to be able to work with them. If I don't appreciate them for just who they are, then my work becomes drudgery; if I maintain my appreciation, then I see my work as a very positive part of my life and my identity.

Gratitude unlocks the fullness of life. It turns what we have into enough, and more. It turns denial into acceptance, chaos to order, confusion to clarity. It can turn a meal into a feast, a house into a home, a stranger into a friend. Gratitude makes sense of our past, brings peace for today, and creates a vision for tomorrow.

Melody Beattie

Appreciation can and should be a conscious choice. When someone gives me something, or when I'm able to buy something I want, I choose how I react to this new thing that's in my life. Any time that I get anything new, I try to remind myself of its source so that I can feel appreciation for it. If I buy something new, I appreciate the work that I have that allows me to purchase things I need. If I go for a long drive, I remind myself that I'm very fortunate to have a reliable car. If someone pays me a compliment, I keep in mind that the person didn't need to do that, and the kind words are truly a blessing to me.

Sometimes we avoid appreciation for various reasons. For years I did so because I simply didn't trust the things I got—I was pretty sure I'd lose them soon enough. Other people that I know take things for granted because they feel that they're entitled to those things, even though there are millions of people on this planet who never will experience the riches that they have— they take for granted things that they're very blessed to have. I know people who don't appreciate their kids because the kids aren't acting in exactly the ways the parents want them to act. And I know many, many people who never really feel appreciation because they simply never stop to think about just how fortunate they are to have the things and people and situations in their lives that they do have.

Living life fully requires that we do think seriously and consistently about the many blessings that we do have (awareness), and that we do bring ourselves to a state of appreciation for our blessings. Of course, we can take things for granted and we can decide not to remind ourselves of the gratitude that we could and should be feeling, but by doing so we most definitely are limiting the blessings that we have and the possibilities of future blessings. Look at and think about all your blessings, feel appreciation and gratitude for it all, and feel just how rich and full your life truly is.

Questions to Consider:

Can you list ten things for which you're truly grateful within the next sixty seconds?

Do you have any established criteria for whether or not you feel gratitude for something? What do people have to do to earn your gratitude?

What kinds of things do you feel entitled to? Your job? Your home? Your family? From where does the feeling of entitlement come?

Some things to be thankful for, here and now:

I believe that this list should follow very closely the Awareness list. When we become aware of our blessings, won't gratitude naturally follow?
One of the things that I like to do when I think of such a list, though, is to extend it as far as I can. For example, I love having a bowl of cereal with milk in the morning. Now I can be grateful for that bowl of cereal, and that's fine, but there's so much more to be grateful for in that simple meal. Concerning the cereal, I can be grateful for the people who developed it, the people who grew the grains necessary to make it, the people who harvested the grains and shipped them to the places where they were converted into my cereal, the

people who made the highways on which the grains were transported, the people who made the trucks in which they were transported, the people who made and transported the other ingredients of the cereal, such as the sugar, the raisins, the nuts, etc.—and you can see how this list can be almost never-ending, going all the way back to the people who first thought of eating grains, and who first started cultivating them. And we haven't even addressed the milk yet! Almost anything that we have can be seen through the lens of a long list of gratitude such as this one.

Journal Entries

Day One: Why do we tend not to teach our young people the importance of appreciation in making our lives more fulfilling?

Day Two: Think about something that you would have appreciated years ago, but that doesn't spark that feeling now. What has changed?

Day Three: How often do you tell other people that you appreciate them and the things that they do? Could you do it more? What would happen if you did?

Day Four: Think of a particular person, and write down several things about that person that you appreciate. Why do you appreciate these things? How do they affect you personally?

Day Five: What would our world be like if no one appreciated the things they have or the things that other people do for them? What would it be like if everyone did so?

Three

Attitude

I will be the first to admit that my own attitudes have caused much of the stress and many of the problems of my life. While I've always tried to keep a positive and caring attitude, I haven't always been successful in doing so.

I'll also admit, too, that much of my attitude in the earlier years of my life was the result of my upbringing—things that I learned from parents and relatives and other elders, through things that they taught me and ways that they treated me and others. While I don't blame those people for any of my problems, it would be silly to think that they had no effect at all on my attitudes towards life and living.

What has been the most important thing of all that I've learned, though, is that my attitude is my choice. I used to think that it just was as it was, and I didn't see the connections between my attitude and how other people treated me. I saw myself as more of a victim than anything else, and I felt completely helpless about changing my circumstances. This perspective led to pretty constant and extremely painful bouts of depression that were absolutely debilitating—and the depression was something else that I just didn't recognize as being related to my own attitude.

Our attitudes control our lives. Attitudes are
a secret power working twenty-four hours a day,
for good or bad. It is of paramount importance
that we know how to harness and control this great force.

Tom Blandi

All that changed, though, as I learned of the importance of my own attitude on my life. But learning its importance was only the first step, and a pretty easy step at that—there were plenty of people around and books that I could read that told me this fact. What I needed to do was accept the fact that I was causing much of my own pain by holding on to attitudes and ideas that were very destructive to me. And once I accepted this fact, it was important that I learn how to actually change my attitudes, a task that isn't at all easy.

The acceptance came as I started to look for cause and effect relationships between my attitude and things that happened to me. One good example was how I approached potential relationships. While growing up, there were no positive relationships in my life for me to witness. I grew up in a military family, so we moved constantly, staying nowhere for more than a couple of years. In my family, relationships were marked by addictions and anger and frustration and mistrust. In my extended family, virtually every one of my elders whom I saw regularly had had failed relationships and were alone in life.

Without any truly and fully positive role models in life, is it any wonder that I developed an attitude towards relationships that was basically, "This probably isn't going to work out?" I always felt that people were doing me favors by spending time with me, and that is not a positive way to see things.

In short, my attitude towards my relationships and friendships—an attitude that said "This is going to fail"—caused my relationships and friendships to fail. My attitude was based on fear and a lack of trust, and I approached things with an attitude of fear, and that fear caused me to pay heavy prices.

The greatest discovery of my generation is that
people can alter their lives simply by
altering their attitude of mind.

William James

Obviously, William James is right here. It isn't an easy process, that of changing attitudes, but it is one that can be undertaken successfully.

The biggest problem for me, and the thing that made progress so very slow, was that in order to change my attitude, I needed to see evidence that doing so was going to do me some good. That evidence didn't come very often. If I acted more positively for a week and didn't see any positive results from the attitude I was showing the world, I would be hit with a bout of discouragement, and it became even harder to carry that new attitude with me. We as people tend to need to see positive results if we're going to continue to try to change.

What worked best for me was constantly reading books and articles from people who actually had changed their attitudes and whose lives had been changed for the positive because of their changes. It was clear that the changes they had experienced had taken a significant amount of time to show up, so it gave me hope that if I were to do something with a lot of patience, I could trust that the positive changes would happen to me, too. And I also realized that if I made no effort at all, then I was dooming myself to the dark and dismal life that I so often experienced—and it would probably get worse if I made no changes.

It did take time, but I did make changes. I started to see relationships as a normal part of life, and I started to have the attitude that people did want to get to know me. I started to realize that I had value, and I showed that in my attitude. I started to not take life too seriously, to not take setbacks too seriously, because I realized that my attitude towards setbacks changed how they affected me. If I saw them as drastic and terrible, then guess what they were to me? But if I saw them as bumps in the road that I was already over, then guess what?

Your attitudes are your choice. It's that simple. "Yes," you say, "but what about when people do bad things to me no matter what my attitude is?" Simply enough, your attitudes towards what they've done or said also is your choice, and your attitude will determine whether you work your way quickly past the pain or dwell in it and let it keep hurting you long after it's happened.

Your attitudes are controllable. They are changeable. And they are one of the key factors in whether or not you're happy with life. If you're having trouble changing them for the better, then find a role model to observe, someone who has the type of attitude that you'd like to have. Emulate that person, and watch carefully how they approach their lives. We all have a lot to learn in life, and we can learn a lot about attitudes by watching other people in our lives.

Questions to Consider:

Think about one particular attitude of yours—perhaps your attitude towards work, for example. What factors have contributed to this particular attitude? Is it positive or negative? What would you need to do to change it if you felt it necessary to do so?

What kinds of attitudes do you value and respect in other people? Do you show similar attitudes yourself? What kinds of attitudes do you dislike? Are any of yours similar to those?

Do you know someone whose attitude(s) hold him or her back from achievement, positive relationships, fulfilling work, or other things? How does that person's attitude affect his or her life in observable ways?

Attitude Keywords

positive upbeat negative self-defeating triumphant realistic celebratory winning accepting demanding destructive loving hopeful defeatist helpful cheerful morose sunny amazing persevering condemning curious inclusive exclusive arrogant humble dismissive affirming

What kinds of words can you come up with that would describe attitudes you'd like to have?

Journal Entries

Day One: How much attention do you pay to your attitudes about different things in your life? Are you aware of what your attitudes are and how they affect you?

Day Two: How do your attitudes affect other people? How often do you consider whether or not your attitudes are positive parts of other people's lives?

Day Three: Write a letter to a young person telling him or her why it's important to have a positive attitude in life if they want to be happy.

Day Four: How can you change your attitudes if they're not serving you well now? How can you recognize which attitudes of yours are holding you back?

Day Five: Can you help other people to change their attitudes if they're not serving them well? How might you be able to do so?

Four

Giving

Most of us spend our days going through life trying to figure out how we can get things. I'm no exception—I focus on things like how I can earn more money, what new music I'd like to hear, whether I can afford something right now, how to get someone to do something I want (or think I need) them to do.

There are others, though, who go through their lives focusing on what and how they can give. Their lives are characterized by how they've contributed to the lives of others, not by what they've taken from others. I've met many people like this, and I'm constantly amazed at just how happy they tend to be. Yes, they do have their down times, but that's a fact of life for all of us. These people tend to be bright and shining lights who do what they can to lighten the loads of other human beings rather than focusing on what they can get for themselves out of the circumstances they encounter.

We make a living by what we get,
but we make a life by what we give.

Winston Churchill

Much of my problem with giving in life has had to do with the idea that somehow entered my mind and stuck in there for a very long time that others simply didn't want what I had to give. This was a silly idea, to put it mildly, for I've since found that what I do have to give is very useful and valuable to many people. The interesting part of this reality, though, is that they often don't recognize its value until much later, they very often don't appreciate what's been given to them, and they usually don't thank me for what they get. And these truths have caused me to completely redefine my giving.

I used to give with the expectation of thanks, for example. Heck, if I give you something, it's only common courtesy for you to thank me, right? But that type of giving, I've found, isn't at all useful or helpful. Any giving that I do must be done without any expectations of return at all if it's to be true giving. If it's not done this way, then it's more a chance for me to manipulate someone else than it is for me to share my own gifts with others. Giving with the expectation of return—even of a simple "thank you"—is barter, not giving.

I also used to give very little of myself, due to the idea that I had that other people weren't interested in what I was or what I thought. As a teacher, for example, I stuck only to the information that I had been hired to teach. After all, no one could be interested in my ideas about the subject, right? I've since learned, though, that what most students remember about my classes more than anything else is the information and ideas that I shared with them that I had come up with myself, the focus on life and living that I've used to complement the writing and reading that we've had to do. They really have valued my thoughts and my perspective, even though I used to spend tons of time convincing myself that they really wouldn't, so I'd better not share them.

Simply give others a bit of yourself; a thoughtful act, a helpful idea,
a word of appreciation, a lift over a rough spot, a sense
of understanding, a timely suggestion. You take something
out of your mind, garnished in kindness out of your heart,
and put it into the other person's mind and heart.

Charles H. Burr

What I have to give in a classroom is one thing, of course, but there are many, many more things that we can give with a cheerful heart and no expectation of return. Encouragement, love, a piece of chocolate, a smile, acceptance, a special book or movie, listening, a bit of knowledge, a flower, a few hours to oneself—the list is very, very long indeed.

Giving is one of the best ways there is to augment our own awareness of what we really do have in life, and when we see the effects of what we give on others—even if the effects aren't immediate, we have to trust that there will be effects—then we can appreciate more the many gifts that we do have, as well as our power to contribute positively to the world. When we're able to look at something that we have and realize that someone else could probably use it more or in better ways, then we can start to see the power of letting go of things in our lives.

After all, what are you doing when you give? You are contributing to the well-being of someone else, and when you do that, you're contributing in a very real way to the community in which you live or the community in which that other person lives. You're adding positive energy to the world, and you're diminishing the power of someone else's negative situation. After all, our main purpose for being here on this planet at all is to learn to share love and then to share it, isn't it? And we simply can't share anything if we do not learn how to give it to someone else.

True religion. . . is giving and finding one's happiness
by bringing happiness into the lives of others.

William J.H. Boetcker

Our culture teaches us things quite backwards, sometimes, and it definitely teaches us wrong when it comes to giving. We are taught that we'll find happiness through getting and buying, and if we do give, we should get something back for it. This is simply a recipe for frustration and unhappiness, though. We find our own happiness through making others happy, and when we give of our own gifts and talents and even material goods, we can most certainly—at the very least—put ourselves on the road to happiness, and that's a great road to be on.

Questions to ponder:

How do you define giving? Does your definition include expectations of something in return? Are you willing to give a second time to a person who fails to acknowledge the first thing(s) that you gave them?

How predominant is the concept of giving in your culture? How much do you follow your culture's norms?

What kinds of things might you give today to someone in your life? How might your giving affect the other person?

Do you ever think that you'd be willing to give more if only others would give more to you? What's the major flaw in that line of thinking?

The Golden Ladder of Giving

1. To give reluctantly, the gift of the hand, but not of the heart.
2. To give cheerfully, but not in proportion to need.
3. To give cheerfully and proportionately, but not until solicited.
4. To give cheerfully, proportionately, and unsolicited, but to put the gift into the poor person's hand, thus creating shame.
5. To give in such a way that the distressed may know their benefactor, without being known to him or her.
6. To know the objects of our bounty, but remain unknown to them.
7. To give so that the benefactor may not know those whom he has relieved, and they shall not know him.
8. To prevent poverty by teaching a trade, setting a person up in business, or in some other way preventing the need of charity.

~Maimonides

Journal Entries

Day One: What kinds of things are you afraid to give away because you might need them one day? Why do you have this fear?

Day Two: Are you in a society that values giving more, or getting? How does it feel to be a part of that culture?

Day Three: Some cultures value teaching their children to be generous givers so that their children don't become attached to material things. Are we like that? Are we attached to the things that we own?

Day Four: Make a list of things that you currently own that you would be fine giving away. Then write the best recipient you can think of for each thing, and tell why it would be good to give something to them. Then do so.

Day Five: The other side of giving is receiving. If someone wants to give you something, what message are you sending if you refuse it? How do you feel if someone refuses something that you want to give them?

Five

Love

Most of us look at love in the same ways that we look at God—as something that is out there, something that we must search for and try to find. Most of us live in cultures and societies that tell us that this approach is true, and that if we want to "find" love, we'd better start looking. I grew up learning this approach, and it ended up causing me years of misery and depression because I had a very flawed vision of what love really is.

The simple truth is that love is a part of who we are, not something that others "give" to us if we're worthy of it. We're taught that if we just find that right person, and that person "falls in love" with us, everything will be fine. We're not taught about recognizing the love that is a part of our spirits, the love that we radiate when we recognize the beauty and need in all the people that surround us. Love is ours to share, at all moments and in all situations, but for some reason we fear doing so.

Our fear causes us to withhold our love for several reasons. We may think that we have only so much love to give, and we'll wither and die if we give too much without enough coming back to us. We may have a strong sense that we should only give love to others if they meet certain criteria of if they live up to certain standards. Or we may feel that our love is something that belongs in our families, to be given only to those people who are close to us.

When you commit yourself to living love, you feel
at peace with yourself because you are at harmony
with the flow of life. . . . You're not looking for love,
but for opportunities to love.

Susan L. Taylor

Unfortunately, though, this approach to love is one that keeps us from feeling love fully, from making it one of the most important elements of our lives in *all* situations. When we see love as something that comes from the outside, then we deprive ourselves of much of the power that we have as human beings, as the spirits that we are, living amongst so many other wonderful spirits who are in dire need of love in their lives. When we spend our time waiting for love to "show up" because we've finally somehow "earned" it, then we spend our time in a kind of nether world, refusing to live our lives to their potential because we're refusing to share the greatest gift that we've been given as human beings.

In my life, here's how love has worked: I've always been afraid to love others for several reasons: they wouldn't love me back and I'd suffer rejection; I'd somehow make myself feel worse because I'd be giving all this love and not getting any back; or I'd show love to the wrong person and end up in a relationship that wasn't at all good for me. What I didn't understand, though, was that love was something that I needed to give unconditionally—and I also had no idea what it meant to "give" love.

Over the years, though, I've been able to work my way towards a healthier perspective on love. I no longer expect anything in return when I show love—I simply show it. If something comes back, fine. If nothing comes back, fine—I know that love shared is always out there, and it will come back to me at a different time, in a form that I never would have expected.

Agape means love for another self not because of any lovable qualities which he or she may possess, but purely and entirely because it is a self capable of experiencing happiness and misery and endowed with the power to choose between good and evil. The love of humans is thus more than a feeling, it is a state of the will.

Obert C. Tanner

Learning how to love was quite a struggle for me. I never really saw love as an action verb—I always thought of myself as "showing" my love. Very often, this meant things like buying gifts or doing favors for others, sometimes committing myself far too much and ending up hurting myself because of it. And ironically enough, what I did very often wasn't at all helpful to that other person, mostly because it wasn't really love at all, but a desire to be loved and appreciated that motivated me. Strictly speaking, my love was a form of manipulation that wasn't in any way healthy.

What I see love as being now, though, is more like a process that involves getting to know the other person—his or her true wants and needs—and then finding ways to fill those needs without thought of being repaid; sometimes, even, without that other person even knowing that I was the one who did what I did.

For example, my daughter might need a kind word if she does something wrong instead of a harsh judgment. My wife may need some encouragement if something she's doing isn't going all that well. One of my students may need me to be inflexible on a due date because he or she is having issues with fulfilling responsibilities, while another student may need that due date to be pushed back because of personal issues going on in his or her life. The woman in the supermarket may feel much better if she gets a smile and a warm greeting, and I myself may feel much, much better after a good cup of coffee and an unexpected piece of chocolate.

The key, though, is often awareness—getting to know other people and learning to recognize when these *signs* of my love may be appropriate or needed.

Notice that I say "signs," for none of these things are actually love. I've learned to love in a couple of ways. First of all, I try to pull myself into awareness of my love by telling myself in all situations, "I love this person." When I tell myself that, I realize that it's more important for me to listen than to talk, more important to help people find their own answers than it is to give them mine.

Secondly, I try to ask myself "what would love do in this situation?" or "what would the loving response here be?" Sometimes I truly dislike the answer, because my ego is also telling me the response that it wants to see and feel. But acting in spite of the ego is very important if we're to act in loving ways. When someone insults me, the loving response is almost never to insult them back, even though the ego wants you to believe that that's the only appropriate response.

You must act in your friends' interests whether it pleases them or not; the object of love is to serve, not to win.

Woodrow Wilson

Finally, I try to remind myself constantly that everyone is fighting their own battles and doing the best they can, and that everyone is certainly deserving of love (though many refuse to accept it and live life as though they weren't deserving of it). It's only by reminding myself of this that I keep in mind that my major reason for even being on this planet is to love others, and if I'm not doing so, then I'm squandering a whole lot of opportunities for doing so.

The love that is a part of me is here for others to benefit from. I need to be aware of the need for love and of my ability to share it, and I need to be willing and able to give it at all moments if the love that is me is going to affect others by strengthening the love that is them.

Questions to ponder:

How do you define love outside of its "romantic" implications? How do you express your love to people with whom there's no possibility of any sort of romantic involvement?

Why do so many companies spend so much money trying to get us to focus on the idea of "romantic" love? How much money do they earn if they can get people to believe that romance is a necessary element of love?

What would this world be like if all people were able to love all others unconditionally? How many people would not act in unacceptable ways because they feel unloved? How many people would have stronger self-esteem and self-worth?

Something to Consider:

Because the word "love" is often loosely used to describe a variety of feelings and relationships, it can be easy to become confused about love's real meaning. Society today tends to define love as a romantic expression for someone of the opposite sex. But it's possible to think of love in much broader terms: the basic feeling of goodwill for another, care for their health and well-being, and the desire to have only good come to them. This includes our parents, siblings, friends, and everyone! . . . . Sometimes when we think we love someone, we're actually loving what we think the other person may be able to give us. This can be an aspect of "conditional" love. Love at its highest level demands nothing in return. It loves for the sake of loving. It is not concerned with *what* or *whom* it loves, nor is it concerned with whether or not love is returned. Like the sun, its joy is in the shining forth of its nature.

Love is an inner quality that sees good everywhere and in everybody. It insists that all is good, and by refusing to see anything but good, it tends to cause that quality to appear uppermost in itself and in other things. Love takes no notice of faults, imagined or otherwise. Love is considered the great harmonizer and healer in life.

John Marks Templeton
Worldwide Laws of Life

More Questions to Ponder:

From whom do we learn our lessons about love? How do we learn them? Are the lessons thorough, or do we try to make sense of mixed signals? How did the people we learned from learn their lessons about the nature of love?

What does the word "unconditional" mean to you? Is the love that you share with others unconditional, or do you expect something in return (such as the person loving you back)?

What would the world be like if everyone felt loved, and didn't doubt that others loved them for just who they are, nothing more and nothing less?

Journal Entries

Day One: From whom have you learned your lessons about what love is and how we should approach it and show it? Were they effective teachers? Were they good at loving and showing it themselves?

Day Two: Why are we so often reticent to show our love to others? Why do we have such a hard time accepting love? How much fear is involved before love is given and accepted?

Day Three: Why do so many people limit love to the feelings between a man and a woman who are attracted to each other? What are some of the results of this limitation?

Day Four: Write a letter to a young person telling them how to show love to other people. Give them many ideas of loving things they can do to show love without saying anything about love, and without expecting anything in return.

Day Five: Someone has said that there's no such thing as unconditional love—that it isn't love at all if there are conditions attached. Do you agree with this idea? Why or why not?

Six

Character

When I started *Living Life Fully* many years ago, character was one of the first pages that I created. It seemed very important to me to acknowledge the fact that the characters that we develop for and in ourselves is one of the most important determining factors in whether or not we're happy in life. If our characters are seen by others in our honesty, our perseverance, our love, and our giving, then the chances are great that we are living full and happy lives.

If, on the other hand, our characters are reflected in our fear, our greed, our conflict, and our insecurities that cause us to hurt others, then the chances are that the lives that we're living are shallow, painful, and unfulfilling.

The most common misperception about character, though, is that our character is simply what we are, instead of what we build. Our character is not thrust upon us by genetics—rather, it is crafted by decisions we make on everything from our actions to our purchases to whether or not we're going to do something dishonest or harmful or loving or risky.

Material possessions will rust away, wear away,
or depreciate, but your inner resources—character—
must never depreciate. In seeking success you must
also seek fulfillment. Ask yourself not only what
you want to be, but who you want to be.

Elizabeth Dole

What kind of person do people know us as? Do they know us people they can trust, people they want to be around, people on whom they can depend, people with whom they would trust their children? If they do see us as this kind of person, then the chances are that we emanate a strongly positive sense of character. People know that we're not in life to get what we can out of it and hurt others in the process, and they know that we are aware of the needs and wants of others, not just ourselves.

And that kind of character doesn't just happen. It's something that is built bit by bit, a part of ourselves that develops slowly and steadily all through our lives. If we're focused solely on getting material things and competing with others and trying to put ourselves above others by insulting them or putting them down, then we're building a character that's not only useless to others, but actually harmful to them, and it would make perfect sense for those people to avoid us. When we decide to drink to excess, to take drugs, to cheat to try to get ahead, to tell lies to people who trust us, to misrepresent ourselves or the truth, then we really are defining who we are, and who others see us as being.

No, we should not live our lives dependent upon the approval of others. If we follow a course that is honest and joyful and productive but that doesn't meet someone else's approval, that disapproval really is their problem, not ours. But when others disapprove of us because of actions that we've taken that prove that we don't deserve approval, then that most certainly is a different story.

Character is the product of daily, hourly actions, words
and thoughts: daily forgiveness, unselfishness, kindnesses,
sympathies, charities, sacrifices for the good of others,
struggles against temptation, submissiveness under trial.
It is these, like the blinding colors in a picture, or the
blending notes of music, which constitute the person.

John MacDuff

It's funny sometimes how we can meet a person who's kind and honest and giving and forgiving, and tell ourselves that that's what that person is like "by nature." We assume that he or she was born that way—or raised that way—and we don't often think about whether or not that person has faced a series of difficult struggles to become that way. But the chances are that many of the people whose character we admire didn't come into that character by mistake.

Jim Rohn told the story of being so broke that he lied to some little girls, Girl Scouts who had come to his door to sell cookies. His own hard times had put him into a position in which he lied to some kids, and that was a turning point in his life—he didn't want to be that person.

Which person do you want to be? Will the very next decision that you make—the next ten decisions—be indicative that you actually are that person? Will the thoughts that you share two hours from now with someone else expose you as a kind and loving person who would make a wonderful friend, or as a self-centered gossip who's after all you can get and is willing to hurt others to get it? Will they show you as a person who tries to build others up through encouragement and compliments, or as a person who tries to tear others down through insults and criticism?

Your character really is a result of choices that you make whenever you speak and act. And as those choices become more centered on love and giving and sharing and unity, you'll find that your life becomes fuller, richer, and much more satisfying. The work we do on ourselves and our own character is the most important work that we can do in our lives, and should not be neglected.

Happiness is not the end
of life; character is.

Henry Ward Beecher

Questions to ponder

1. How often do you undertake a task or make a decision thinking "No matter what else happens, this will help to develop a strong and positive character within me"?

2. How do you feel about people who have what we might call "questionable" characters? What causes us to see their character in this way? Does your own character have any similarities to the ones you don't see as positive?

3. What can you do right now, in this moment, to strengthen your character? (For example, not eat a food you're supposed to avoid, volunteer for a task you've been avoiding, come clean with someone about something you've been less than honest about, forgive someone who could use your forgiveness, etc.)

An excerpt on character

Sweeter than the perfume of roses is a reputation for a kind, charitable, unselfish nature; a ready disposition to do to others any good turn in your power. "The mind's sweetness," says Herbert, "has its operation on the body, clothes, and habitation." So Cervantes spoke of one whose face was like a benediction. "Good looking," as Horace Smith remarks, "is looking good." "Be good," says our Amesbury poet, "be womanly, be gentle, generous in your sympathies, heedful of the good breeding of all around you,—and you will not lack kind words of admiration."

Was there ever an unselfish person, of charitable and generous impulses, sociable, loving, kind, of tender spirit, thoughtful for others, who was not universally beloved? He, indeed, is the light-bearer.

Some people are born happy. No matter what their circumstances are, they are joyous, content, and satisfied with everything. They carry a perpetual holiday in their eyes, and see joy and beauty everywhere. When we meet them they impress us as having just met with some good luck, or as having some good news to tell. Like the bees that extract honey from every flower, they have a happy alchemy which transmutes even gloom into sunshine. In the sick-room they are better than the physician and more potent than drugs. All doors open to these people. They are welcome everywhere.

The most fascinating person is always the one of the most winning manners; not the one of greatest physical beauty.

We do not need an introduction to feel his greatness, if you meet a cheerful man on the street on a cold day you seem to feel the mercury rise several degrees.

Orison Swett Marden, from *Character: The Grandest Thing in the World* (available as a free ebook at livinglifefully.com)

Journal Entries

Day One: What do you know for sure about your character, versus what do you think others know about it? Are all the things that you think you are also things that others think you are?

Day Two: What kind of person do you wish to be known as? What kind of character would you need to have to be known in this way?

Day Three: How do we develop character? What have been some of the most important incidents and lessons in your life that have developed your character as it is right now?

Day Four: Whom do you know who has a very strong character? What kinds of things does this person do to make his or her character known to others?

Day Five: Is character as important as it used to be to us? Do we see character or personality as more important now? What are some differences between the two?

Seven

Principle

No matter what we do or where we want to end up in life, we have to decide eventually upon what we want to build our lives. We've all read the parable about the man who built his home on sand versus the man who built his home upon a foundation of stone. We all have decisions to make in our lives concerning the bases that we're going to build upon, and our principles become some of our strongest bases that can withstand the worst storms—or our weakest foundations that are washed away by the slightest of rainstorms.

While I was growing up I saw this dynamic in action many times. There were people in my life whose major principles seemed to be self-indulgence and self-gratification, and they did everything they could to fulfill their needs and desires, including stepping all over others, stealing from others, betraying others, and letting others down. What I learned from watching them was that they were on a constant spiritual roller-coaster ride, and their highs were much less common than their lows. The people they treated poorly stopped trusting them, and some even did their best to hurt them back, and these people couldn't truly depend on anything in life to turn out in positive ways, all because the principles they followed were destructive and harmful.

I did see other people, though. These were the people who lived quiet, peaceful, fulfilling lives because they knew that they were always working towards their best, and doing their best for others. Their principles had to do with helping others, with being steady and trustworthy, with contributing to life instead of taking from life. These people were rarely flashy, and they rarely showed off or made themselves the center of attention. But these people attracted me because of their steadiness and their reliability—and those were two things that were sorely lacking in my life as I was growing up.

The principles we live by, in business and in social life,
are the most important part of happiness.

Harry Harrison

I believe that principle is one of the qualities of the novel To Kill a Mockingbird that makes it truly timeless. Atticus Finch has become an undying character because he lives by his principles, and he knows that if he violates them, he would lose the respect of his children. Therefore, he's a man who does what he knows to be right, no matter what the cost. He's not a perfect man by any means, but he is truly admirable because he sticks to his principles.

If we're to live truly happy and fulfilling lives, then it is important that we choose carefully which principles we live by, and that we stay faithful to them. It's also important that we don't let our principles become nooses, which can happen very easily if we never allow for change of mind or change of heart. As a college teacher, for example, there were certain principles that I always took into the classroom with me; as a high school teacher, though, those principles have changed to fit my situation—many things that are appropriate to expect from college students simply shouldn't be expected from younger kids.

If I do choose my principles carefully and I do live by them, then I am creating my own world that is either very positive or very negative. I am giving myself rules to live by, and when I live by them I make my life. Personally, I want my life to be defined by things like honor and honesty, fairness and kindness, love and peace, and I try to adopt principles that allow those aspects of my life to shine through consistently. Am I a person who criticizes others constantly, or am I someone who encourages? The answer to this is found in the principles I live by.

The principles you live by create the world
you live in; if you change the principles you
live by, you will change your world.

Blaine Lee

Many people are frustrated and confused and unhappy not because they've chosen the wrong principles to live by, but because they haven't chosen any principles at all to live by. This is a recipe for disaster, because then we go wandering through the world without any sense of purpose or direction. We may be striving towards goals, but on whose terms? History is full of examples of people who have turned out to be miserable because they've adopted their bosses' greed, their peers' willingness to step on others to advance, their spouses' fears and insecurities, and have gone on to live their lives without ever deciding on which principles they'd live by, which principles they'd use to determine what they would do in any given situation.

What do you stand for in life? The answer to that question can be found in the principles you live by. It can also be found in your actions when you either base them on your principles or don't base them upon any principles at all. Who you are and what you contribute to this world are completely up to you, after all, and we all make decisions constantly about what kind of face we show to the world. What person do you show? You'll find that if you're consistently true to the principles that you hold near and dear, others will know you better, trust you more, and be willing to share more with you. Your principles give your life clarity and direction, and it's worth your time to make the effort to consider clearly just what principles will define your life.

It's important that people should know what
you stand for. It's equally important that they
know what you won't stand for.

Mary H. Waldrip

Questions to ponder

1. Where do principles come from? How do we develop them? Are there universal principles of goodness and honesty, or do they depend on things like culture and societal norms?

2. Which principle is the most important for you? How, specifically, do you make that principle an integral part of each day?

3. Think of someone you know who doesn't seem to allow any principles to be guiding forces in his or her life. How would you describe that person? What advice would you give to that person?

4. When do we use our principles as excuses, or as rationalizations for things that we do that we know inside aren't the right things to do?

A Passage on Principle

The place to take the test of a man is not the forum or field, not the marketplace or the amen corner, but at his own fireside. There he lays aside his mask and you may judge whether he is imp or angel, king or cur, hero or humbug. I care not what the world says of him, whether it crown him with bays or pelt him with eggs; I care never a copper what his reputation or religion may be; if his babes dread his homecoming and his better half has to swallow her heart every time she asks him for a five dollar bill, he's a fraud of the first water, even though he prays night and morn until he is black in the face, and howls hallelujah until he shakes the eternal hills. But if his children rush to the front gate meet him, and love's own sunshine illumines the face of his wife when she hears his footsteps, you may take it for granted that he is true gold, for his home's a heaven and the humbug never got that close to the great white throne of God.   -William Cowper Brann

I present this passage because I think we've all known people like this, and they've affected all of our lives in some way. I think the last sentence tells us what we need to know about principle—the ways that we treat other human beings will work to create the lives that we live, and those lives can be either heavenly or hellish—it truly does depend upon us.

Journal Entries

Day One: Do you live according to your principles? Which are harder to live by, and which are easier?

Day Two: How do we go about developing principles? How do we choose which ones we wish to develop?

Day Three: What do you feel like when you violate some of your principles? What do you usually have to do to put things right after you do so (if putting things right is possible)?

Day Four: Write a letter to a young person telling him or her why it's important to live by principles. Explain what they are and how to develop them.

Day Five: Do our young people have a lot of examples of people with strong principles in the public eye these days? If not, where do they find them? Are you one of them?

Eight

The Present Moment (aka, Now)

Over and over again, we read about the importance of living in the Now, in the present moment, because the future isn't here yet and the past is done and gone. We have no guarantees of what will come in the future, so we can't depend upon our plans and ideas for it; we can have no effect at all on the past, so dwelling on mistakes and successes of the past is a futile waste of our time. Only right here and right now can we hope to have any effect at all upon our lives and the lives of others.

The principle behind this idea, of course, is very sound—many of us spend much of our time worrying about things to come and thinking about things that were instead of looking around ourselves to see our present situations and to find ways to improve them. We all have things that can and should be done, and eventually we need to make sure that they get done—things that include rest and relaxation and nice conversations with friends and many other positive, fun things. Sometimes the best thing to do in any given moment is simply to enjoy ourselves, for that enjoyment helps to rejuvenate and reinvigorate us, making us more effective when we do the many things that we're called to do each day.

How, though, do we go about making sure that we get the most out of our present moments? In many ways, it's a question of awareness—having the ability to know what's going on in our lives, what needs to be done, and what can wait. We need to be able to make decisions that are sound and that we trust, even if that decision means that we take an hour-long walk in the woods instead of tackling that new set of tasks that we need to deal with.

Begin doing what you want to do now. We are not living in eternity. We have only this moment, sparkling like a star in our hand. . . and melting like a snowflake. Let us use it before it is too late.

Marie Beynon Ray

I used to be completely out of tune with the present moment. I would have moments of clarity when I was able to appreciate and enjoy what was in my life, but for the most part my mind kept me out of the present because it was focused on what wasn't there rather than what was in my life. I would be worried about the relationships I didn't have, the money I needed, the problems that might be coming up. I was successful in what I did because of the pressure that came from deadlines and the expectations of others and my sense of responsibility, not because I was getting the most out of my life and giving my all to what I was doing.

Our awareness and appreciation of the present moment is a mental issue, after all. It's tied in with where and how we place our attention, with what we're thinking of and what we choose to focus on. That person might have just insulted me, but the sun is shining and a warm breeze is blowing and there are really nice people with me—so why do I spend my time and energy being angry and worrying about what that person said to me? What I focus on is, after all, my choice.

More important than awareness of the present moment, though, are our actions in each present moment. I know people whose first action when they return home is to turn on the television, which then stays on for hours, never allowing the person to experience the amazing qualities of silence and reflection. I know people who have the chance to go and talk to someone really interesting, but who instead pay more attention to their fears than to their curiosity or desire to know someone new and choose not to have that conversation. I know people who sit down to relax, but who choose to answer their phones instead of relaxing—and they're suddenly spending their time dealing with someone else's stress and problems.

I live now and only now, and I will do what I want to do this
moment and not what I decided was best for me yesterday.

Hugh Prather

In his book *Island*, Aldous Huxley wrote of a society that had trained birds to repeat the words "Attention," and "Here and now." These birds were wonderful reminders to the people of the importance of keeping our minds and our spirits attuned to the present moment, of paying attention to all that is around us, right here and right now. We're virtually surrounded by thousands of amazing things all the time, but we tend to allow ourselves to ignore the wonder of the world because we're so caught up in all the little things our minds are doing. When we pay attention only to what is in our minds, we lose what else there is in life at this very moment.

Living in this moment takes a lot of effort. Existing in this present moment takes very little. The effort involves making decisions—decisions to pay attention, to appreciate, to notice, to feel, to allow ourselves to ignore our own egos that are telling us to pay attention only to ourselves in the ego's own petty little ways. Decisions we make right now will affect us in an hour, in a day, in a year, and in a decade. Sometimes the decision is to do something we don't want to do, like the dishes or the homework or the phone call to that difficult person. But sometimes the decision is to do something wonderful or remarkable or just really, really fun.

We can smile, breathe, walk, and eat our meals in a way that allows us to be in touch with the abundance of happiness that is available. We are very good at preparing to live, but not very good at living. We know how to sacrifice ten years
for a diploma, and we are willing to work very hard to get a job, a car,
a house, and so on. But we have difficulty remembering that we are alive in the present moment, the only moment there is for us to be alive. Every breath
we take, every step we make, can be filled with peace, joy, and serenity. We need only to be awake, alive in the present moment.
Thich Nhat Hanh

Right here and right now, where are you? What's going on in your life? Are your steps filled with peace, or with strife? Do you see the wonder, or is your mind focused on a future outcome, a past mistake, or someone else's "wrong" actions? You are able to make your choice to return to the present moment, to the now. And when you do make that choice, you have the choice to view it with jaded eyes that tells you what's worthy and unworthy, or with wondering eyes that notice the amazing things and let your mind know that life is an amazing experience. Right here and right now, there are tons of opportunities all about us. It's a shame that we so often ignore them, isn't it?

Questions to Ponder

1. Right here and right now, you're obviously reading, which we all know to be a very positive use of time. But in the back of your mind, are there other things that are preventing you from being fully present in the here and now, things such as some task that you have to do soon, or some job that needs to be done, or some argument you've had recently with someone? How might you push those things out of your mind to be able to focus fully on the here and now?

2. How many times have you missed what's happening right in front of you because you've been thinking about something else that wasn't a part of your here and now?

3. Is our present-day world of cell phones and computers helping us to be more present in the here and now, or making it more difficult to do so? If you're on the phone talking with someone about something that's happening in a different place, are you fully present in your own "here"?

Things that make me sad

When I see parents who are with their children, but having conversations on their cell phones instead of paying attention to their kids. So often, the kids look lost and bored, and they look like they need a hug. Right here and now, those parents are with their kids physically, but miles away mentally and emotionally.

I remember going for a winter hike with a small group of people many years ago. We were in a beautiful New England forest, and everything was snow-covered and beautiful. Two of the women were talking in very loud voices about stores that they liked to shop at. On a still winter day, of course, voices seem to be louder, and they're very difficult to ignore—eventually I had to drop back from the group just to be able to take in my surroundings without having my mind distracted by the descriptions of shopping.

I had a friend once who lived so deeply in the past that she never seemed to be present in the present. Every conversation that she started had to do with things that had happened years earlier; when I tried to shift the conversation to something that was current, it was only a matter of minutes before she would redirect the conversation back to her past (which I had not been a part of, so it was completely irrelevant to me). This was her safety zone, something that she knew intimately, so it was what she wanted to talk about.

Journal Entries

Day One: Right here and right now, what are five things that are going on around you that you hadn't been paying attention to?

Day Two: Why do so many of our religious teachers teach the importance of being present in the moment? Why isn't this taught in schools?

Day Three: What's the relationship between being present in the now and awareness? Mindfulness? Do you practice either enough to be truly present each moment?

Day Four: How would you respond if someone you know said that being present in the moment is an overrated concept and isn't very important at all?

Day Five: Practice being here and now with all five senses—what is available to you in life right now that you can touch? Taste? Hear? Smell? See?

Nine

Letting Go

This is a concept that took me many, many years just to understand, much less put into practice. I grew up thinking that I needed to control situations to the very end, that I needed to make sure that results were what I wanted them to be and expected them to be. Because I saw life in that way, I set myself up for much unnecessary and unhelpful disappointment, over and over again. It was rather silly of me, but I didn't know any better.

Letting go of things is one of the most liberating actions that we can take in our lives. More importantly, letting go is also a very effective way of making sure that things turn out the ways that they're supposed to instead of the ways we want them to. That's the concept of letting go of outcomes. In another meaning, letting go is liberating because it allows us to be free from those things that often possess us when we think that we possess them. In both of these meanings, the act of letting go allows us to breathe freely, to see life with new eyes, and to get on with our lives and move on to new things instead of being tied down to and with the old.

We must be willing to let go of the life we have planned,
so as to accept the life that is waiting for us.

Joseph Campbell

Much of letting go is the ability to allow ourselves to stop trying to control our lives. Yes, we do have decisions to make and choices to weigh, but once we make them it's important that we let them play out on their own. I used to think that if I did that, then things would go terribly wrong and that they would never turn out the ways that I wanted them to. In some ways, I was right— things very often didn't turn out the way I expected them to or wanted them to. That wasn't a bad thing, though. Even though I didn't realize it at the time, things were turning out in the ways that were better for me. That woman with whom I wanted a relationship wasn't as nice of a person as I had thought; that job I wanted would have made me miserable; the people I wanted to spend time with turned out to be rather toxic.

Nowadays, I know that it's important to try to do what I want, but not to have too many expectations based on what I want something to be. I left my last job because I needed to let it go—it wasn't what I had been led to believe it would be, and though I loved the kids I worked with, I felt that I was contributing to a situation that was detrimental to them, not helpful. So I had to let go of the security of the income and let go of my relationships with the kids and my colleagues and move on, and the change has turned out to be extremely positive. Years ago I would not have been able to see that a change was best—I would have held on, hoping against hope that things would change there, even though change really was not in the cards based on the leadership that was in place.

One of the most important things that I've ever learned to let go of are my beliefs, especially those to which I've held on for many years. Such beliefs can be especially limiting and very inaccurate. Beliefs that we've had since our childhood years tend to be reflections of the beliefs of our parents and other adults and authority figures who have had an influence on our lives. They are not accurate reflections of what we know in our hearts and spirits to be true, and they keep us from uncovering our true beliefs simply because we hold on to them without letting go.

Let go. Why do you cling to pain? There is nothing
you can do about the wrongs of yesterday. It is
not yours to judge. Why hold on to the very thing
which keeps you from hope and love?

Leo Buscaglia

Another thing that I've learned to let go of is that which Leo talks about above: pain from the past in the form of grief, resentment, anger, pain and the like. When someone else does something that hurts us, it's very easy to allow ourselves to wallow in the negative feelings that are caused by that hurt. Sometimes we spend weeks, months, or even years feeling awful because of someone else's actions, and we're simply unwilling to let go of the feelings that we somehow think make us feel "better," for if I resent something, then I'll show that person, won't I?

The truth is, though, that these feelings are self-destructive. They don't destroy anyone else, nor do they send an important message to anyone else about what happened—rather, they send a message about what kind of person I am to hold on to anger and resentment for such a long time. It's important that we move on with our lives, and if we don't let go of these feelings, it's pretty much impossible to move on. After all, I can't move to a new city until I leave the city I'm in, can I?

Simply put, when I hold on to such feelings, I'm making myself miserable. When I choose to accept that I'm doing that to myself, then I can let go of those feelings and make myself feel much, much better.

*Once we see that everything is impermanent and ungraspable
and that we create a huge amount of suffering if we are
attached to things staying the same, we realize that
relaxing and letting go is a wiser way to live. Letting
go does not mean not caring about things. It means
caring about them in a flexible and wise way.*

Jack Kornfield

Life is not about control or making things happen in the ways we think they should happen. In fact, it's rather arrogant for us to be on this planet that's been here for so long and expect to be able to control life on it. If we want to see changes, then our task is to set things in motion, not to micromanage and make them happen in the ways we think they should. If we have something that is possessing us, such as alcohol or our television sets or our cell phones, then it could be time to let it go and move on with our lives. If we're holding on to resentment and anger, we're simply raising our own stress levels and blood pressure, but we're not contributing anything positive to the situation—and it's time to let it go.

We have to decide if we're going to spend our time fighting life, or living life. Are we contributing to life, or are we telling life what we think it should do and be? Are we at peace when life shows us something we didn't expect, ready to deal with it on its own terms, or does such a thing knock us for a loop, making us fearful and upset? Too many of our disappointments are caused by our own expectations, and until we can let go of those expectations, we can be sure that we're going to experience many more stressful, difficult moments in life, moments that we've caused ourselves.

Questions to Ponder

1. Name one thing that it would benefit you to let go of. How would it benefit you? How is it holding you back now?

2. Why is it so difficult to let go of certain things? How can they become "safe" for us even as they affect us in negative ways?

3. Stephen C. Paul said, "Every time you let go of something limiting, you create space for something better." If you were to let go of something limiting in your life (remember question one), what kinds of new things might be able to come into your life?

A Short List of Things That We May Need to Let Go of

Resentment, anger, jealousy
A need to be in control of situations
Fears
Expectations of others (especially our unrealistic ones)
Beliefs that have proved to be harmful to you
Prejudices and biases
Negative thoughts
Ideas of how things should be

Journal Entries

Day One: Sometimes it's easier to see something that someone else needs to let go of in order to be happier. Think about such a person and write them a letter encouraging them to let go of something limiting in their life.

Day Two: Many people say that letting go of something that's limiting us makes room for something that's much better for us in our lives. What can you think of in your life that's limiting you, and that would be better for you to let go of?

Day Three: How is letting go related to acceptance? Why do we need to accept that some things just aren't helping us at all?

Day Four: Why is it so difficult sometimes to let things go?

Day Five: What's the most important thing that you've let go of in your past? How has that affected your life?

Ten

Action

You really do have to do something if you want to see change in this world. And you need to do it sooner rather than later—the more time we spend putting things off, the less time others in the world will have to benefit from our actions. And even if you feel that your actions simply don't matter in this world, that there's nothing you can do that makes a difference, it's important that you take action anyway, for you'll never see any results of your actions in life until you actually take some sort of action.

I speak as someone who has been fortunate enough to have the willingness and desire to take action, even if the circumstances have not been ideal, so it is sometimes difficult for me to understand what happens to people who shy away from taking action. On the other hand, I grew up without much self-confidence and with very few positive role models in my life, so I do know what it feels like to face the possibility of taking action with no real trust in myself or the possible outcomes of my actions. And I've taken many actions that have "failed," but few actions that have not caused me to learn something—or to verify something that I had learned before.

We should be taught not to wait for inspiration to
start a thing. Action always generates inspiration.
Inspiration seldom generates action.

Frank Tibolt

I had a student once, a college freshman, who shared his philosophy with the class one day—he was sure that if he just sat in one place long enough, life would bring him all sorts of wonderful things. Anything good that could happen in life would happen to him, simply because he was patient enough to wait for it. While it was a pleasant thought, it definitely ignored some of life's most important laws, such as "life gives back to you exactly what you give to life" and "a body in motion tends to stay in motion." By sitting around and doing nothing, one isn't contributing a single thing to life, and therefore it's almost impossible to have other people react to us, to put things into motion that will have positive effects later, or to accomplish things that will give us (and others) a sense of accomplishment or opportunities to do more.

I believe quite strongly that in today's world, we've come to a point at which we value action too much and we undervalue the concept of rest and rejuvenation. We often get so caught up in doing things that we forget to *be*, and the things we do suffer from our lack of focus — because we're focused on doing so many things, we don't put our absolute best into any of them. In this sense, action sometimes becomes almost another dirty word as we find just one more thing to do to keep us from reflecting upon ourselves and our lives.

But this is what happens when we take action to an extreme, and it's similar to what happens when we take almost anything else to extremes. It's not our actions that are hurting us, it's our inability to keep ourselves from stretching ourselves too thin, to moderate our own lives and keep ourselves from taking on too many actions to be healthy.

Having the world's best idea will do you no good unless you act on it.
People who want milk shouldn't sit on a stool in the middle
of a field in hopes that a cow will back up to them.

Curtis Grant

So what keeps us from doing those actions that could have very positive effects on our lives? What are we so afraid of that we allow our fears to keep us from doing things that will be beneficial to us and to other people? Of course, there's the fear of failure, which tells us that if we fail, then that failure will define us as people. This fear is simply silly, as we can look at any successful person and find in his or her history actions that they took that did not have their desired effects—but that they learned from and moved on from, continuing to take actions that helped them to grow and develop and become successful.

I think there's also the fear of success in many people. If my action is successful, then perhaps much will change in my life, and I'm not quite sure that I'm ready for much to change. Expectations will be higher, there will be more work to keep up with the new expectations, and with new expectations come many more chances to fail. The status quo feels safe and easy, while actions could lead me to a more challenging life—and not everyone relishes the idea of facing more challenges in their lives.

If we want to do things that will affect our lives positively, though, we must face those fears and not allow them to keep us from doing what we know to be important. Sometimes an action is as simple as telling someone hello or asking for directions or apologizing to someone; even the most complicated things that we do are little more than an aggregation of smaller actions that all work together towards one goal. Baking a cake, for example, starts with the action of taking things out of the cupboard, and includes actions such as breaking eggs into a bowl, measuring water and oil, and so on. When you say "I just baked a cake," you're including all those many actions into your statement.

*I got the blues thinking of the future, so I left off and made some marmalade.
It's amazing how it cheers one up to shred oranges and scrub the floor.*

D.H. Lawrence

I love Lawrence's quotation here, for it's a truth about action that is almost universal: being active keeps our minds busy, and then we don't spend so much time thinking about the things that we see as bad or negative. Being active allows us to focus on doing something rather than sitting around pondering something. When we ponder, we often allow our minds to run away with thoughts and ideas, exaggerating them and turning molehills into mountains—the hill is the same size, but because our minds aren't occupied with something more productive, they often turn small problems and minor occurrences into huge issues that make us feel awful. Much of our misery, unfortunately, is our own doing.

I hope that I'm always able to be active in my life. I hope that I never refrain from acting because I think it will be useless, as the vast majority of our acts are never noticed by anyone else, though they do add up to something much, much bigger and more important: a life that's been spent doing what we know is right when we know it's needed. The key word there is "doing"—not thinking, not wishing I could do, but doing. My major actions today may be encouraging someone, picking up some litter, petting a dog, sharing a candy bar, calling a friend to get together, and writing one page of a novel. And there will be nothing earth-shattering about any of that, but each of those things most certainly will contribute to this world in very positive ways.

Questions to Consider

1. Most of the time when we fail to act on something, we fail because of fears that hold us back. Think of one time when a fear of yours kept you from acting. Would it have been better to act and face the outcome your fears told you might occur, or to not act? What didn't become a part of your life because of your lack of action?

2. Right now, in this moment, is there some sort of action you can take that can help you or someone else in some way? It could be something as simple as calling or texting a friend an encouraging message or as complicated as writing the next page of the novel you're working on, or even just making a cup of tea to share with someone, or apologizing to someone you need to apologize to.

3. Think of one action you can do today that will make someone else feel much better, even if only for a short time. What keeps us from thinking about such things more often?

Some of the Most Important Actions in My Life

Applying for college; going to college
Enlisting in the Army
Asking my wife to marry me
Buying a one-way ticket to Spain after my bachelor's degree
Quitting a job that was going nowhere
Signing up for an ultramarathon—and then running it
Writing my first novel—which brings up an important point. This was an action that took repeated decisions to sit down and write, over and over and over again. Some actions take dedication over time, and the decision to act must be made each day, not just once.
Finishing my dissertation
Moving to a new place (quite a few times, actually!)
Telling someone I was sorry for something I did (also quite a few times!)

Journal Entries

Day One: Think of an important action that you've taken in your life that led to positive results. Why was it a significant action? What were some of the obstacles to taking it?

Day Two: You know someone who talks a lot about wanting to do things, but who doesn't take any actions to make them happen. Write a note to this person telling him or her why it's important to act on desires.

Day Three: Is there something that you've been delaying on acting upon? If so, what would it take to make you stop delaying?

Day Four: "Action always generates inspiration," according to Frank Tibolt. Do you agree? Do you tend to act first, or wait for outside inspiration to do so?

Day Five: What kinds of things do you know of that are accomplished without someone acting to get them done, or at least get things started?

Eleven

Peace (Be with You)

As I grow older and older, I start to feel that there's something behind all of the things that we're doing—all of the giving and loving and hating and controlling and manipulating. More and more I get the feeling that our actions while we're here on this planet are designed to try to give us a sense of peace in our lives, a sense that we can live without fear of things like rejection and conflict and hurt. We feel that if we can avoid these things, our lives will be nice and pleasant, and gaining these things will give us the peace of not having to worry.

Life, though, doesn't work that way. It's when we learn to have and feel and make peace even with the trials that come to us in life that we're able to live our lives more pleasantly, that we're able to accomplish things that we want to accomplish and give more love and be more generous people.

Peace isn't about elimination—peace is about acceptance. Peace isn't about making others into what we think they should be—it's about accepting them as they are. Peace comes from us, from our inner spiritual lives, not from outside influences. If we want to have peace of mind and peace of heart, then we must work to develop our own ability to accept and even celebrate differences in the ways that people look, talk, feel, dream, relate to others, and live their own lives. If we want to have peace, then we must focus on getting our own lives straight, and not worry about straightening out others.

Ultimately, we have just one moral duty: to reclaim large areas of peace in ourselves, more and more peace, and to reflect it towards others. And the more peace there is in us, the more peace there will be in our troubled world.

Etty Hillesum

I wrote once a long, long time ago that if I could give any gift possible to everyone in the world, that gift would have nothing to do with riches or possessions or even relationships—that gift would be peace. It's only when we're coming from a place of peace in our lives that we're able to make the most of all of our opportunities and relationships. If we were to have widespread peace in our world instead of widespread anger and insecurities and ignorance, we would see a huge change in our world as more people would be able and willing to love others unconditionally, for they would have the peace inside themselves that would allow them to accept others unconditionally.

A person at peace isn't going to make decisions that promise the illusion of peace—decisions such as getting intoxicated, taking drugs, stealing, spending their money on useless toys and trinkets, and committing acts of supposed power over other people (robbing, raping, beating, etc.). No, crime would not disappear from our world, but with peace in our hearts, our inclination towards actions that undermine the social order would be much, much weaker. If we're at peace, we don't feel the same needs to challenge, to criticize, to try to lessen others.

Peace comes from living a measured life. Peace comes from attending to every part of my world in a sacramental way. My relationships are not what I do when I have time left over from my work. . . . Reading is not something I do when life calms down. Prayer is not something I do when I feel like it. They are all channels of hope and growth for me. They must all be given their due.

Joan D. Chittister

But how do we find peace? How do we cultivate it and make it a dominant force in our lives? If it's so important to us, then why do we not have many more teachers available to us who will help us to create peace in our lives and help it to grow? In addition to <u>acceptance</u>, I believe that one of the key areas that we must strive to develop is our sense of awareness. I know that in my life, until I actually became consciously aware of the ways in which I was sabotaging my own peace, I was unable to develop that peace until it became stronger than my senses of unrest and frustration.

Thich Nhat Hanh tells us below that peace is all around us right this moment, yet we tend not to see it or feel it. We tend not to let it into our lives because we're so busy with the things that we think will bring us success and control that we don't even see that this peace is right here, right now. All the time. You have peace in your life—peaceful people, peaceful situations—yet you tend to avoid them because you're searching out something else. And most of the time, we're not even sure what that something else actually is.

Joan Chittister tells us some of the things that we can do to bring peace into our lives, even if it's little by little. Personally, I value peace very highly, but I find that when I'm doing peaceful things like reading a book, I start to get antsy, as if I needed to be doing something productive instead of what I was actually doing. At those times, I have to take a deep breath, close my eyes and remind myself, "what I'm doing is productive, for it's allowing me to relax and feel peace, which are much more important than accomplishing that one more task."

Peace is present right here and now, in ourselves and in everything we do and see. The question is whether or not we are in touch with it. We don't have to travel far away to enjoy the blue sky. We don't have to leave our city or even our neighborhood to enjoy the eyes of a beautiful child. Even the air we breathe can be a source of joy.

Thich Nhat Hanh

My world is different when I feel at peace. It doesn't just feel different—it is different. It's slower, it's easier to understand, it's more believable. When I'm at peace with other people's actions—no matter what they are—I can understand the motivations, positive and negative, behind those actions. When I'm at peace with myself, I don't judge myself harshly and make myself feel awful. When I'm at peace with what I have, I don't feel any need to spend time and effort trying to get more possessions and to use my money for material goods, other than those that are needed.

I would love to give peace as a gift, but unfortunately, it's not something that we can pass on to each other. Peace is the result of introspection, awareness, acceptance, and compassion, and it's something that only we can achieve for ourselves. Your peace is inside of you, just waiting to be set free once you get rid of all the other stuff that's covering it up—those many mental traps into which we all fall, such as holding on to things, resentment, jealousy, anger, and especially the expectations we have of events and other people.

Find your peace and free it. When you do, you'll find that so many of the things that you consider to be drastic and worth stress and worry suddenly don't have the hold over you that they used to, and you'll be able to begin living a balanced life that's focused on making the most of your own life and gifts instead of striving constantly to achieve the peace that already resides in your spirit.

Thoughts to Consider

1. How important do you make your quest for peace in your life? Is it more important than your job or your relationships? Would your job and relationships benefit if you were to find peace in your life?

2. How do you define peace? Why isn't peace a concept that's taught to us when we're young as something that's very important?

3. What's the difference between a moment of peace and a deep peace that isn't disturbed by outside circumstances? Which do you pursue more often?

Are You an Ocean Person?

The surface of life is also in a state of constant flux, with good days and bad, victory and defeat. To maintain, as the ocean does, a deep inner calm, while the storms of misfortune, reverses, fears and worries lash at the surface of life, is to discover the secret of serenity.

Years ago, when Thomas Edison's factory burned down, he wasted no time bemoaning his fate. Immediately after the disaster the reporters found a calm, quiet man already at work on plans for a new building.

When Emerson's home was destroyed by fire and his precious books were being reduced to ashes, Louisa May Alcott came to console him. The great philosopher said, "Yes, yes, Louisa, they are all gone, but let us enjoy the blaze now. Isn't it beautiful!"

Some people are ocean personalities. In their inner depths they are not defeated by what happens to them.

The towering waves of circumstances cannot reach us when we go deep within to seek the peace that passes all understanding. While the surface of life is in turmoil we can find an inner calmness to see us through.

Wilferd A. Peterson

Journal Entries

Day One: In what ways do I see that peace is missing in my life? (I get frustrated at little things that really shouldn't bother me.)

Day Two: How can I go about bringing more peace into my life? (I can talk more to Fred, who seems to have a lot of peace, and find out how he views peace.)

Day Three: What kinds of changes might I see in my life if I develop more peace? (My daughter might not be so nervous around me, wondering when I'm going to get upset over something trivial.)

Day Four: What is the greatest potential source of peace in my life? (God, self-confidence, allowing myself to let go of things, etc.)

Day Five: How can I help others to find more peace in their lives? (I can help with things that are frustrating them, I can listen when they need to talk.)

Twelve

Living with Nature

One of the most important elements of living a full and happy life is available to us all the time, to varying degrees, and it doesn't charge us a cent to use it. The natural world is all about us, all the time, though for people who live in cities it can be far less obvious and more difficult to access—but that doesn't mean that it's not there to one degree or another.

The natural world makes many contributions to our lives, many that we accept without even thinking about, and many that we must allow to do so by paying attention to the world. For example, that oxygen that you're breathing and that's keeping you alive came from the trees that are on this planet—the same trees that "inhale" carbon dioxide and act as living air purifiers for us. The beauty of the flowers and the mountains and the sea, the wonder of the snowfall and lightning and wind, the feel of grass and sand under our bare feet, the thrill of the sounds of the birds singing and coyotes howling, all contribute to our lives in very real and very remarkable ways.

People are incomprehensible without Nature, and
Nature is incomprehensible apart from people. For
the delicate loveliness of the flower is as much
in the human eye as in its own fragile petals, and the
splendor of the heavens as much in the imagination
that kindles at the touch of their glory as in
the shining of countless worlds.

Hamilton Wright Mabie

For some reason, though, we tend to put nature off more and more, focusing instead on "doing" things, being busy, and trying to manage our lives without trying to make any real connections with the natural elements of our world. Thoreau once said that if we spend a day walking in the woods we're considered loafers, but if we spend the day cutting down trees in order to sell the lumber, then we're considered to be industrious. He said that almost two hundred years ago, and while much has changed in the meantime, things haven't changed for everyone—most people still hold the same perspective. Nature is something for our spare time, something that we get to when we can—not something that we see as essential for our well-being.

I know that in my life, I need nature. When I've lived in large cities like Barcelona, I felt a definite lack of nature and I spent as much time in parks as I could. Obviously, the lack wasn't debilitating and it didn't keep me from living my life, but there was a missing spiritual element that felt like an emptiness that was hard to define or describe. It would become clear to me when I did get out of the city to a place where the natural world dominated just what it was, as I realized how much I missed the "real" world.

I believe that many people experience that emptiness but still don't understand what it is because they never do take the time to visit a nearby lake, river, or forest, and they never do get the feelings that such places bring out in us.

Climb the mountains and get their good tidings. Nature's peace will flow into you as sunshine flows into trees. The winds will blow their own freshness into you, and the storms their energy, while cares will drop away from you like the leaves of Autumn.

John Muir

The time that I spend in nature teaches me much, also. I've learned incredible things about life and living from noticing trees that have branches only on one side because of winds that keep them from growing on the other side—yet the trees still survive and thrive in their own ways. I've learned about patience and perseverance from watching seedlings push their way through the soil towards the sun and its light; I've learned about the cycles of life by watching the seasons come and go and feeling those changes in my heart and in my spirit. I've learned about acceptance from the plants that go dormant when it becomes too hot or too cold, only to come back and thrive when conditions are more amenable to their needs. And I've learned about giving by watching how the dead things in the forest become part of the new forest, the one that goes on without them, as they deteriorate and contribute to the new plants and animals.

So many of the scientific advances that we've made have come about because scientists observed nature and have asked themselves, "How it this animal able to repel that other one?" "What allows this plant to survive when the other ones don't?" "Why does this flower grow here, but not there? And why do no other flowers grow there?" Our history is rich with cures and remedies that come from plants, or even from animals. Just ask any birder how therapeutic their hobby is for them.

After all, I don't see why I am always asking for private, individual, selfish miracles when every year there are miracles like white dogwood.

Anne Morrow Lindbergh

The natural world is an amazing source of energy, perspective, learning, spiritual development, peace, and hope—but only if we make use of it. And making use of it doesn't have to mean taking a week-long camping trip into a mosquito- infested wilderness area—it simply means taking the time to notice, accept, and appreciate all that nature gives us. It doesn't mean doing heavy-duty research on a particular area or animal (though that can be helpful in many cases), but it does mean opening our eyes and our hearts and our spirits to the natural world in order to recognize the amazing connectedness that exists between us and the natural world. And when we feel that sense of being connected, then perhaps we'll finally know for sure that we really do belong in this world on an equal footing with all of nature—equal, not superior or inferior—and realize that there is no reason for us to play small and consider ourselves inferior or alone, or to let a superiority complex grow in us that will keep us feeling separate.

Nature is, indeed, a beautiful and inspiring gift. And when we make use of that gift, our lives, too, will become beautiful and inspiring.

Thoughts to Consider

1. Nature is omnipresent, around us all the time. Why do we so often not even notice it? Why and how do we get so used to it that we don't see it anymore?

2. Almost everything that keeps us alive, from oxygen to food to water, as well as most of the things that inspire true awe, from sunsets to mountain ranges to powerful storms, are of the natural world. Why, then, do we make so little effort to preserve nature and all that's a part of it (including us)?

3. How are you connected to nature? How do you feel when you're out for a walk in a forest, or on a day with a crisp, clear breeze and bright sunshine?

A Passage from Long Ago

I was utterly alone with the sun and the earth. Lying down on the grass, I spoke in my soul to the earth, the sun, the air, and the distant sea far beyond sight. I thought of the earth's firmness—I felt it bear me up: through the grassy couch there came an influence as if I could feel the great earth speaking to me. I thought of the wandering air—its pureness, which is its beauty; the air touched me and gave me something of itself. I spoke to the sea: though so far, in my mind I saw it, green at the rim of the earth and blue in deeper ocean; I desired to have its strength, its mystery and glory.

Then I addressed the sun, desiring the soul equivalent of his light and brilliance, his endurance and unwearied race. I turned to the blue heaven over, gazing into its depth, inhaling its exquisite colour and sweetness. The rich blue of the unattainable flower of the sky drew my soul towards it, and there it rested, for pure colour is rest of heart. By all these I prayed; I felt an emotion of the soul beyond all definition; prayer is a puny thing to it, and the word is a rude sign to the feeling, but I know no other. By the blue heaven, by the rolling sun bursting through untrodden space, a new ocean of ether every day unveiled. By the fresh and wandering air encompassing the world; by the sea sounding on the shore—the green sea white-flecked at the margin and the deep ocean; by the strong earth under me.

Then, returning, I prayed by the sweet thyme, whose little flowers I touched with my hand ; by the slender grass; by the crumble of dry chalky earth I took up and let fall through my fingers. Touching the crumble of earth, the blade of grass, the thyme flower, breathing the earth-encircling air, thinking of the sea and the sky, holding out my hand for the sunbeams to touch it, prone on the sward in token of deep reverence, thus I prayed that I might touch the unutterable existence infinitely higher than deity.

Richard Jefferies

Journal Entries

Day One: What are the most easily accessible elements of nature in my life? (The fresh air, the park two blocks over, the trees and bushes in our yard.)

Day Two: In what ways do I see that I don't connect enough with nature? What might I do to remedy this situation? (I haven't seen a sunset in ages; watch a sunset or three.)

Day Three: In what ways might my life be happier or more fulfilling if I do develop a stronger connection with nature? (I might be more at peace, I might feel myself more a part of the bigger picture.)

Day Four: Many aspects of our lives keep us from nature by keeping us in an office or a home or a store or a factory. How might I develop strategies for connecting with nature more even if I do have such limitations? (Walk home from work through a park now and then, devote a weekend day to hiking or a long walk by a lake or the ocean.)

Day Five: Nature has provided my food, my oxygen, my water. How can I give back? (Plant a tree or three each year, support ecologically friendly businesses, pick up litter when I see it.)

Thirteen

Oneness/Unity

I spent my growing-up years thinking that life was about independence, about getting along by yourself, for yourself. Because my parents never really had any friends to speak of, I never got any sort of example to show me just how connected we as human beings truly are. Over the last pair of decades I have come to realize and appreciate the fact that we as human beings are completely connected—to each other, to this amazing world of ours, and to everything else on this planet.

When we go to school, we continually receive messages that focus on our differences rather than our similarities and connectedness. We need to wear the coolest clothes, we need to hang out with cool people, we're given grades that separate us from the others, for good or for bad. We're usually not taught the beauty of working together to achieve certain goals and to create beautiful things—rather, we're taught that our work is our work, and we're going to be judged for that work. We're put into grades, and we focus on whatever number that happens to be as part of our way of identifying ourselves—you're in fifth grade, but I'm in sixth; you're just a freshman, so what do you know?

We find many, many more ways to separate ourselves—the cities, towns, states, and countries that we live in; the religions that we follow; the type of music we listen to; the places we shop at; the things that we study; the jobs that we do—the list goes on and on. And with each new thing that we find that we're able to look at as something that separates us from our fellow human beings, we step farther and farther from being able to see the unity that should unite us all "fellow passengers to the grave," as Charles Dickens so aptly put it.

*It's only in our minds that we are
separate from the rest of the world.*

Gay Luce

When we separate ourselves from the rest of the world, the world becomes a lonely and difficult place to live in. When we see ourselves as completely separate, we cannot call upon the power and strength that comes from unity, from being part of a greater whole. In today's world, we buy into the lie that if we do see ourselves as—or make ourselves into—a part of the greater whole, then we'll lose our identity and become nothing more than another face in the crowd, a lemming who does nothing but follow others and never creates his or her own life. Nothing, though, could be further from the truth.

In unity there is a freedom that most can only dream of—the freedom of belonging to something greater than ourselves, to which we must contribute, obviously, but for which we are not entirely responsible. Realizing our connectedness to the rest of the planet and accepting our place in this world gives us an entirely different perspective, and our value as an individual actually increases rather than decreases. Have you ever seen a digital television screen with just one pixel that doesn't work? The entire picture is affected rather negatively by the loss of this one pixel, and we're just like that—the communities of which we're part lose their integrity and wholeness when members are not able to see themselves and act as part of the whole.

Your life and my life flow into each other as wave flows into wave, and unless there is peace and joy and freedom for you, there can be no real peace or joy or freedom for me. To see reality—not as we expect it to be but as it is—is to see that unless we live for each other and in and through each other, we do not really live very satisfactorily; that there can really be life only where there really is, in just this sense, love.

Frederick Buechner

We do belong together, and we are meant to be with each other—there really is no other logical explanation as to why we've been created just as we are. And when we see ourselves and each other as part of the same team, our world becomes much brighter, much easier to bear. This team, though, is not set up to compete, for there is no other team against which we must compete. Rather, the team that we're on is a team that thrives on cooperation, the cooperation necessary to help ourselves and each other attain the greatest possible level of self-actualization that we can. We can come much closer to reaching our full potential by contributing to the whole than we can by scratching and clawing to get by completely on our own.

If you hurt, I hurt. And that man on the news that just killed someone else? As unpleasant as it sounds, he's a part of humanity, too, and while his actions have caused horrible pain to others, those actions are also the result of pain that we cannot even imagine if we haven't walked in his shoes. The cashier at the supermarket and the man who just smiled and said hello and the little kid who's a bit too noisy sometimes—they're all integral parts of our world, not separate entities living in separate worlds. And perhaps it's about time that we start treating them that way—perhaps it's time that we start extending our love to everyone and everything with which we share this planet.

Unconditional love is the experience of being; there

is no "I" and "other," and anyone or anything it touches
is experienced in love. You cannot unconditionally love
someone. You can only be unconditional love. It is
not a dualistic emotion. It is a sense of oneness with all
that is. The experience of love arises when we surrender
our separateness into the universal. It is a feeling of unity.
You don't love another, you are another.
There is no fear because there is no separation.

Stephen Levine

Our separateness is a myth, after all. Our ego likes to tell us that we're on our own, for then it's able to be in charge, to convince us that it's extremely important to us, when the fact is that it really is more destructive than helpful. Our ego likes us to feel separate, for then we depend on it rather than on the other people and elements of our world that can help us when we need it. But when we let go of our separateness, when we let go of the feelings that we are not connected to the rest of the world, then we can start to live truly, to feel truly, and to love truly.

We are one with the world. We are a part of the world, and all in the world is a part of us. If we wish to live our lives fully, then we must acknowledge and accept—even celebrate—this great truth. Once we do so, then we can begin to live a life that sees our connections with others as one of the greatest blessings in our lives, and we'll know that all that we do to contribute to the world has a reason behind it and inherent value within it. Let your separation go, and thrive in the unity that's already there, waiting for you to embrace it.

Thoughts to Think About

1. Why does our society teach us more about independence than about unity? Which concept would be the most beneficial to society as a whole for more people to learn?

2. What kinds of fears arise in us when we think about being one with the rest of humanity? Why might we spend so much time and energy fighting this reality?

3. Does the concept of unity make more demands on us as people? If we lived as if we believed we are all unified, what would our responsibilities be? What would the benefits to us be?

A Poem by John Donne

No man is an island,
Entire of itself,
Every man is a piece of the continent,
A part of the main.
If a clod be washed away by the sea,
Europe is the less.
As well as if a promontory were.
As well as if a manor of thy friend's
Or of thine own were:
Any man's death diminishes me,
Because I am involved in mankind,
And therefore never send to know for whom the bell tolls;
It tolls for thee.

Journal Thoughts

Day One: What are some benefits of focusing on unity rather than independence? (I can help more people with their needs, there may be more people there for me when I need help.)

Day Two: What are some ways that I can express my knowledge and acceptance of my unity with the rest of the world? (Be less judgmental, share more of what I have, ask more if my help is needed by others.)

Day Three: How will my life change if my personal focus shifts to unity, without creating any false expectations of how others should react to my shift? (I'll be more tolerant of others, I'll start to understand others better, I'll feel less alone.)

Day Four: How does the concept of unity fit in with my religious and spiritual ideas and ideals? (Am I one with God, or separate from God?)

Day Five: How can I be a beacon of unity to others? How can I act in ways that respect the unity that I feel and also show others the benefits of doing so?

Fourteen

Perspective

We see the world how we see the world—it's as simple as that. Unfortunately, though, we somehow grow to believe that the ways in which we see the world should be universal, should be the same for everyone. Only when we grow to accept and appreciate the fact that each human being on this planet sees the world in a unique way can we grow to be at peace with the fact that other people aren't doing things the ways that we think they should do them.

While I see a beautiful rainstorm, someone else may be looking at nasty weather. Where I see a building that's an eyesore, another person may see a building that's full of tradition and history. The piece of art that I love may be a boring painting to the person standing right next to me at the exact same moment. There really is no accounting for perspective, and we all definitely have the right to see the world in the ways that seem most accurate to us.

Problems arise, though, when others want us to see the world their way, or when we get disappointed that others don't see the world our way. This tendency of ours shows a lack of respect for the perspectives of others, and this lack of respect seems to have become the norm in our debates about politics, finances, environmental issues, education—you name it. And we spend a lot of time being stressed out and feeling bad because others simply don't see things our way; we try to plan ways to convince them to agree with us instead of saying quite simply, "Of course they don't see things our way—nor should they!"

It is the mind which creates the world around us, and even though
we stand side by side in the same meadow, my eyes will never
see what is beheld by yours, my heart will never stir to
the emotions with which yours is touched.

George Gissing

We can make our lives much simpler and much more agreeable if we can keep in mind that another person's disagreement with us is simply that—a disagreement, and something that is completely natural. Sometimes we complicate life by reading things into another person's perspective that really isn't there. When we allow ourselves to try to understand another person's perspective rather than judging their actions based on our perspectives, then we can keep ourselves from trudging down the road of disappointment and judgment.

We can also help ourselves in our lives by remembering that our perspectives are not chiseled in stone—they're the result of dealings that we've had with other people, and things that we've learned from them. The fact that we've learned something from our parents, for example, doesn't make that something the gospel truth, and eventually we may meet someone else who teaches us something completely new that our parents never knew, and that changes our perspective significantly as long as we allow the changes to come.

We can also help ourselves by realizing that our perspectives sometimes can be flawed. We may see an occurrence as a tragedy when it may be simply a bump in the road. An obstacle may look to be overwhelming, but it may be quite manageable if we just look at it in a different way. Our own perspectives often keep us from living our lives fully and completely, for they keep us thinking negative thoughts and keep us focused on the impossibilities that we think we see rather than on the possibilities that are always before us.

A child on a farm sees a plane fly overhead and dreams of a faraway place.
A traveler on the plane sees the farmhouse and dreams of home.

Carl Burns

Sometimes we get so caught up in what we think we want that we're unable— or we refuse—to see just how positive things are in our lives. Carol Burns points out that two people can look at each other or their situations and wish for what the other one has, while not keeping in mind that what they have is pretty positive, too. The person who is lonely and wishes for companionship doesn't keep in mind that the ability to be alone is something that others long for; those who are in relationships but long for the independence to spend time on their own, traveling or reflecting or doing some of the many other things that are best done on one's own, often undervalue the positive side of the relationship.

Envy often arises out of a flawed perspective. We may think that the person who has tons of money or fame must be happy, but that's not necessarily the case. We simply think that what we believe about that person must be true, even though we haven't had the opportunity to walk a mile or two in that person's shoes—something that if we were able to do it might teach us a thing or two about just how flawed our perspective can be.

Before we set our hearts too much upon
anything, let us examine how happy
they are who already possess it.

Francois de la Rochefoucauld

I like to be an observer. I like to observe more deeply than the surface shows, for it's only when we look past the superficial that we realize what lies in the depths. Our perspectives, unfortunately, are too often developed by watching the surface and making judgments based on what we see there. Only when we realize that we don't know the whole picture and that other people might see the picture completely differently will we be able to have some peace with the fact that what we often see as reality is only our version of reality, based on a limited and incomplete perspective. And that's okay—we don't need to know everything about everything, and we can't.

But when we do realize that we shape reality by how we see it, we also realize that reality shifts in nature as our perspectives grow and develop, and that we can live in a beautiful world that is giving and caring just by changing the way that we see this world, and by accepting the fact that others see the same things that we do in completely different ways—and that's okay.

A Few Questions about Perspective

1. Who taught me that the ways that I see things are "right"? Why do I believe that my perspective is necessarily accurate, even though I've been proved to be wrong many times before in my life?

2. How do other people see the world? Since they've had different teachers, different experiences, and different lives, what are the chances that they see it exactly as I see it? And if their perspective is just as valid as mine, who's right when we disagree?

3. Why do we hold so fast to our own ways of seeing the world and the things that happen to us and around us?

An Interesting Lesson on Perspective

If we could shrink the earth's population to a village of precisely 100 people, with all the existing human ratios remaining the same, it would look something like the following:

There would be

57 Asians; 21 Europeans
14 from the Western Hemisphere, both north and south; 8 Africans
52 would be female; 48 would be male

70 would be non-white; 30 would be white
70 would be non-Christian; 30 would be Christian
89 would be heterosexual; 11 would be homosexual
6 people would possess 59% of the entire world's wealth, and all 6 would be from the United States.
80 would live in substandard housing
70 would be unable to read
50 would suffer from malnutrition
1 would be near death; 1 would be near birth
1 (yes, only 1) would have a college education
1 would own a computer (this would probably be higher now than when this was written)

When one considers our world from such a compressed perspective, the need for acceptance, understanding and education becomes glaringly apparent.

Journal Ideas about Perspective

Day One: Where did most of my thoughts about other people and different aspects of life originate? (I learned them from my parents or other authority figures, I developed them myself, I adopted them to fit in.)

Day Two: What can I do to broaden my perspective? (Read more and different books and magazines from different sources, listen to other people without trying to argue with them to defend "my side.")

Day Three: What might happen in my life if I were to develop my perspective into a broader and more open one? (I might be able to accept others more easily, I might judge less.)

Day Four: Choose one thing that you've believed for a very long time, and challenge your own belief based on the limitations of your perspective. (I've always considered my uncle to be a very unpleasant person, but I never had considered. . . .)

Day Five: Thing of one topic on which you have very strong feelings one way or another. Write down an argument that goes against your feelings. (If you feel that children shouldn't be allowed to read certain books, write an argument telling why they should. You don't need to change your own mind, of course—just examine the other side of the story to know it better.)

Fifteen

Failure

It truly is a shame that so many people "learn" so early in life that failure is a negative thing. After all, failure is one of the most important elements of our lives, for it's through failure that we do our best learning of all. A lack of success teaches us what doesn't work and allows us to focus on other strategies that may prove more successful. Yet we demonize failure, and we treat it as a terrible part of life—we even allow it to contribute to our self-perception and self-esteem, two places where failure doesn't even belong. We cannot and should not define ourselves ourselves by something that we tried and didn't succeed at, especially if we've learned from the failure.

Personally, I'm very grateful for the failures in my life, for they've shown me some very important aspects of myself that I hadn't known about before. In fact, I often put myself in situations in which failure is probably, first to see if I can avoid that failure, and second because I want to learn how to deal with failure if it does come to pass. It's only when I enter situations with a true respect for the possibility of failure that I can put my all into them without having the illusion that my all isn't necessary.

It is a common mistake to think of failure as the enemy of success.
Failure is a teacher—a harsh one, but the best. Pull your failures
to pieces looking for the reason. Put your failure to work for you.

Thomas J. Watson, Sr.

As much as we may hate to admit it, failure very well could be what Thomas Watson calls the best teacher in our lives. Let's face it—as much as we like to succeed, we don't learn a whole lot from our successes, because we usually have a very good idea how to proceed before we succeed. When we undertake a task that's truly daunting, though, we face a greater possibility of failure, and we pay much closer attention to all that we do. If I'm setting up a stereo out of a box, there's very little chance of failure, for all the wires are color-coded or they have connections of unique shapes. If I'm building something of my own that I've never built before, though, it's important that I pay close attention to every step so that I maximize my potential for success, and minimize my potential for failure.

So many of what we call failures, though, have to do with other people. Do we fail if we lost a basketball game because the other team played better? Do we fail as a salesman if that couple that were just in decided not to buy my product after all? Other people make decisions in life, and their decisions usually don't have anything to do with us. Someone may decide not to buy a car from us not because we failed at selling it to them, but because their financial situation doesn't allow them to afford it right now. I may lose a tennis match not because I failed to defeat my opponent, but because my opponent is better than I, or because he or she simply had an awesome match.

In either case, defining our lack of success as "failure" is inaccurate—those were just the ways that things turned out. If the customer is having money problems, do I truly want to sell him or her something that could add to those problems? And when I lose a match, I really look forward to the next one to see how and if I improve.

Failure is a reality; we all fail at times and it's painful when we do. But it's better to fail while striving for something wonderful, challenging, adventurous and uncertain than to say, "I don't want to try, because I may not succeed completely."

Jimmy Carter

The most tragic part of failure that I witness, though, is when people allow the fear of failure to keep them from even trying something important. I see this very often in the schools where I teach—students who don't even start to do the work because they're afraid they're going to do it poorly and thus fail. These are students who are fully capable of doing the work at a "C" level, at least, but who end up failing not because of their efforts, but because they don't allow themselves even to try to do the work.

In this situation, "failures" of the past have led to criticism and/or ridicule, and the person has had a hard time dealing with the ways that other people have treated him or her. So they just close themselves off to possibility and never even try something that may turn out to be actually easy, or at least something that they definitely can accomplish. Almost everyone on this planet, for example, can write a simple five-paragraph essay with the right training and practice, yet I've seen many, many students not even try to do so because of their fear of failure. And when they do that, they keep themselves from finding the small successes in life, the ones that build upon each other to make a pattern of success that will help them eventually to eliminate or greatly lessen their fear of failure.

You need the ability to fail. I'm amazed at the number of organizations that set up an environment where they do not permit their people to be wrong. You cannot innovate unless you are willing to accept some mistakes.

Charles Knight

"Failure" is not a dirty word. In fact, it may be one aspect of our lives that's absolutely necessary if we're ever to live fully, meet our potential, and learn the lessons that we're supposed to learn in life. Of course, there are exceptions to this rule, mostly dealing with people who fail because they simply don't care about what they're doing, but when we redefine failure as a positive in our lives, we can actually learn from it and allow it to help us to grow and become better people because of our failures than we would have been had we succeeded.

Some Questions on Failure

1. Why do so many of us consider failure to be a negative result?

2. What would your life be like if you weren't afraid of failure in any field?

3. What kinds of things have your learned from failure in your life?

An Interesting Poem on Failure

Failures

'Tis better to have tried in vain,
  Sincerely striving for a goal,
Than to have lived upon the plain
  An idle and a timid soul.

'Tis better to have fought and spent
  Your courage, missing all applause,
Than to have lived in smug content
  And never ventured for a cause.

For those who try and fail may be
  The founders of a better day;
Though never theirs the victory,
  From them shall others learn the way.

Edgar Guest

Journal Entries

Day One: Do I fail enough? If I don't, am I taking enough risks?

Day Two: How do I see failure? Is it a reflection of who I am as a person, or something that I actively risk achieving?

Day Three: What kinds of things might I try in order to achieve failure more often?

Day Four: Are all failures equal? Is failure in a relationship similar to failure in a business venture? Is there even such a thing as failure in a relationship, or is a finished relationship an inevitable outcome of people who are incompatible in significant ways?

Day Five: What has been my most positive failure? What have I learned from it? How has it affected me?

Sixteen

Work

Work is something that I've always been good at, given the fact that I have an innate drive to do well in whatever I do. When I was working at a hamburger place in high school, I always did my best to make sure that what I cooked looked good and was cooked just right. Nobody had to remind me that I was making people's food, so it was important that it was cooked well. When I was in the Army, I always tried to do well whatever my current task was, even if it was sweeping the floor or cleaning my M-16. Because of this trait, I think that I've gotten a lot out of the jobs that I've done—I've learned from them and grown while doing them.

I'm always surprised—and a little dismayed—at how often I hear people complain about their jobs and the work that they do at them. It dismays me because it seems that these people aren't very happy at all. How can they be if they have to spend so much time at a job that they don't even like? The shame of it is that so much of their time each week is spent at work, and if they don't enjoy their work, then a huge part of their lives is spent doing something unpleasant.

Our work should be something that we take pride in and enjoy doing. If neither of these conditions are true, then we really need to reconsider what we're doing. Most of us, though, feel somewhat trapped by our jobs—after all, this is how we earn our pay, and leaving the job would mean leaving the security that a paycheck brings to us. For many of us, that lack of security is something that we're not willing to face, especially if we have a family and the welfare of others is also dependent upon those checks that we bring in.

I studied the lives of great men and women, and I found that the people
who got to the top were those who did the jobs they had in hand,
with everything they had of energy and enthusiasm and hard work.

Harry S. Truman

So how do we try to make sure that our work contributes to living our lives fully? First of all, it's important that we give our all to the work that we do. If we don't make this effort, then we always will know that the work that we do is basically second-rate, for if it's not the best that we can do, it's not our first-rate work. This is important because one of the best feelings that we can have is one of satisfaction from having done a job well. This feeling is also strongly related to the pride we can feel when we not just succeed at what we're doing, but excel. Meeting the minimum requirements almost never results in a sense of satisfaction or pride, and can very often make us feel dissatisfied—even ashamed—of ourselves.

I'm sure we all have the experience of going to a store and asking where something is located. The workers there who do their jobs well know exactly where things are—that's part of their job. Someone who comes to work and only does the minimum, though, never makes the effort to get to know the store, and they usually say things like "We don't have any of those," or even "I'm not sure, but I think it's in aisle 12." (And of course, we have to make allowances for people who are new to the job.) I do a lot of painting, and I can't tell you how often I have to replace outlets and switch plates that were simply painted over—the previous painter couldn't take the 30 seconds necessary to unscrew them and take them off before painting. These are people who aren't doing jobs that they can be proud of.

It's important, though, that we set ourselves up for feeling pride in our lives. Work is one of the places where this can be done rather easily, but it depends upon our attitudes. There have been some days when I've been walking to school feeling tired and unmotivated, and I always tried to reframe the day and my work by telling myself that I had another opportunity to work with some amazing young people and help them to learn some things that could be helpful to them later in life. This helped me to start the day with a positive attitude, and it kept me from letting my job get me down.

The beauty of work depends upon the way we meet it, whether we arm ourselves each morning to attack it as an enemy that must be vanquished before night comes—or whether we open our eyes with the sunrise to welcome it as an approaching friend who will keep us delightful company and who will make us feel at evening that the day was well worth its fatigue.

Lucy Larcom

I was fortunate because I was working with young people who inspired me, but I've also spent four years in the Army, where I did work that wasn't nearly as fulfilling as teaching. But I had a choice to make—do the work well and be proud of what I accomplished, or let the work get the best of me and make me feel miserable, which would lead to a vicious cycle in which because I felt miserable, I would do a crappy job; because I did a crappy job, I would feel even more miserable. I didn't want to get into that sort of reality.

Work can help us not only to feel a sense of pride, but it can also provide us with a sense of purpose. This is especially true because most of the work that's available in the world provides us with a chance to serve other human beings. There are jobs that allow us to serve directly, such as being a doctor, teacher, or travel agent, for example, but there are also many jobs that allow us to serve indirectly, such as being a janitor or working in a factory or assembly line. We may never see the people who receive the benefit of our work, but that's okay. If we do the work well, we'll know that the people who receive the benefit of our work will be satisfied with what we've done.

Few persons realize how much of their happiness is dependent upon their work, upon the fact that they are busy and not left to feed upon themselves. Blessed is the person who has some congenial work, some occupation in which to place one's heart, and which affords a complete outlet to all the forces that are in him or her.

John Burroughs

One of the most important things that we can do is to choose work that is good for us—work that we truly enjoy doing, and work for which we have talents that make us better at it. Many people choose their jobs simply by staying at the first job that they're hired for, whether it's satisfying and fulfilling to them or not. And once the paychecks start coming in, it can become very difficult to leave a job that helps us to pay our bills. We have to make a conscious effort to choose work that can help us to grow and to learn, and that can help us to serve other people in ways that we're good at. Our work should be in areas of our strengths, not our weaknesses. I'm a good teacher, but I'd be a terrible doctor. I'd probably earn more money as a doctor, but I would not be as happy a person if I chose work that I know for sure that I would not be very good at.

Work is not a minor part of most of our lives. In many cases, work comes to define us as people, even. When someone asks us what we do, we often start with our employment rather than anything else. Near the end of our lives, we often find that other people know us more by our profession than by anything else. If we make our work something that we're proud of, we can use it to help us build a life that is satisfying and fulfilling.

Questions on Work

1. Is your work something that fulfills you and satisfies you, or does it simply provide a paycheck in return for time served?

2. How do most people you know choose the types of work they do?

3. Have you ever worked with someone who hated their job? How did that make you feel to have to work with them? How did they do on the job?

On Work

Khalil Gibran
from *The Prophet*

Then a ploughman said, "Speak to us of Work."
And he answered, saying:
You work that you may keep pace with the earth and the soul of the earth.
For to be idle is to become a stranger unto the seasons, and to step out of life's procession, that marches in majesty and proud submission towards the infinite.
When you work you are a flute through whose heart the whispering of the hours turns to music.
Which of you would be a reed, dumb and silent, when all else sings together in unison?
Always you have been told that work is a curse and labor a misfortune.
But I say to you that when you work you fulfill a part of earth's furthest dream, assigned to you when that dream was born,
And in keeping yourself with labor you are in truth loving life,
And to love life through labor is to be intimate with life's inmost secret.
But if you in your pain call birth an affliction and the support of the flesh a curse written upon your brow, then I answer that naught but the sweat of your brow shall wash away that which is written.
You have been told also life is darkness, and in your weariness you echo what was said by the weary.
And I say that life is indeed darkness save when there is urge,
And all urge is blind save when there is knowledge,
And all knowledge is vain save when there is work,
And all work is empty save when there is love;
And when you work with love you bind yourself to yourself, and to one another, and to God.
And what is it to work with love?
It is to weave the cloth with threads drawn from your heart, even as if your beloved were to wear that cloth.
It is to build a house with affection, even as if your beloved were to dwell in that house.
It is to sow seeds with tenderness and reap the harvest with joy, even as if your beloved were to eat the fruit.
It is to charge all things you fashion with a breath of your own spirit,
And to know that all the blessed dead are standing about you and watching.
Often have I heard you say, as if speaking in sleep, "He who works in marble,

and finds the shape of his own soul in the stone, is a nobler than he who ploughs the soil.

And he who seizes the rainbow to lay it on a cloth in the likeness of man, is more than he who makes the sandals for our feet."

But I say, not in sleep but in the over-wakefulness of noontide, that the wind speaks not more sweetly to the giant oaks than to the least of all the blades of grass;

And he alone is great who turns the voice of the wind into a song made sweeter by his own loving.

Work is love made visible.

And if you cannot work with love but only with distaste, it is better that you should leave your work and sit at the gate of the temple and take alms of those who work with joy.

For if you bake bread with indifference, you bake a bitter bread that feeds but half man's hunger.

And if you grudge the crushing of the grapes, your grudge distils a poison in the wine.

And if you sing though as angels, and love not the singing, you muffle people's ears to the voices of the day and the voices of the night.

Journal Entries

Day One: What advice would you give to someone who is considering what type of work to go into as a career? Write a letter to a young person you know giving them guidance based on your experience.

Day Two: Why do so many people end up in jobs that aren't satisfying to them? Do they take pride in work that they don't enjoy?

Day Three: Why do many people in our society look down on certain types of work and the people who do them? How does that affect the people who do those jobs?

Day Four: Pick three different kinds of work that you would love to be doing, and write down why these jobs are attractive to you. Then consider whether or not it would be worth pursuing jobs in these fields.

Day Five: How do you imagine life would be if we didn't have any work to do at all? How would we feel about ourselves and our lives?

Seventeen

Success

It's such a shame that most of us allow others to define success for us. It's especially a shame that we allow others in the media and entertainment and sports worlds to define it for us, for usually then our definition of success has to do with fortune and fame, two things that the vast majority of us never will achieve, thankfully. The truth is that if we wish to be successful in life, it's important that we take the time to define success for ourselves, that we decide what's important for us in life and strive to attain that, rather than trying to attain things that other people value.

Success has much to do with our values. When we define success for ourselves, our definition will be true to the values we hold dear—that is, if we've made the effort to consider just what we value, too. Some of the most successful people I've ever met haven't had much to show as far as material wealth is concerned, but they've been happy and fulfilled people. They enjoy their lives and the people in them, and they take every chance they get to serve others in whatever ways they can.

On the other hand, I've known people who earn good wages and who have plenty of material toys, but who have been grumpy and selfish and very unhappy. While they expect the world to see them as successful because of their paychecks, they're living lives that show to the world their lack of success. One particularly "successful" man whom I've met had a miserable marriage and stress-induced health problems that demanded several surgeries—very high prices to pay for maintaining a paycheck, no matter how much money might be involved.

A successful life for a man or for a woman seems to me to
lie in the knowledge that one has developed to the limit
the capacities with which one was endowed; that one
has contributed something constructive to family and
friends and to a home community; that one has brought
happiness wherever it was possible; that one has
earned one's way in the world, has kept some friends,
and need not be ashamed to face oneself honestly.

Eleanor Roosevelt

Each of us is gifted with a unique set of talents and skills, and if we take the time and make the effort to develop them, we'll find that our lives become much more successful. When we're functioning in areas that are our strengths, we can contribute more to the world, and we can give more of ourselves to others. When we develop our strengths, they become much more effective and useful, and they can bring better things to other people in our lives.

Whenever we contribute something positive to someone else's life, we are successful. Whenever we create something that is special to us, we are successful. Whenever we help someone else to learn, to grow, to think, to bear a burden, or to overcome adversity, we are successful. Whenever we do something that helps ourselves to grow, to learn, to think, to bear a burden, or to overcome adversity, we are successful. Whenever we develop our own skills in an area in which we're gifted, we are successful.

The unsuccessful people are the ones who allow other people to define their success, and who take all they can from life without giving back. A person who hoards money without ever using it to do any good for anyone is unsuccessful. One who constantly expects others to do things for them, but who isn't willing to do things for others, is unsuccessful.

If my goal is to run a marathon, and I've never run more than five miles, can I be successful even if I don't run the marathon? Absolutely. If race day comes and I make it 17 miles, that's a huge success on the road to the ultimate success. It only becomes something negative if I perceive it to be a failure, but running 17 miles is a great achievement by any measure. If my goal is to raise $1,000 and I raise $850, I've still raised more than eight hundred dollars that weren't there before.

The successful person is the
individual who forms the habit
of doing what the failing
person doesn't like to do.

Donald Riggs

After we define success, we have to pursue our goals. As Donald says here, it's important that we make ourselves do the things that may not be as easy to do as some other things. If I'm training for that marathon and it's cold and wet outside, I may still have to go out and run while I would prefer to stay at home in the cozy warmth. If I need to raise the money, I may have to come home and do some more work instead of resting and relaxing. If I want to make a certain team, I'll need to practice more than other people do. If I want to get a new job or a raise or a promotion, I may have to do more work than the people around me do, and I may have to spend more time at work than they do.

Success, though, often takes its time, and it may take longer than we think it should before our efforts are rewarded. Colonel Sanders faced hundreds of rejections from restaurant owners before he finally found someone to use his recipe. Richard Bach received eighteen rejection letters for *Jonathan Livingston Seagull* before he found a publisher. Many other people have succeeded because of perseverance and hard work, and they deserve all the success they get. Even more people taste success very rarely, mostly because they're not willing to do the things necessary to be successful.

You are a process, not a product. Your job is to discover
what you are and create that creature. You still won't be
perfect, but success isn't about perfection—it is
about authenticity. You are a success if you are
being your real, authentic self.

Bernie Siegel

In the end, though—when we reach our final day on this planet—the true measure of our success will be just how true we are to who we are, and just how authentic the lives we've led have been. When we look back on the lives we've lived, the chances are that we're going to be focused on the people to whom we've given, with whom we've shared, whom we've helped. And how we feel about ourselves today has a lot to do with how much success we feel that we've had so far—and I'd be willing to bet that we've had much more that we give ourselves credit for, if our definitions of the term are realistic.

And for next week and next year? Well, let's get into the habits of doing everything that we need to do and persevering when others stop, and we can be sure that our future and current endeavors will end up successful, too— even if they don't seem to match up with the ways we thought they'd be.

Questions to Ponder

1. Where have your concepts of success come from? Have you developed them yourself or have you borrowed those of other people?

2. How do you see the relationship between success and failure? Are they mutually exclusive, or are they related?

3. Why do so many people have a fear of success? How does that fear affect them and the things that they attempt to achieve in life?

Ideas about Success

Success

They have achieved success who have lived well, laughed often, and loved much;
who have enjoyed the trust of pure people,
the respect of intelligent men and women and the love of little children;
who have filled their niches and accomplished their tasks;
who have left the world better than they found it
whether by an improved poppy,
a perfect poem or a rescued soul;
who have never lacked appreciation of Earth's beauty
or failed to express it;
who have always looked for the best in others and
given them the best they had;
whose life was an inspiration;
whose memory a benediction.

—Bessie Anderson Stanley, 1904

("Success" was written as the winning entry in a contest run by Brown Book Magazine in 1904. Bessie won a cash prize of $250 which paid off the mortgage on the house, among other things. It was included in Bartlett's Book of Quotations for decades, and if you can find an old edition from the 30's or 40's, it should be in there. They dropped it, I think in the 60's, but I don't know why.
The family isn't sure how the poem got mangled and attributed to Emerson, but it was further confused by Ann Landers and her sister Abby. Ann Landers used to (mis)quote it all the time and cite Emerson as the source. My great-uncle Art, a retired federal judge who died last March, and she had a decade-long correspondence as he argued for a public correction. She finally conceded and in her book, *The Ann Landers Encyclopedia*, prints the whole story.
-Bethanne Larson, a granddaughter of Bessie Stanley) (Thanks to robinsweb.com for this info.)

Journal Entries

Day One: How do you define success in your life? What are some of the most important indicators that something you've done has been successful?

Day Two: Why do so many people allow society to define success for them? Why do they strive to be successful on those terms rather than on their own terms?

Day Three: Bernie Siegel says that success isn't about perfection, but about authenticity. What does that mean to you? Do you agree with him?

Day Four: What have been some of the most important successes of your life? Would you do anything to improve them if you could do them over again?

Day Five: What do you want to be successful with in the future? What will you do to make sure you succeed?

Eighteen

Self-Love

Of all the topics that are covered on the Living Life Fully website, this is the one that has given me the most difficulty of all in my own life. I grew up being my own worst critic, and I rarely gave myself the benefit of the doubt in any area of my life. There are specific reasons for this that I've learned later in life, but they aren't necessary to go into here. What is important is that I've finally learned the importance of loving myself, being good to myself, and taking good care of myself so that I'm in a better position to do good for others.

After all, that's the bottom line on self-love: how can you possibly love others well if you're not able to love yourself? How can you treat others in ways in which you're not even willing or able to treat yourself? We can fool ourselves and try to convince ourselves that we can treat ourselves poorly yet still be better to others, but that simply isn't true.

Most of the terrible things we see people doing to others comes from people who aren't able to love themselves. It's sad, but it's true.

You can explore the universe looking for somebody
who is more deserving of your love and affection than
you are yourself, and you will not find that person
anywhere. You, yourself, as much as anybody
in the entire universe, deserve your love and affection.

the Buddha

Sometimes it's hard to convince ourselves that we are just as deserving of our love—and the love of others—as anyone else on this planet. When Jesus said, "Love others as you love yourself," there are two commands in that sentence, yet we somehow tend to ignore the second one. And because we do ignore it, we treat ourselves with less dignity and grace and caring than we really should. We deprive ourselves of rest and relaxation, we come down hard on ourselves for every little mistake that we make, and we criticize ourselves ruthlessly for almost anything that we do. This isn't loving behavior, and in fact, many of our problems in life result from our own treatment of ourselves, though we may blame them on the way that others treat us.

But others can treat us only as well as we treat ourselves. This is one of the cardinal rules of life that most of us refuse to accept, for it doesn't make sense to us. Can't we be loveable even if we don't love ourselves? After all, our mothers love us unconditionally, so why won't others?

But we must remember that a lack of self-love sets us up with neediness—we need more love than others because of our lack of self-love, so we become more demanding, often in ways that we don't even notice. We may drop hints to others in an effort to make them express their love, trying to reassure ourselves but ending up making them uncomfortable around us. If we don't love ourselves, we may make more self-deprecating statements, and those make anyone uneasy—after all, if we're able to cut ourselves down, what might we say about others?

When you love yourself you feel worthy and deserving
of claiming the gifts of this world. Self-love gives you
peace of mind and balance. Self-love gives you self-
respect and the ability to respect others. It gives you the
confidence to stand up and ask for what you want.
Self-love is the main ingredient in a successful, fulfilled life.

Debbie Ford

When we do feel comfortable with who we are and how we approach life, when we do feel the love and compassion for ourselves that we're meant to feel, we approach life in different ways—as Debbie says, we approach life with a confidence that we simply can't have without self-love. When we can respect ourselves, then we can extend that respect to others with little effort, and we won't feel the hopelessness of not being loved. And we won't be spending much time and effort trying to be loved, which makes our relationships much less stressful and much healthier.

So many things in life cannot fall into place without a sense of self-love. When we don't love ourselves, we put ourselves in positions in which success is much more difficult to achieve, in which fulfillment is an underground spring that we cannot find without the divining rod of love. When we tell ourselves that we are not even worthy of our own love, how can we possibly feel worthy of the love of others?

We receive mixed messages about taking good care of
ourselves. Love thy neighbor as thyself means to love
thyself and thy neighbor.
Yet, self-love often is confused with selfishness and
conceit. We are selfish when we do not love and accept
ourselves, and attempt to take from others to fill
the emptiness.
Conceit indicates low self-worth and an attempt to

conceal it. It is difficult to extend to others what you
have not been able to give yourself.
  Take good care of yourself so you can care
about the rest of us.

Jennifer James

Self-love is not hedonism, and it is not conceit. Self-love is a necessary quality if we want our lives to work, if we want to be able to reach our potential in any of the most important areas. We cannot be afraid to love ourselves if we want to live the full and fulfilling lives that we are meant to lead—we cannot let what we think other people would think of us change the ways in which we treat ourselves. What have you done today to show yourself love? Doing so isn't a question of indulging in every whim or desire; rather, it's a question of giving to yourself the same love, respect, and compassion that you know is important to give to others.

Questions about Loving Ourselves

1. Do you truly love yourself? Do you show it?

2. Why do so many people put a negative slant on the idea of loving ourselves? Why do they try to discourage other people from doing so?

3. What is one thing that you can do in the next hour that will be a reflection of your love for yourself?

Why It Used to Be Hard to Love Myself

  I grew up hearing lots of messages about how selfish it was to do things for ourselves, about how important it was to make other people happy before we try to make ourselves happy. I also heard a lot of criticism of me whenever I would make a mistake or do something "wrong." The result of these messages was that I became very critical of myself. Once I developed the self-criticism, I started to criticize myself pretty harshly, even in situations when the criticism wasn't warranted. For example, if I heard someone say "that guy is so nice," the little voice inside my head would say, "that must mean that I'm not as nice as he is."
  In all probability, the other person meant no criticism of me at all, but my lack of love for myself caused me to interpret their words as criticism. After all, it was easier for me to justify my own lack of self-love if I knew that others were

critical of me, too!

It took me a long time to realize what I was doing. This trait, in conjunction with other things going on in my life (such as having an alcoholic parent), caused me to sabotage myself in many ways. If I could teach young people anything at all useful, I would teach them to love themselves and to treat themselves well and to engage in positive self-talk as much as they can. I would want to do this to help them feel better about themselves and their lives, and to make it more likely that they will be able to help others in their lives by loving them fully.

Journal Entries

Day One: There are many lovable aspects of me: (I'm kind, I try to understand others, I try to do my best whenever I undertake a task.)

Day Two: What are some ways that I can show love to myself? (Take rests when needed, treat myself from time to time, respect my own likes and dislikes (say no to that invitation to something I don't like).)

Day Three: What are some of the obstacles I face when trying to love myself fully and sincerely? (Not knowing for sure what it means to do so, feelings that I don't deserve it, fear that I'm being selfish.)

Day Four: Write about a person you know who has a hard time loving her- or himself. Why does this person have difficulties? How does this difficulty show up in her or his life? (My uncle doesn't treat himself well at all, and he tends to be extremely critical of others as well.)

Day Five: How can I help others to feel more self-love? (Encouragement, sincere compliments, pointing out strengths rather than weaknesses.)

Nineteen

Motivation

I get very concerned about motivation, mostly because of the fact that I teach. I see many, many young people these days with almost no intrinsic motivation at all—they expect all of their motivation and fulfillment to come from outside of themselves. This is what we get, I suppose, from developing a society that thrives on passive entertainment and lack of personal achievement. These days, if it's not on the Internet it's not worth doing, it seems, and most of the young people I work with don't see much value at all in what they do, because there is no admiring world to give them likes or thumbs-ups.

Another big problem is that many young people are becoming convinced that money is the most important thing in the world, and they're motivated only by the desire to make a lot of it, thinking that with tons of money will come tons of happiness. And while money certainly can't cause unhappiness, it can't cause happiness, either—it may lower some stress levels and it may be very helpful in difficult situations, but happiness is something that isn't caused by something like money. Thus the motivation of money is one that is bound to lead to disappointment and a sense of emptiness once one realizes that what he or she has chased for so long really doesn't do what they thought it would.

*People who are unable to motivate themselves must
be content with mediocrity, no matter how
impressive their other talents.*

Andrew Carnegie

One thing that I notice over and over again among my students is that those who are able to motivate themselves are those who end up having a stronger sense of purpose than their peers have, who end up feeling better about themselves and who never sit around bored, wondering what they could possibly do with themselves. To them, there's always something interesting to do next, some new hobby to try, some old task to finish up. They take up things because they want to learn new ways of doing things, new perspectives on life. And they don't need someone else to tell them what to do—they're open to suggestions, usually, but they can find plenty to do on their own.

I spend much of my time as a teacher trying to develop a sense of intrinsic motivation in my students, for I know that if they're able to motivate themselves, they'll be able to accomplish pretty much whatever they wish in life. They'll be able to learn material in school because they want to know it, not because they have an assignment or because they're going to have a quiz on it. And they'll learn well whatever they need to learn; they won't settle for performing on a quiz and then forgetting what they've "learned."

Unfortunately, parents these days seem to be more and more distracted all the time, and they don't spend nearly as much time with their kids as parents used to. Because of this, most of them depend on extrinsic motivation in order to teach their children the life lessons that parents generally teach kids. And their extrinsic motivation usually consists of threats or rewards, neither one of which help the children to learn about motivating themselves, so that by the time they get to school, these kids really don't have any idea of what it means to do things because they really want to get better at whatever they undertake.

You can motivate by fear, and you can motivate by reward.
But both those methods are only temporary.
The only lasting thing is self motivation.

Homer Rice

How do you motivate yourself to do the things that you need to do? If you're filing, do you want to keep the files as clear and neat and accurate as possible, or do you simply want to get an annoying task out of the way? When you're cleaning, do you want the area to be as clean as it can possibly be, or do you just want to get done so that you can move on to something else? When you're finishing up a report, do you want to make it as accurate and effective as you possibly can out of personal pride, or are you just doing the bare minimum that you need to do to get by?

I've sat through presentations that obviously were the results of someone who wasn't at all motivated to give us the best they had, and I've sat through others to which someone obviously took a lot of pride in what he or she was doing. As a participant, I really appreciated the fact that someone was motivated enough to give us his or her best, for it helped me, too. The other presentations are usually nothing more than a handout or a Powerpoint presentation that I could have read myself and gotten everything out of the presentation.

If you hire someone to work for you, do you want someone who is self-directed and who is able to find work to do even during slow times? Most of us want to have the self-motivated person who isn't going to be coming to us all the time trying to find something to do, or who finishes one assigned task and then starts texting their friends or just hanging around doing nothing. And if you're the self-motivated person, you'll find that doors open to you because people appreciate not having to monitor you constantly—they can leave you on your own and do the work they need to do.

Where did we ever get the crazy idea that in order to make
children do better, first we have to make them feel worse?
Think of the last time you felt humiliated or treated unfairly.
Did you feel like cooperating or doing better?

Jane Nelson

What's going to motivate you today? Are you going to do your work because you want to do it well and have some pride in it, or is your paycheck going to be your major motivation? The answer to that question tells you a lot about yourself, and it tells others a lot about you. It also indicates your relationship to life, too, and just how much you're getting out of life. Our lives are full of opportunities and wonderful chances to do wonderful things, and it's only the self-motivated person who's going to find and enjoy most of those great opportunities. The person whose motivation has to come from outside him- or herself is only going to uncover the treasures that others direct them to—and believe me, others won't direct us to too many treasures when they could keep them for themselves.

Questions to Consider

1. What motivates you most? Why?

2. Among the people who have raised you, what do you notice are their major motivations for the things they do? How has that come to affect you?

3. Is most of your motivation intrinsic, or are you motivated more by the idea of rewards for your actions and behaviors?

A Short List of Possible Motivators

The desire to do a good job at something (intrinsic)
The desire to be praised for what I've done (extrinsic)
Earning money
The chance to learn something new
The desire to have other people admire you or what you've done
The desire to have a new experience or two
The desire to "pay someone back" in a positive way
The desire to "pay someone back" in a negative way
The desire to have peace of mind and feel good about myself

The hope of improving my life
The hope of improving the lives of others

Journal Entries

Day One: When you were growing up, how did the adults in your life try to motivate you? What was the result? (They offered rewards, I often expect rewards for things I shouldn't.)

Day Two: Think about someone you know who expects a reward of some kind for everything they do. What is that person's life like? (My brother seems very insecure and seems to be very dissatisfied, even after being praised for something.)

Day Three: What would life be like if we all had the desire to help others as our primary motivation, as opposed to trying to impress others?

Day Four: Is it possible to adopt new motivators if the ones we have now aren't effective? (My desire for praise isn't fulfilling, so I'll choose to be motivated by a desire to do well.)

Day Five: Is it possible to help others to recognize their own motivators that aren't effective, and to help them to adopt ones that are?

Twenty

Learning

I sincerely hope that I never stop learning until the day I die—and who knows what will happen from there on? More importantly, though, I hope that I never learn the desire to learn, and to actively seek out situations that will help me to do so. I definitely do not want to be a person who keeps doing things the same way just because I've always done them that way—that would be very similar to being dead for me, for then I would be stagnating without any growth or development at all in my life.

Because of our experience in public schools, unfortunately, most of us view learning as a passive activity—somebody tells us some information, and we "learn" it. Unfortunately, though, learning is actually an active process that we truly have to pursue if we're going to come anywhere close to actually reaching our learning potential. The good news is that learning is actually pretty easy— we've been doing it since infancy—and there are plenty of worthwhile and fascinating fields in the world about which we can learn an almost unlimited amount.

One of our most important decisions, though, is whether we want to learn only information, which involves memorization and which allows us only to repeat information, or we want to learn more productive ways of thinking critically and processes that will allow us to do many things other than spewing forth information and random facts.

Learning is not attained by chance. It must be sought
for with ardor and attended to with diligence.

Abigail Adams

No matter what we want to learn, we are blessed to be living in an era in which learning is possible at almost any level on almost any subject. We have libraries full of books and an Internet and foundations developed for certain fields and an incredible communications web available whenever we decide to use them. There are more college courses available on more subjects than we could ever really count. Unfortunately, as the availability of learning opportunities increases, it seems that the number of excuses for not learning also rises.

We can learn only if we wish to learn, and only if we put ourselves into situations in which we can learn. If we continue to do the same things in the same ways, over and over again, then we can't expect much learning to happen at all. As a teacher, I witness many students who come to class unwilling and not ready to learn—they think the ways they do things already are fine, and they don't see or feel any need to change anything they do. These are people who will stay at the same level in pretty much everything they do, never growing past their current levels of knowledge and ability—and this is a shame, for they're ensuring that they never reach the amazing potential that they have.

You know that I don't believe that anyone has ever taught anything
to anyone. I question the efficacy of teaching. The only thing
that I know is that anyone who wants to learn will learn. And maybe
a teacher is a facilitator, a person who puts things down and shows
people how exciting and wonderful it is and asks them to eat.

Carl Rogers

Another problem that we have with learning, though, is that we seem to assume that we learn naturally if we're in the right situations. Learning, though, usually takes work, and it often takes a systematic effort that most people haven't learned how to apply. It's a process of paying attention to what we want to learn, and then finding ways to internalize that information so that we don't simply forget it. We all have the potential to learn, but not all of us have the tools available to do so, for we either haven't been exposed to those tools, or we didn't pay much attention when they were introduced to us.

In many ways, our school systems hurt our learning abilities more that they help them. We've set up a system that for many young people is a social experience rather than an educational one, and one that often relies on the punishment of bad grades as a threat to "encourage" learning. We don't tend to teach effective study skills there, nor do we help young people to develop the intrinsic motivation necessary to be successful and effective learners. Our school systems also regularly assume that everyone can learn the same material in the same way, and really, nothing could be further from the truth. We each learn effectively in our own individual ways, and many of us are turned off of learning because of our "failures" in learning in ways that someone else has determined that we should learn.

But no matter what school did to us or for us, we always have the opportunity to redirect ourselves and our efforts towards more effective learning in areas that truly interest us—but we have to want to do so if we're going to learn.

Place yourself among those who carry on their lives with passion,
and true learning will take place, no matter how humble or
exalted the setting. But no matter what path you follow, do

not be ashamed of your learning. In some corner of your life,
you know more about something than anyone else on earth.
The true measure of your education is not what you know,
but how you share what you know with others.

Kent Nerburn

Our ability to learn new things and new ideas and new information is one of the greatest gifts involved with being human. It's a tragedy that so many people choose not to learn because they're afraid that they may find out that what they know already hasn't necessarily been right. They choose instead to hold on to their mistaken beliefs and ideas, afraid to let them go and move on to new knowledge and new ways of seeing and doing things. If we're ever to reach our potential as human beings and as a race, we must make learning one of the highest priorities of our lives, and we must allow people to learn what they will in the ways that they learn most effectively themselves.

Learn today, and enrich your life. It doesn't matter what you learn, just be sure that you allow something new into your thoughts and your knowledge base. If you're looking to make your life richer and fuller and more fulfilling, then actively pursuing learning is one of the most effective ways of expanding your perspective, your tolerance, your compassion, your understanding, your love, and your life.

Questions to Think about

1. In what situations do we actually reject learning in order to hold on to beliefs that we've held for a long time?

2. In which ways do you learn best? Do you try to do your learning in those ways, or do you simply try to learn in the ways that are offered?

3. What can happen to us in life if we stop learning?

How Do You Learn?

Many people give up on learning because they find it so difficult when they're in school—what they're supposed to learn just doesn't stick, and they receive punishment in the form of low grades for that fact. When they start playing a game, though, they're able to pick up on the rules quickly and easily—because a different learning style is called for, one that doesn't ask them to read and to memorize and to repeat information back to others.

Many a young person has learned a valuable trade through apprenticeships, where they're learning in a completely hands-on way, actually doing the task that they're learning. I learned how to lay carpets this way over the course of a month one summer, and the lessons have never left me. I learned how to make a lamp in wood shop, and now, several decades later, I could still easily make a lamp if I needed to (and I find it very easy to repair them now that I know how to make them).

Some learn best kinesthetically, some learn best by listening, some learn best by seeing. I love to read books, but I absolutely hate listening to audiobooks. I like watching movies, but I don't enjoy watching plays. If everything I wanted to know in life were set to music, I could learn it all quickly and easily (as long as it was music I liked!).

So what's the point? It's quite simple—never give up on learning something until you've tried to learn it in several different ways. You may read ten books on a subject and still not get it, but understand it completely after an hour-long conversation with someone who knows the subject well. Give yourself a chance. Re-try one strategy after you've tried others; perhaps the extra information that you've learned will help you to learn better in that way.

Anyone who tells you that everyone learns in the same way is selling a lie. You have your own unique ways of learning, and you owe it to yourself to explore them. Find your strengths and work from there. Give yourself the best chance to learn that you can. Then, if you finally still can't learn something, move on. Personally, I've never learned advanced mathematics like calculus, and though I tried for a long time to learn to play the piano, it never came to me. And I'm okay with both facts. There are many other things that I do very well, so not learning in those two fields isn't a great loss by any means.

Journal Entries

Day One: What have been some of your most frustrating learning experiences? What made them frustrating? How could they have been better?

Day Two: Write about something that you've learned that was extremely easy for you. What made it easy? Could you use that learning strategy for other things? (I learned how to play baseball by joining a team and playing when I was a kid. Some things could be learned that way, but others can't.)

Day Three: Write about how your life could change if you were able to learn things more quickly and easily. What kinds of things would you try to learn?

Day Four: How might you help other people to recognize how they best learn?

What would some advantages be, for example, if you were to help your child explore different strategies for learning until you found his or her most effective method?

Day Five: What do you want to learn? Why aren't your learning it now?

Twenty-One

Hope

I've always had a bit of an adversarial relationship with hope. I used to not believe in it at all, except to consider it as an impostor, something not trustworthy and not smart to entertain. Given the situation in which I grew up, this perspective isn't surprising to me. Thankfully I've grown through that perspective, and I now consider hope to be one of the most important parts of my life, as well as of the lives of everyone I know. Hope allows us to grow, to move forward, to seek, and hope allows us to make our lives richer by having something to strive for outside of and beyond our normal daily existence.

I think that most of us remember more the hopes that have been dashed to pieces rather than the hopes that have come to be reality in our lives. After all, it seems to be much easier to remember the disappointments because we remember hurts much more strongly than we remember good things. When we get hurt, we try to develop strategies for avoiding hurt in the future, but if things turn out well, we don't necessarily need to develop any strategies at all, do we?

This is a shame, because our hope is something that we should actively nourish, just as we should feed any part of ourselves that needs nourishment, from our bodies to our spirits. The fact that we don't do this hurts us, even though it's something that should be very easy to do. I've hoped to get work and I've found it; I've hoped to be able to see different places, and I've been able to visit them; I've hoped that good things would come for loved ones, and good things have, indeed, come to pass. So why do I not remember these good things and allow them to bolster my hope, to build it up to be stronger than ever?

Take from people their wealth, and you hinder them;
take from them their purpose, and you slow them down.
But take from them their hope, and you stop them.
They can go on without wealth, and even without purpose,
for awhile. But they will not go on without hope.

C. Neil Strait

I think that part of our problem is our need to see verifiable evidence that our hope has been justified. We need to KNOW that what we hoped for has come to be, and we need to be able to point our fingers at the evidence and say, "Look, there's proof that my hope wasn't useless!" But we can't usually do that, can we? And this is where faith comes in—not necessarily religious or spiritual faith, but faith in life and the laws of life. Faith that when we do good, we're inviting more good into our lives. Faith that even though we can't see positive results, those positive results still have occurred.

It's much easier said than done. In fact, hope is one of the easiest things in our lives to lose, because it is so hard to define and impossible to quantify. When we hoped that today would be a better day and it's turned out to be even worse than yesterday was, what does that tell us about hope? That it's misplaced and misguided and not at all helpful? Or that no matter what we hope, life is going to go ahead and do what life wants? These are easy traps to fall into with our thinking, and it's usually that thinking that causes us to lose hope.

Whenever I feel my hope starting to wane, I have several things that I remind myself that help me to hold on to it. First of all, I remind myself that the tide will not turn until it's reached its lowest point—in fact, it *can not* turn until then. And I stop thinking in terms of days—I know that things will turn when they're supposed to turn, and I will be okay sometime soon. There will be signs that I need to look out for that things will be okay, and I can't ignore those signs (something that I tend to do when I'm feeling a lack of hope and thus am more prone to feeling self-pity).

Hope is both the earliest and the most indispensable virtue
inherent in the state of being alive. . . . If life is to be sustained
hope must remain, even where confidence is wounded, trust impaired.

Erik H. Erikson

I also remind myself that untold numbers of people have gone through similar situations to those I'm going through, and they've come out of it fine, even better than before. And I'm really not at all different from them—I go through difficult situations and I experience the loss of hope, but eventually I will be fine. When we read about how people have kept their hope in the worst of times and how their lives have turned out because they didn't lose their hope, we have role models who have taught us the value in maintaining our hope, no matter what. Many people have gone through far worse experiences than I'll ever imagine, and they've come through bruised and battered, but they've made it because they didn't give up on hope.

When we have hope for the future, hope for change and for better things, we have an indispensable tool that can act as a catalyst to help us to act in hopeful ways. When we're distressed because we were laid off and we've filled out twenty job applications with no luck, hope is what makes us fill out applications twenty-one and twenty-two, because we know that even if it takes thirty, we'll never get that job unless we do fill out thirty. Hope is what has us go to marriage counseling instead of giving up; it's what has us start that novel even though we're not sure we can write that much; it's what allows us to buy all the ingredients to that dinner that we've wanted to try to make.

Hope works in these ways: it looks for the good in people
instead of harping on the worst; it discovers what can be done
instead of grumbling about what cannot; it regards problems,
large or small, as opportunities; it pushes ahead when it would
be easy to quit; it "lights the candle" instead of "cursing the darkness."

unattributed

Hope changes our perspective, but only when we let it. When we allow hope to be an important part of our lives, we give ourselves a real chance to see the beauty and the opportunity in life, and we give ourselves a real chance to find opportunity in what seem to be even the most dismal situations. We have to be careful what we hope for, of course—hoping for a win in the lottery or for a new relationship to start tomorrow are two things that are bound to lead to disappointment. We also have to be careful not to have unrealistic expectations, especially of other people, for those will usually lead to disappointment. But when we combine our hope for what may be in our lives with the action necessary to make those things happen, we develop a strategy of life that will definitely lead to fuller and richer lives.

Questions to Consider

1. When in life have you felt the most hopeful about life in general? Least hopeful? What contributed to these two extremes?

2. Is hope a friend that you keep close by, or an enemy that you keep at a distance?

3. Why is it so easy to give up on hope for good after only one or a few disappointments?

Thoughts on Hope

We all have hope. Sometimes, oddly enough, we don't want to admit it—to others or to ourselves—but no matter how bad things get in our lives, we have hope. It's one of the greatest gifts that we've been given, for out of hope come all of our scientific and medical advances — why even start trying something new if there's no hope for a successful outcome? Hope is what keeps us going on those dark, dark nights in our lives when it seems as if the sun never again will shine, but we have to give hope its due; we have to let its light shine in our lives if it's to do any good. We have to tell ourselves that things will get better, that life will radiate its beauty in our lives once more, if we but let it.

Hope never dies in us, yet often we cover its light, or we cover our ears so that we won't hear it sing its song. But that's like turning off a lamp when we most need its light, or shutting the door on a best friend when we most need company. We were created to be hopeful creatures, to look at the possibilities in the world and in ourselves, yet many of us aren't willing to do so, and we deny that there's even hope in the world, and once we deny the existence of hope, we start living dull, lightless lives that serve no one — ourselves or those who surround us. To live is to hope, and to hope is to live.

Personally, I remember that even during my darkest depressions, I've always felt the flame of hope, no matter how tiny it seemed to be. The problem was that all of the negative thoughts that were my depression kept arguing against the hope, calling it stupid, telling me that it was unrealistic and unjustified. The hope inside of me was like the one person who is willing to stand up with a voice of reason against a mob, only to be attacked by that mob and left for dead. Thankfully, it didn't die, or I might have.

When the voice of hope speaks inside of you, listen closely. The voice of hope is the voice of God, the voice of all the wonderful people with whom we share this world, the voice of truth and reality. It's those other voices inside of you, the voices of despair and condemnation and hopelessness, that are the liars. Call them what they are, and give them no credence. It's hope that springs eternal. These other things are temporary parts of ourselves that we have to learn to reject, like someone renting our house who not only isn't paying their rent, but who's destroying the house. To restore peace and equilibrium, we have to get rid of the renter and restore the hope of better days to come.

Journal Entries

Day One: Write down what you would tell a child if that child asked you what hope is. What would you tell that child if he or she asked you if they should have hope for his or her future?

Day Two: Explore the ways that you either foster or destroy hope in other people. Do you have the power to strengthen or weaken another person's hope? Which do you do? How?

Day Three: Religions are supposed to bring hope to us. How can they do so? In reality, do they usually actually do so?

Day Four: How do you feel when other people try to undermine your hope? When has it happened? What did the others do? (It frustrates me because I feel that the person is more interested in bringing me down than helping me; it's happened to me when people have said things like "Be more realistic," or "That's never going to happen.")

Day Five: Is it possible to build hope in small increments? Explore how you might do so.

Twenty-Two

Prayer

I've always had a strange relationship with prayer in general, probably because I learned early the "religious" perspective on prayer, the perspective that tells us that prayer "should be" this and should be that. Religions, unfortunately, have put so many rules on prayer that it's almost impossible to be a part of a religion and feel the freedom of prayer as a dialogue between us and God (whatever we perceive God to be) rather than as a highly structured, highly stressful set of rules and regulations that probably will fail because of our own lack of piety. It's rather sad, really, just how many people are disappointed in prayer because the rules that they've followed haven't provided the desired results.

One of the greatest obstacles that I felt to my prayer life was the idea that if you pray for anything, if your faith is strong enough then you will get it. I can't begin to list the things I used to pray for but didn't get—any list would be completely inadequate. But when I prayed for something and didn't get it, then the fault had to be mine, according to religious teachings, because my faith wasn't strong enough. It was a Catch-22 situation, especially when I prayed for stronger faith: of course my faith wouldn't grow because my faith wasn't strong enough for my prayer to be answered.

Fortunately I've grown out of that without any real lasting damage. I've learned that the most important element of prayer is not what words I use or what form I use or what position my body is in when I pray, but my sincere desire to connect with God and life and my willingness to be open and honest, both in what I say and in the ways that I listen.

Never will I pray for the material things of the world. I am not calling to a servant to bring me food. I am not ordering an innkeeper to provide me with room. Never will I seek delivery of gold, love, good health, petty victories, fame, success, or happiness. Only for guidance will I pray, that I may be shown the way to acquire these things, and my prayer will always be answered.

Og Mandino
The Greatest Salesman in the World

Personally, my favorite form of prayer is simply to go for a long walk and have a talk with God. It's nothing dramatic and I don't follow any scripts or formulas, but it does keep my mind conscious of the fact that there truly is more to life than what I see around me and what happens to me. When I talk to God, I'm reminded always of the qualities that we ascribe to God—love, hope, peace, compassion—and how those are qualities that I should be striving to show to every person in my life. During my walks, I tell God what I'm feeling, what I'd like to accomplish, things I'd like to be able to do, and other things like that.

Most importantly, though, I don't ask God for any of those things. I don't ask God for the money to do something—I simply ask God to be with me to help me to be able to do the things I need to do to accomplish my goals. God's a pretty good companion to have, for focusing on his presence helps us to stay focused on hope, and when we focus on hope, we can accomplish almost anything we set our minds to.

Prayer is not a manipulative strategy. I remember reading a book once in which a man on a plane prayed about a woman he knew, telling God that if she was the right one for him, God should have her bake a pie for him. When the plane landed, she was waiting there with a pie that she had baked just for him. I remember feeling very uncomfortable with this attitude—that God is a servant for us, that we can get him to do special things for us just by asking. My guess is that he had heard her mention baking a pie, but that he had forgotten it, or that he had heard her tell someone else that she was going to bake one, but had been focusing on something else at the time so the fact didn't make its way into his conscious mind.

When we consider God to be a servant who's supposed to do things for us, then we're setting ourselves up for disappointment. Yes, we are supposed to ask for specific things, but why would God give you that job but not the other three people who have applied? Praying for God to "give" us something like that over other people isn't going to have the effect of God making a decision that you're more deserving. It may come to pass, but it doesn't do so because God favors you over others—God loves all of us equally, and there will be something else waiting in the wings for those others.

When you embrace the mystery and open yourself to it, a new life is created, resistant to the old problems. You will notice at times that the new life isn't what you asked for. But asking for specific items or for particular events to occur isn't how I define prayer. I cannot guarantee that the orders you place with God will always be filled. Prayer is not a test of God, but a call for help to find your inner strength and talent.

Bernie Siegel

It's been well said that prayer doesn't change God, but it changes those of us who pray. Making prayer an important part of each day helps to remind us that there is more to life than our senses tell us, and that we actually do have the ability to tap into the universal consciousness that is God—we can become stronger people and more compassionate people by asking for the strength and the courage to live our lives right, to live our lives in ways that are beneficial to others, to be role models that other people can see and hope to emulate themselves. If we're peaceful people, others will want to know how we've become peaceful. If we're compassionate, they'll want to tap into that compassion, too.

Prayer does change us, as Alexis says below. It does give us strength, and that's something important to keep in mind. Some people grow frustrated and stressed out when they forget to stay in touch with their higher power, because they try to do everything themselves without any guidance. It's like having a book of directions and never opening it—it does us no good at all unless we access its contents. Likewise, our relationship with God has amazing potential, but if we never tap into that potential, it all will be completely lost—tons of potential that's simply wasted.

Prayer is the most powerful form of energy one can generate. The influence of prayer on the human mind and body is as demonstrable as that of the secreting glands. Prayer is a force as real as terrestrial gravity. It supplies us with a flow of sustaining power in our daily lives.

Alexis Carrel

And of course, one of the most important elements of prayer is listening to and recognizing the answers that come to us while we pray and after we pray. Sometimes our prayers are actually answered for us, yet we don't recognize the response because it comes in a form that we didn't expect—or we simply wanted it in some other way. We must be aware that responses to prayer may seem to be completely different than what we think we want, but will be what's best for us, and better for us than the way we expected to see the response.

There really are no rules to prayer. It's kind of astonishing that some people can tell us that they ways that they pray are the ways that we should pray— we're all unique individuals with unique ways of thinking and seeing the world, and it only makes sense that our relationships with God will be different, too. There are some prescribed prayers that we definitely can use to help us to get focused, or that we can use when things are hectic and we just want to take a quick prayer break, but for the most part, our prayers should come from our hearts, not from our heads. And when we learn to pray that way and trust our prayers, then we'll see how our prayer lives can positively affect our lives overall, and we'll find that life becomes a more beautiful experience overall.

Questions to Consider

1. What did Mohandas Gandhi mean when he said that prayer is "the most potent instrument of action"?

2. What would your life be like if your prayer practices were stronger? If they were weaker?

3. Why do so many people teach that a strong prayer life is important if we want to live our lives fully?

A Pair of Poems on Prayer

1. I asked God for strength, that I might achieve;
I was made weak, that I might learn humbly to obey. . .

I asked for health, that I might do greater things;
I was given infirmity, that I might do better things. . .

I asked for riches, that I might be happy;
I was given poverty, that I might be wise. . .

I asked for power, that I might have the praise of men;
I was given weakness, that I might feel the need of God. . .

I asked for all things, that I might enjoy life;
I was given life that I might enjoy all things. . .

I got nothing that I asked for—but everything I had hoped for;
Almost despite myself, my unspoken prayers were answered.
I am, among all people, most richly blessed.

unattributed

2. I got up early one morning
And rushed right into the day;
I had so much to accomplish

That I didn't have time to pray.
Problems just tumbled about me,
And heavier came each task;
"Why doesn't God help me?" I wondered.
He answered, "You didn't ask."
I wanted to see joy and beauty,
But the day toiled on gray and bleak;
I wondered why God didn't show me.
He said, "But you didn't seek."
I tried to come into God's presence;
I used all my keys in the lock.
God gently and lovingly chided,
"My child, you didn't knock."
I woke up early this morning,
And paused before entering the day;
I had so much to accomplish
That I had to take time to pray.

unattributed

Journal Entries

Day One: Pretend that a friend has asked you about your prayer life. Explain it to that friend, completely honestly. Is it what you want it to be? If not, how could it be improved?

Day Two: What do you know about prayer now that you didn't know while you were growing up? How have you learned these things?

Day Three: A young child has asked you how he's supposed to pray. Write a response.

Day Four: How much of the time that you devote to prayer do you spend listening for responses from God? Do you believe that such responses come?

Day Five: What, to you, is the main value of prayer? (It helps me to focus my thoughts in a positive way on needs that I have.)

Twenty-Three

Beauty

This world is full of beauty. It's full of things and places and people and animals who share their beauty with us each day—but unfortunately, we've been conditioned over the course of our lives not to see that beauty any longer, if we ever noticed it in the first place. And therein lies the problem with beauty: it has tremendous potential to make our lives richer, yet it can only do when and if we notice it and appreciate it. So the problem with beauty lies not in the beautiful object or person, but in ourselves and our lack of awareness and gratitude.

Beauty is, they say, in the eye of the beholder. But this isn't necessarily true. While there are some works of art or industry, for example, that one person may find beautiful and another may find horribly ugly, the fact that I don't see something as physically attractive does not mean that it is devoid of beauty. This is especially true in people—our society teaches us that certain types of looks are more beautiful than others, so it's very easy to miss the beauty in a person whose looks don't match the societal "ideal." And this is a huge shame because if we're unable to see the beauty in other people who are, indeed, beautiful, then our lives are much, much poorer.

The fact that we can't see the beauty in something doesn't suggest
that it's not there. Rather, it suggests that we are not looking carefully
enough or with a broad enough perspective to see it.

Richard Carlson

Seeing beauty isn't necessarily all that easy, though. I've known many people who do their best to hide their beauty, often simply because they don't think they're beautiful at all. They hide their talents and abilities, and they show the world their hardness or their anger, and that's a facade that is very often difficult to see through. Some young girls who have been made to feel ugly learn to dress and act in unattractive ways; some young boys who don't feel at all beautiful do their best to make themselves ugly, either through their actions or their clothing or their hygiene.

But beauty is an important part of our world, and thus an important part of our lives. And beauty is something that we all share, both in its possession and in the enjoyment we get from it. If I'm able to see your beauty clearly—in your eyes or your smile or your words or your actions, then my life is richer. If you're able to see mine, your life is richer. If I hide my beauty, though, I won't be making your life even the slightest bit more positive.

Most of us need to make an effort to be able to see beauty more easily. It makes me feel awful to think of how often I've taken people for granted as just "ordinary" people with no real beauty, only to see later that their beauty was amazing—it was just somewhere that I hadn't even thought of looking. My own judgmental attitude and inability to recognize something that was right in front of my eyes kept me from experiencing some amazing things. It's taken me a long time to learn to actively seek a person's beauty, or a town's beauty, or a work of art's beauty, but nowadays I think that if I don't see the beauty immediately, that's a sign that the beauty is probably going to be more extraordinary than superficial beauty usually is.

People should hear a little music, read a little poetry,
and see a fine picture every day of their lives, in order
that worldly cares may not obliterate the sense of the
beautiful which God has implanted in the human soul.

Johann Wolfgang von Goethe

Far too often, we consider superficial beauty to be the true indicator of beauty, and that's far from the case. Yes, the spectacular sunset is beautiful, but the less dramatic sunsets have their own subtle beauty, too. Some trees don't seem to be nearly as beautiful as others, yet what they contribute to the planet is necessary and, therefore, beautiful. Sometimes we need to look very closely at things to see the beauty of their intricacy, while other times we may be looking too close and we should back up a bit to see the beauty in the bigger picture.

The appreciation of beauty is a gift that we should not squander. But it's also a gift that we should not allow to be affected by the superficial mores of our culture—we should not let other people define beauty for us. If we do so, we're making our lives poorer, for then we will lost out on much beauty that remains unrecognized and unappreciated. When we're able to recognize beauty, we then allow wonder and awe to be an important part of our lives, and these two attributes also contribute much to a healthy and fulfilling life.

If we actively make an effort to allow beauty to be an important part of our lives, then we can enrich our lives ourselves. And if we make sure that we define beauty ourselves, based on our instincts and our personal tastes, we won't spend a lot of time wondering why we don't feel the same way about a particular object or person that other people feel. As Jean says below, the appreciation of beauty opens doors to our souls, and those are doors that always should be open.

*As I experience it, appreciation of beauty is access to
the soul. With beauty in our lives, we walk and carry
ourselves more lightly and with a different look in our
eyes. To look into the eyes of someone beholding beauty
is to look through the windows of the soul. Anytime we
catch a glimpse of soul, beauty is there; anytime we catch
our breath and feel "How beautiful!," the soul is present.*

Jean Shinoda Bolen

I've reached a point at which I can see beauty in almost everything, even litter
on the highway (in its texture or shape or form) or other things that don't seem
to have any inherent beauty. (Of course, I pick up all the litter I can, because
even if it does have some beauty, the natural state of a place is usually better.)
In being able to recognize and appreciate the beauty in the world in which I
live, I've given myself a tool that can help me to feel better when I feel down,
that can help to elate me when I need to feel elation, that can brighten a dull
day or make even brighter a day already bright. Seeing and appreciating
beauty is a gift that I can give to myself whenever I feel the need. And when I
do this, my life is brighter and my spirit soars, knowing that I'm not neglecting it
at all.

Questions to Think about

1. Why is beauty so important in our lives? Do we really appreciate that
importance as much as we could or should?

2. Why do so few people seem to believe that beauty isn't relative, that each
person considers different things to be beautiful?

3. What effect does something that's truly beautiful have on you?

A Poem on Beauty from Ella Wheeler Wilcox

The search for beauty is the search for God,
*   Who is All Beauty. He who seeks shall find;*
And all along the paths my feet have trod,
*   I have sought hungrily with heart and mind*
*   And open eyes for beauty everywhere.*
*   Lo! I have found the world is very fair.*
The search for beauty is the search for God.

Beauty was first revealed to me by stars.
　Before I saw it in my mother's eyes,
Or, seeing, sensed it beauty, I was stirred
To awe and wonder by those orbs of light,
　All palpitant against empurpled skies.
They spoke a language to my childish heart
Of mystery and splendor and of space,
Friendly with gracious, unseen presences.
Beauty was first revealed to me by stars.

Sunsets enlarged the meaning of the word.
　There was a window looking to the west:
Beyond it, wide Wisconsin fields of grain,
And then a hill, whereon white flocks of clouds
　Would gather in the afternoon to rest.
And when the sun went down behind that hill,
What scenes of glory spread before my sight—
What beauty—beauty, absolute, supreme!
Sunsets enlarged the meaning of that word.

Clover in blossom, red and honey-sweet,
　In summer billowed like a crimson sea
Across the meadow lands. One day, I stood
Breast-high amidst its waves, and heard the hum
　Of myriad bees that had gone mad like me
With fragrance and with beauty. Over us,
A loving sun smiled from a cloudless sky,
While a bold breeze kissed lightly as it passed
Clover in blossom, red and honey-sweet.

Autumn spoke loudly of the beautiful,
　And in the gallery of Nature hung
Colossal pictures hard against the sky,
Set forests gorgeous with a hundred hues,
　And with each morning some new wonder flung
Before she startled world—some daring shade,
Some strange, new scheme of color and of form.
Autumn spoke loudly of the beautiful.

Winter, though rude, is delicate in art—
　More delicate than summer or than fall
(Even as rugged Man is more refined
In vital things than Woman). Winter's touch

On Nature seemed most beautiful of all—-
That evanescent beauty of the frost
On window-panes, of clean, fresh-fallen snow,
Of white, white sunlight on the ice-draped trees.
Winter, though rude, is delicate in art.

Morning! The word itself is beautiful,
    And the young hours have many gifts to give
That feed the soul with beauty. He who keeps
His days for labor and his nights for sleep
    Wakes conscious of the joy it is to live,
And brings from that mysterious Land of Dreams
A sense of beauty that illumines earth.
Morning! The word itself is beautiful.

The search for beauty is the search for God.

Journal Entries

Day One: Define beauty in your own words. Make a list of things that you find beautiful, through all your senses (flowers, music, the feel of a dog's fur, etc.).

Day Two: If the world is completely full of beauty at every turn, why do we see so little of it? List a few of the obstacles that keep you from seeing and appreciating beauty. (Being busy or in a hurry, my own prejudices and judgmentalism.)

Day Three: How might we go about teaching children to recognize and appreciate beauty? (Spend time with them pointing out beautiful things, letting them know that it's okay to think that something's beautiful (especially boys!).)

Day Four: Make a list of things that you can do to add to the beauty of the world in your own small ways.

Day Five: How might my perspective on the world and life change if I make a conscious effort to focus on beauty?

Twenty-Four

Today

To me, the beauty in each day lies largely in its potential. Each day comes to us new and fresh, with a huge number of opportunities to do with the day as we will, to make the best of all the situations that we're given, to create new situations and to begin new projects and friendships. Sure, very often we try to do these things and they don't work out, but that truly doesn't matter—we've had the chance to try, and in trying we've learned and grown and made it more likely that tomorrow—when our newest today enters our lives—we'll be able to do something new and different and exciting based on what we learned today.

Sometimes my todays are quite run-of-the-mill, but I've learned to really like those, to be honest. Days when I have chores to do like laundry and filing bills and cleaning a room can be very relaxing and productive, for they usually leave me feeling relieved that a job that was hanging over my head is now done, leaving me free to do something else without thinking about whatever it was that was hanging over my head. Sometimes a day in the park isn't as fun when I know that there's a whole bunch of laundry or dishes just waiting for me to take care of them.

Somehow, we start to think that for a day to be special, we have to do something special—we have to go someplace we've never been, meet someone new, read a book we've been wanting to read for years, see the brand-new movie that everyone's talking about. But that's not the case at all. Some of our todays are in our lives to give us some rest, or to help us to get ready for the other todays that will include those special things. Some of my best days ever have been days that I've spent completely alone, puttering around the house, listening to music or enjoying the silence, maybe taking a nap now and then.

You wake up in the morning, and lo! your purse is magically filled with twenty-four hours of the unmanufactured tissue of the universe of your life. It is yours. It is the most precious of possessions. No one can take it from you. It is unstealable. And no one receives either more or less than you receive.

Arnold Bennett

Some of my other best days have been spent at amusement parks with my family, riding bikes with friends in Spain, climbing mountains in New England and eating wild blueberries that we've found there.

You see, there is no such thing as a "perfect" day. Almost any day can be perfect, depending on how we look at it and how we take what comes during its course. Sometimes we feel a bit of pressure to "make" today special, but often the day is special because of what it brings to us and how we accept that. Some days are hard because they bring us work or situations that are difficult to get through, but if we remember that our lives are defined by each present moment that passes and what we choose to do with it, then even the difficult days are very special days.

Today, I woke up in a bed, in a room that sheltered me from the outdoors and provided me with a safe and comfortable place to sleep. I had breakfast in a comfortable living room, I listened to music, I read a book, I did work on my computer and work in the yard, I spent time talking to my wife, I went to the store and bought food for dinner—I did many, many things that other human beings on this planet don't have the chance to do, and I realize that my today was very special, and I very much appreciate it.

It's very easy, though, to take a day like today for granted and not see the specialness in the ordinary, in the regular things that I do almost every day.

Live for today. Multitudes of people have failed to live
for today. . . . What they have had within their grasp
today they have missed entirely, because only the
future has intrigued them.

William Allen White

So if you can appreciate the gift of today, you're ready for the next step: deciding what you're going to give for today. This is where we start to create very special lives—when we decide that we're going to give to the world each day that we're alive. What will you contribute today? Kind words? Encouragement? Your best effort on the work that you do? Listening to someone who needs to be heard? A bit of money to someone who can use it?

What about love? Can you give some of that today, especially to people who aren't expecting it and who need it the most? You could also help to boost someone's sense of hope if you want to, or show appreciation for something that's been done well or done specifically for you.

One question that must be addressed always is the way we approach our days. Do we go through each day with no sense of direction, just allowing things to happen to us; do we allow our jobs and our responsibilities to determine what's going to happen each day; or do we take the time to make sure that we know what we're going to do with our day, making a plan—no matter how basic— that will guide us through our days and allow us to be productive on our terms? Sometimes having that basic plan can make our days much more fulfilling as we accomplish the things that we set out to do.

Anyone can radiate love for a day. Anyone can rise
above fear for a day and meet each new situation with courage.
Anyone can be kind and thoughtful and considerate for a day.
Anyone can endeavor to learn something new each day
and mark some growth. . . .
The supreme art of living is to strive to live each day well. . . .
Live a day at a time and remember that tomorrow is another today.

Wilferd A. Peterson

Today is a wonderful gift for each of us. Within its hours we have many chances for sharing, for giving, for loving, for being entertained, for sitting quietly and reflecting, for going for walks and appreciating the world around us. Let us make the most of today, for if we can do so each day, we'll find that we have weeks worth remembering, months to treasure, and years that we can look back on with great satisfaction. Your today still stretches out before you— what shall you do to make it special?

Questions to Consider

1. Why are we generally not taught how to seize our days?

2. How do we manage to focus more on yesterday and tomorrow than on today? How do fears and regrets play into the mix?

3. How much does your first hour of the day influence the rest of it?

Ancient Wisdom Concerning Today

Look to this day!
For it is life, the very life of life.
In its brief course lie all the verities
and realities of your existence:
The bliss of growth
The glory of action

The splendor of achievement,
For yesterday is but a dream
And tomorrow is only a vision,
But today well lived makes every yesterday
a dream of happiness
And tomorrow a vision of hope.
Look well, therefore, to this day!
Such is the salutation to the dawn.

from the Sanskrit

Journal Entries

Day One: Write a list of things that today offers that yesterday did not offer. How will you take advantage of those offers? (I can get something done that I couldn't do yesterday, I can call a friend I didn't call.)

Day Two: Explore the possible effects of focusing completely on today's needs and possibilities instead of thinking about the past or future. (Getting more done and doing it better and enjoying it more.)

Day Three: A friend has told you that someone just told her that she should focus on living each day fully, but she doesn't understand what that person meant. Write her a note explaining in your words what that means.

Day Four: What kinds of things can you do today to make your tomorrow better when it becomes today?

Day Five: Pay attention to your thoughts for one day, and then write down as many of them as you can remember. How many of them were on the past and how many on the future? Can you do anything about those thoughts of the past or future?

Twenty-Five

Friendship

Friendship has always been one of the weakest areas of my life, mostly because I grew up with parents who were pretty individualistic and who didn't value friendship all that much. I also grew up moving from place to place regularly (my father was in the military), so whenever I ended up making friends as a kid, we would eventually move away and I would lose all of my friendships. I learned not to trust that friendship would be lasting, and I learned that if I did become attached to people, I would just lose them. So by the time I hit young adulthood, I didn't really have any friend-making skills developed at all.

This, of course, has made life difficult for me in many ways, as friendship is one of the most important elements of a healthy and fulfilling life. I can't help but feel, though, that there's also been a blessing hidden in my past—the ability to truly value the friendships that I do have, and the ability to distinguish between a friendship and an acquaintanceship. Both of these abilities are very helpful to me, and I don't know that I would have them if I had grown up with steady friendships over long periods of time.

Be courteous to all, but intimate with few, and let those few be well tried before you give them your confidence. True friendship is a plant of slow growth, and must undergo and withstand the shocks of adversity before it is entitled to the appellation.

George Washington

Sometimes "friendships" form simply out of convenience, because we end up living next to someone we like or working with someone with whom we get along well. When this happens, it's a very good feeling, but one that we need to be careful of. When a friend falls into our lives like that, it's important that we remain discerning, and that we're careful of just how far we take a friendship of convenience. We need to be careful because with true friends we're able to make ourselves vulnerable and willing to share much that we don't share with others. As George Washington says, though, true friendship takes time to develop, but when we feel a quick friendship with someone, we tend to risk much more if we share things that should be shared only with good friends.

Many a person has been burned by supposed friends who very soon move on to someone else after they get tired of being with someone. And once they move on, they take with them the trustworthiness, the compassion—and everything that you've shared with them.

Friendship is so important to us, though, that we want to consider people as friends; we want to have the feeling that another person is close enough to us and cares enough for us that we're able to share important thoughts and feelings that we can't share with others. But we don't want what we've shared to come back and haunt us later because we've shared it with the wrong person.

A friend is one who joyfully sings with you when you are on the mountaintop, and silently walks beside you through the valley.

William A. Ward

True friends are people who accept us just as we are without harshly judging us, and they are people who stand beside us when we need support. There are plenty of people who are willing to spend time with you when things are going well, but there are very few who will be willing to share your difficult times with you, too. I believe it was Oprah Winfrey who pointed out the difference between the people who will ride in your limo with you and the people who are willing to ride the bus with you when the limo is gone. They're not all the same people.

When we go through difficult times, it's very comforting to have someone there with us, someone who can comfort us and help us to deal with whatever's going on in our lives. That kind of friendship, though, generally doesn't just happen—it's something that we have to work at if we want it to be strong. Friendships are just like anything else that's valuable to us—we need to care for them and give to them for them to grow. Just as a plant doesn't survive if we don't provide it with nutrients and water, friendship can't survive if we don't give to it.

It's been well said that in order to have friends, it's important that we make an effort first to be a friend. So all of the things that we feel we should be able to expect from friends are also things that they have every right to expect from us. A friend is someone who listens, who makes time for their friends, who tries to understand without judging, who wants the best for his or her friends. Joseph Levine wrote about a time when he was having health problems and many of his acquaintances sympathized with him, but his friends were the people who pushed him hard to adopt a healthy lifestyle that would take care of his issues. The true friends were the ones who took the risk by pushing him to improve himself, and who made the consistent effort of reminding him what he needed to do, even when he didn't necessarily want to do it.

*You can make more friends in two months by becoming
interested in other people than you can in two years of
trying to get other people interested in you.*

Dale Carnegie

Some people use the word "friend" to refer to everyone they know. While it can be a nice feeling to have someone call me "friend," I think it's not very helpful to overuse the word. Some people are acquaintances, and they should stay as such. And it's not an insult not to consider them as friends, as long as we know that we can generally expect much more from our friends—and that we're willing to give more to our friends. There are people to whom I would give unlimited amounts of my time, while there are others to whom I wouldn't give nearly as much.

The biggest barrier in my life to having friends is a feeling inside that people don't want to be friends with me, that they already have enough friends, that I'm somehow someone with whom they don't want to spend time or share their lives. Now that I'm older, I recognize these feelings as a result of my upbringing, but the feelings definitely have caused me to miss out on many potential friendships. It's a battle that I still fight, as I still struggle with these feelings regularly.

If I want to make friends, I need to be a friend. I need to listen more than I talk, and I need to truly learn from the listening—it can't be just polite listening, and I can't forget all that I hear five minutes after our conversation. I need to know about the other person's likes and dislikes, fears and dreams, hopes and frustrations. Being a friend involves really knowing someone else, and if I want to have friends in life, then I will make every effort to be a friend.

Questions on Friendship

1. What are some of the obstacles to making friends that you face?

2. Is it becoming easier or more difficult to have friends in our current technological age?

3. Who teaches us how to make friends and to keep them? Where did they learn their lessons?

On Friendship
Khalil Gibran

from *The Prophet*

And a youth said, "Speak to us of Friendship."
Your friend is your needs answered.
He is your field which you sow with love and reap with thanksgiving.
And he is your board and your fireside.
For you come to him with your hunger, and you seek him for peace.
When your friend speaks his mind you fear not the "nay" in your own mind, nor do you withhold the "ay."
And when he is silent your heart ceases not to listen to his heart;
For without words, in friendship, all thoughts, all desires, all expectations are born and shared, with joy that is unacclaimed.
When you part from your friend, you grieve not;
For that which you love most in him may be clearer in his absence, as the mountain to the climber is clearer from the plain.
And let there be no purpose in friendship save the deepening of the spirit.
For love that seeks aught but the disclosure of its own mystery is not love but a net cast forth: and only the unprofitable is caught.
And let your best be for your friend.
If he must know the ebb of your tide, let him know its flood also.
For what is your friend that you should seek him with hours to kill?
Seek him always with hours to live.
For it is his to fill your need, but not your emptiness.
And in the sweetness of friendship let there be laughter, and sharing of pleasures.
For in the dew of little things the heart finds its morning and is refreshed.

Journal Entries

Day One: Write down a list of things that you expect from your friends, and then write a list of things that you think your friends should expect from you. Are the lists the same?

Day Two: Think of a friend who has been there for you when you've needed him or her. Write a note to this friend thanking him or her for the friendship.

Day Three: What are some of the differences between how you saw friendship as a kid and how you see friendship now?

Day Four: Why do so many people seem to be afraid to have friends? Why would someone avoid friendship?

Day Five: Imagine that you just met someone with whom you'd like to be friends. What kinds of steps would you take to try to make the friendship work?

Twenty-Six

Balance

It took me a long while to realize that much of my early life was characterized by a lack of balance in almost all things. As a child, I had no one around who was able to teach me the lessons I needed to know about balance, so I grew up without knowing just what balance is or how important it is in our lives. What I've come to learn is that balance is a result of my thinking and my decisions, and a life in balance is entirely within reach if I make an effort to keep this life of mine balanced.

Of course, we live in cultures in which advertising is one of the strongest influences in our lives, and one of the last things that advertisers want is for us to live balanced lives—if we eat moderately, for example, they sell us less food. If we buy a modest car and use the savings in another area of our lives, they make less profit. As we grow up, we learn lessons about acquiring and consuming more and more—and those lessons definitely do not encourage us to seek out balance. So one of the first things that we need to do if we want to lead balanced lives is to recognize the messages that we receive regularly and deal with them appropriately, modifying them or rejecting them in order to bring more balance to our own experiences on this planet.

You are one of the most important people you need to look
after and love. Balance your time, your energy, your life with
those around you. You'll be able to give more freely and joyfully
as a result, and you'll be more open to the gifts of the universe.
It's not wrong to give to others. But it's okay to say
yes to ourselves, too.

Melody Beattie

A lack of balance can be extremely detrimental to us for many different reasons. When we go too far toward one extreme or another, we set ourselves up for making huge mistakes or paying very high prices for our actions. How many people end up with problems like diabetes or heart disease because of a lack of balance in their diet? How many people are terrible stressed because they always make time for other people, but not for themselves? How many people pay a heavy price physically because they don't balance their days sitting in an office with physical activity?

It's important that we recognize our need for balance, first of all. Balance in our lives gives us a sense of peace, for when we know that we're balanced, we don't feel strong needs to extend ourselves past comfortable limits in order to feel better about ourselves or to fulfill needs that we perceive, but which possibly aren't legitimate needs at all. Perhaps we feel a need for acceptance, so we take on more tasks than we're comfortable with to try to fill that need, when the truth was that we already were accepted just as we are by most of the people in our lives. That's a typical example of putting ourselves out of balance for a perceived need rather than a legitimate need.

According to Chinese medicine, it is accepted as natural that we fluctuate from being in balance to being out of balance. Peace of mind comes from not attaching a great deal of significance to either state. We simply note our moods and physical states and gently move toward balance as best we can, accepting it all as part of the flow of life.

Charlotte Davis Kasl

Many people who take up sports, for example, respond to the initial rush of positive feelings from it by suddenly devoting huge portions of their time and money to the sport. They buy all the equipment that they didn't need at all just a few days before, and they commit themselves to hours of practice that weren't at all necessary just recently. Their time has suddenly fallen out of balance, and other things that they use to have time for now fall by the wayside and become neglected. I've watched this happen with a friend who took up karate, and two years later, all she had in her life, really, was karate— everything else was sacrificed as she devoted herself entirely to the sport while neglecting to keep her life in balance as she could have done.

"What's wrong with that?" you may ask, "as long as she's happy?" And it's a very good question—in her case, though, she was far from happy. She was quite lonely, and she wondered why the friends she used to have weren't her friends any longer. She turned down invitations to parties and get-togethers and other social activities because of her busy karate schedule, yet she couldn't see that she had lost her connections with her friends because she refused to balance her karate commitments with her other ones, and her social life suffered from a complete imbalance.

We have many areas in our lives in which we could and should strive for balance: finances, relationships, commitments, diet, exercise, television watching, time commitments—the list could keep on and on. But first of all we need to be able to step back and ask ourselves clearly and objectively: Are my efforts balanced in this area?

And if the answer is negative, we need to be willing to make some changes concerning that activity. We need to be able to look at what we're doing and figure out how to reach a greater balance overall. Do I ask too much from relationships, or do I give too much and ask too little? Do I balance my fat-laden desserts each week with other desserts that are healthier? After all, there's nothing wrong with a hot fudge sundae if we don't each one every day, and if we balance our sugar and fat intake with desserts that are better for us on different nights.

*The Amish love the Sunshine and Shadow quilt pattern. It shows
two sides—the dark and light, spirit and form—and the challenge of
bringing the two into a larger unity. It's not a choice between
extremes: conformity or freedom, discipline or imagination,
acceptance or doubt, humility or a raging ego. It's a
balancing act that includes opposites.*

Sue Bender

A balanced life is a rich life, indeed, for such a life is one that allows us to experience peace no matter what our situations, and hope no matter how dark things may seem, for when our lives are balanced, we realize that life, too, is balanced. While things may be difficult for a while, the brighter times will come; and we'll never take things for granted, for we know that days may come that can take those things from us. With decisions that we make about what we strive for and how we strive, we can reach the ideal that Confucius speaks of: the still water that is at peace.

*Balance is the perfect state of still water.
Let that be our model.
It remains quiet within and is not disturbed on the surface.*

Confucius

Questions about Balance

1. How do you define balance? Is your life balanced according to your definition?

2. In which areas of your life could you make the most significant changes in order to bring about a stronger balance?

3. Why is the concept of leading a balanced life not covered in our schools?

Thoughts about Balancing Our Lives

I did a search once for quotations on balance from the Buddha. I thought that if anyone would have talked a lot about balance, he would have. Interestingly enough, I found very few. It seems that the Buddha actually didn't talk much about balance. That's okay, of course, though it was quite surprising—after all, much of what the Buddha taught implies a sense of balance in our lives, a sense of making sure that we don't overdo some things while neglecting others.

And isn't that what balance is all about, anyway? If we spend too much time at work and too little time with family, then those parts of our lives are out of balance. And the problems that we think are "family problems" are actually "balance problems." When family members feel neglected or left out of your life, it's only natural that they'll let you know, one way or another. Since most people haven't been taught to express their feelings and emotions well, their ways of letting us know about this imbalanced state may include acting out, pulling away, starting arguments, feeling resentment, or any other behavior that we may see as problematic. The real problem, though, is not recognizing that the problem is originating in an imbalance.

Here's a small list of some places where imbalances often occur in our lives. Take it for what it is—a starting point. You can add any areas that you'd like, for there most definitely are many, many more.

Work/family; work/recreation; family/self; time with loved ones/time alone; exerting control/letting things go; spending on one thing/spending on others; activity/rest; school/family; time looking at screens/time experiencing the world; time on Facebook/time accomplishing things; time on phone/time with loved ones; eating junk food/eating healthy food; drinking coffee/drinking water; drinking alcohol/staying sober; talking about one topic/talking about others. . . . and on and on and on.

Journal Entries

Day One: In all of our lives, there's something out of balance, if only a slight bit. What's out of balance in your life? How does that affect you? What might you do to change the imbalance (if you even want to)? (I tend to eat more sweets than would be completely healthy for me. I do run a lot to burn off the sugars, so I'm not too concerned about this particular imbalance.)

Day Two: Think of three other people that you know, and write down one area of their lives in which you perceive they're out of balance. Does this imbalance affect them negatively or positively? What effects do you see from your perspective?

Day Three: Consider a relationship you're in. Is it in balance? How is it out of balance? What would have to happen to restore the balance? (In one particular relationship, all of the conversations are 95% about the other person, and they're quite frustrating; redirect the conversations (if possible) or greatly reduce their number.)

Day Four: Think about how your life would be if everything were in balance. Write down how you would feel about life if this were the case. (I would feel more peaceful and less in need of controlling situations.)

Day Five: How might you help other people find balance in aspects of their lives without sounding like you're trying to control them or their lives?

Twenty-Seven

Responsibility

I cannot live my life fully if I do not accept the responsibility that I have for my actions, my words, my reactions, my plans, the ways I treat other people. Our society teaches us often that we aren't responsible for things, that they're other people's fault, that we don't have to take responsibility if we don't want to. But we do have to do so if we want to live happy and fulfilling lives. Without recognizing, accepting, and living up to our responsibilities, we end up as empty shells of people, wondering why the world is treating us poorly.

The good news, though, is that we can start to take responsibility and live up to it at any moment in our lives, no matter what our circumstances. And once we do that, we start feeling better about ourselves, we gain more confidence and self-respect, and we start to learn more and better ways of dealing with life and living in all its pain and glory.

There are several types of responsibility that we need to be aware of. The first is the responsibility for our own lives, for being aware that we ourselves—and no one else—are responsible for ourselves and our own happiness. We can't go through life moaning about how unfair life is or whining about how others get more or better chances than we do. We have to face life full on and if we don't see chances, we need to make them. And if we don't know how to make them, we need to learn how—and there are plenty of books and programs out there that can teach us how to do just that. Money problems? Learn about money and how to make more of it and how to budget it and save it. Relationship problems? Learn how to deal with people more effectively; learn about your own unrealistic expectations of others that may be keeping you from having deep and fulfilling relationships.

The willingness to accept responsibility for one's own life
is the source from which self-respect springs.

Joan Didion

It can be very easy to decide that all of our problems are caused by outside sources, and that we're not responsible for our own misery or unhappiness. When we stop blaming others, though, that doesn't mean that we start blaming ourselves. The blame game is a destructive one, and it doesn't help us to grow or advance at all. Taking responsibility for ourselves doesn't mean that we beat ourselves up for our mistakes—rather, it means that we carefully and thoughtfully examine where we are and how we are, and then make decisions about how we're going to adjust our paths. Mistakes? Don't cry over them or waste time worrying about them—fix them. And then move on. Only when we do this are we being responsible for and about ourselves.

It's also important that we live up to the responsibilities that arise in our worlds, making sure that we fulfill our duties and obligations to others. There are other people on this planet, and just as we depend on them, they should be able to depend on us. We depend on dairy farmers to get milk to distributors; we depend on people to make and repair our roads; we depend on agencies to regulate things that need to be regulated, such as foods and air pollution. In the same way, people depend upon us, and it's our responsibility to make sure that we don't let them down.

Of course, many people take on far too much responsibility, seeing themselves as responsible for much, much more than they really are responsible for. They feel themselves to be responsible for the success of every endeavor, even those that are really the responsibility of others, but they're not. They feel that they're responsible to make sure that other people's problems turn out okay, but they're not. They feel that they're responsible to make sure that everything is and turns out perfect, yet they're not. These people are often running themselves ragged, setting standards that are impossibly high to meet, and dooming themselves to a life full of self-created frustration and annoyance.

The best years of your life are the ones in which you
decide your problems are your own. You do not blame
them on your mother, the ecology, or the president.
You realize that you control your own destiny.

Albert Ellis

We are responsible for our lives and our own attitudes. I've heard many a student tell me, "Of course I see the world as hopeless—life's given me plenty of messages that tell me it's hopeless." Yet I see others who get those same messages and who see beauty, wonder, and hope instead of frustration and hopelessness. Whatever messages life is giving us, we are responsible for the interpretation of those messages and our own reactions to them. We often lean on others when things go badly, and that can be very helpful—we can demonstrate responsibility by asking for help, as contradictory as that may sound. Seeking the aid of another person is a strategy that can help us to see hope and to keep our spirits high, and that's definitely a responsible action.

I am responsible. Although I may not be able to prevent the worst
from happening, I am responsible for my attitude toward the
inevitable misfortunes that darken life. Bad things do

happen; how I respond to them defines my character.

Walter Anderson

Learning responsibility is one of the most important tasks that we can undertake, and living up to our responsibilities in all their different forms is definitely something that can help us to define ourselves as human beings. Our responsibilities to our neighbors, our families, our co-workers, our planet, and ourselves are as important as anything else in our lives, and making sure that we fulfill them can help us to keep our lives on an even keel, and to make our lives something that we're proud of when we look back on what we have done and what we haven't done.

Questions about Responsibility

1. Why do you think that people in the world so often focus on their rights and entitlements rather than on their own responsibility?

2. What kinds of things do you feel you're responsible for that you really might not be?

3. Where do we learn our responsibility? Are the people from whom you've learned responsibility necessarily the best teachers you could have had?

Mistakes I've Made Concerning Responsibility

When you talk about families that have one or two alcoholic parents, you'll find that the children end up with a lot of behavioral traits as a result of having grown up in a household that had little stability. One of the parts of their lives that's affected strongly is their idea of responsibility—they grow up being either extremely irresponsible or quite hyper-responsible. In my case, I turned out to be the latter.

I was too responsible, and that was a trait that sabotaged me through much of my early life and well into adulthood. I felt that everything was my responsibility to make it come out right, and guess what? I failed almost every time I tried. I was terrible with friendships because every time I met someone I liked, I tried to "make" the friendship work. I tried to fix other people's problems for them; I tried to "make" people happy.

There were some benefits to this trait, of course. In more than twelve years of college leading to my doctorate, I don't even need all the fingers of one hand to count the number of papers and assignments I turned in late, or that were of low quality. I'm really good at paying my bills. I've always been good at the work that I do, and I'm one of the people who come in early and stay later than others (though I don't overdo that anymore!). People feel that they can trust me and that they can depend on me, and that's a good feeling for me to have, knowing that fact.

But I also damaged relationships by trying to make them work—I made people feel uncomfortable because I didn't leave them enough space. I damaged myself with my negative self-talk whenever I failed in meeting a responsibility. Not only was I my own worst critic, but I was a very harsh critic of myself, and I didn't give myself any breaks at all.

Now I know, though, that everything is not my responsibility. I'm even able to hear someone talk about problems in their lives without feeling that I should help them fix them—I know that getting through or over those problems is an important part of their own journeys in life. And if something breaks, it's not necessarily up to me to fix it. I know that it may be up to me, but it also may not be. This allows me to be much more relaxed and much more able to enjoy my life.

Journal Entries

Day One: There are many aspects of your own life for which you alone are responsible. List some of them, and explain what you do to meet that responsibility. (I'm responsible for paying my debts, which I've incurred myself; I make sure I have enough money to pay them by not spending my money on other things.)

Day Two: In your life, what has happened when you've taken on responsibility that really wasn't yours? How has that responsibility affected your life? (I volunteered to put on a party that wasn't even for people in my life; it got me stressed and exhausted.)

Day Three: Think of a time in your life when you haven't lived up to a responsibility of yours. How did it make you feel? What were the consequences? (I didn't finish a project that had a strict deadline; it seriously complicated the lives of many other people; I felt guilty and incompetent, among other feelings.)

Day Four: How can I help another person to recognize what are the legitimate responsibilities in his or her life, and which ones he or she really doesn't need to take on?

Day Five: Think of a person you know who is over-responsible, and one who is irresponsible. Which person would you rather spend time with? Why? What are these two people's lives like?

Twenty-Eight

Compassion

When we consider compassion, we look at our ways of relating to other people. We look at the trials and difficulties that others are going through, and we try to put ourselves in their position so that we can come closer to understanding just how they feel and just why they act as they do. And when we understand their conditions and their motivations, we can see them and their actions in a new light. That man might have been rude to us just now, but when we find out that his wife has just left him or that he's afraid of losing his job, then the rudeness takes on a different light. And even more than just understanding where he's coming from, we may even be able to help him out a bit.

But in our societies of today, we seem to be pulling away from compassion and moving towards judgment. As a teacher, it's getting more and more difficult to teach young people about compassion—if we read a story about a character who did something wrong, it's much more common today to hear young people say, "It's his fault—he had it coming," rather than, "I feel bad for him—he made a mistake, but so does everyone." Because they watch so many television programs that are focused around judging other people, this judgment has become their norm, and since they've watched so many people be judged, they have an attitude that says that people actually deserve to be judged, and that they can judge others whenever they want.

Compassion is a sympathetic feeling.
It involves the willingness to put yourself in someone else's shoes,
to take the focus off yourself and to imagine what it's like to be
in someone else's predicament, and simultaneously, to feel love
for that person. It's the recognition that other people's problems,
their pain and frustrations, are every bit as real as our own—often
far worse. In recognizing this fact and trying to offer some assistance,
we open our own hearts and greatly enhance our sense of gratitude.

Richard Carlson

Judgment, though, doesn't leave much room for compassion. When we are compassionate, we recognize the behavior or the act, but we also recognize that we all make mistakes and that a person now has some serious problems on his or her hands. When we're compassionate, we see a starving person and feel deep sympathy inside with that person, and we don't decide that the hunger is somehow that person's fault. When we're compassionate, we sit and listen even if we don't hear what we think we should be hearing. Compassion asks us to leave behind judgment and focus on the suffering that another person is going through so that we can help them.

The best way to feel compassionate is to be completely aware of what people are going through, and simple observation often isn't enough to tell us this story fully. There are times when we have to stop and think deeply about what another person may be experiencing, especially if their experiences are very different from ours. I don't know, for example, what it's like to go through life with a debilitating illness—physical or psychological—so sometimes it's difficult for me to feel compassion for people whose lives and experiences are limited by diseases from which they suffer through no fault of their own.

On the other hand, I know intimately what it's like to grow up with an alcoholic parent and to go through debilitating depression, so it's easier for me to feel compassion when I hear of others going through the same thing. In the former cases, just because I haven't experienced the same things does not mean that it's impossible for me to feel compassion, just more difficult. In the latter cases, compassion comes more easily to me, but my compassion obviously shouldn't be limited to people with whom I have shared experiences.

Shallow observation as an outsider is not enough to see their suffering. We must become one with the subject of our observation. When we are in contact with another's suffering, a feeling of compassion is born in us. Compassion means, literally, "to suffer with."

Thich Nhat Hanh

So why should I even care about being compassionate? I know that personally, I feel much better about myself when I've shown compassion to someone rather than judgment. I feel that I'm being more human when someone tells me of a mistake and I say something like, "I'm sorry you had to go through that, and if there's anything I can do to help you, please let me know," rather than, "That was stupid, and you deserve everything you're getting."

One of the reasons for which many people avoid being compassionate is because they mistake it for being an enabler. They feel that if they're compassionate, they may not be holding people responsible for their actions or inaction. But here's something important—it's not our place to be holding others responsible. It's our place to be responsible for ourselves, not for others. And when we lose our compassion because we've judged someone else, we lose a lot more than just an opportunity to help someone else out.

Most importantly, we lose the opportunity to live from a place that is more deeply human. Some of our most important learning about our own humanity comes when we show caring and love to other people, for that's what being human is all about—caring and loving each other, not judging and harming others.

I am compassionate. I allow my heart and imagination to embrace the difficulties and concerns of others. While maintaining my own balance, I find it within myself to extend sympathy, attention, and support. When they are grieved, I listen with openness and gentle strength. I offer loyalty, friendship, and human understanding. Without undermining or enabling, I aid and assist others to find their strength. I allow the healing power of the Universe to flow through me, soothing the hearts and feelings of those I encounter.

Julia Cameron

So it's important that we do allow our hearts "to embrace the difficulties and concerns of others" if we're truly going to live our lives fully. The compassion that we show to others can contribute greatly to the peace and goodwill of the world, and we can help others to live their lives fully as they realize that they are not alone, and that there are others out there who don't just care for them, but who also are willing to understand them and help them through their difficulties. Our contributions to other human beings are our contributions to the world, and our compassion for others can help us to make those contributions more loving, more helpful, and more lasting.

Questions to Consider

1. Why isn't compassion more of an everyday word for us? Why do we use the word so rarely?

2. What does compassion mean to you? Do you practice it each day according to your definition?

3. What would our world be like if compassion were as common as, say, selfishness?

Relationship of Compassion to Other Principles

Compassion forces me to be aware of what other people are going through—if I understand their situations and trials, I'm able to feel more for them.

Compassion is a sign of love—love for all people, no matter who they are or how different I think they are from me. It also shows my commitment to community when I show my compassion for other people instead of judging them or being indifferent to them. I also feel that my compassion is an indication of my awareness of unity—I am connected to all other people, and because of that connection it would be wrong to simply ignore them or not feel for them and their trials.

Compassion is a sign of my character, too. It's an indication of my integrity, of my kindness and my goodness, and my acceptance and attitude. While pretty much everything in this book is related to everything else in some way, compassion is an element of ourselves that allows us to see exactly who we are. If I see someone else suffering and I don't care, that tells more about me than any words that I may use or any actions that I may take. Love makes the world go round, as we all know, and compassion is one of the most important indications that we love the world and all the people in it.

Journal Entries

Day One: Think of a time when someone has shown compassion to you. How did it make you feel? How can you make others feel that same way?

Day Two: How can your compassion help others to heal?

Day Three: A friend of yours wants to be a more compassionate person, but feels he doesn't know how to do so. Write him a short letter telling him how he can grow in compassion.

Day Four: Who is the most compassionate person you know? Write a note for him or her explaining how you feel about that person's compassion.

Day Five: Write five things that would change in the world if more people were to show compassion to each other rather than judgment or anger.

Twenty-Nine

Kindness

There are few things that can make us feel better about ourselves than kindness. Obviously, then, kindness is an extremely important element of living our lives fully and completely, for our kindness can contribute greatly to the quality of the lives of others, as well as to the quality of our own lives. Most people do desire to be kind, I believe, but find it far too easy to neglect kindness because it's so often "inconvenient" to show kindness to our fellow human beings and everything else on this planet. Often, we don't think of the kind act until the opportunity to show it has passed, such as when we see someone with their arms full of packages finally open that door, and realize that it would have been very easy for us to open that door for that person.

For my part, I find that I neglect kindness far too often. My mind gets caught up with my responsibilities and obligations, and I end up not taking advantage of some very straightforward opportunities to show kindness to others. Sometimes it's easier to give a stock answer than it is to give a kind answer, and sometimes I just don't look hard enough to realize that a certain person really could use some kindness from any source—and here I am, perfectly capable of showing just what they need.

The truth is, of course, that all of us can use kindness in our lives, probably much more than we actually receive it. But since we grow used to getting by without it, we tell ourselves that it isn't really necessary, and that we can get by fine without it. Yes, we definitely can survive without people showing us kindness, but are our lives as rich as they could be without the kindness of others? And if our lives would be enriched by the kindness of others, what effects would our kindness have on the lives of other people in our lives?

All the kindness which a person puts out into the world
works on the heart and thoughts of humankind.

Albert Schweitzer

We have the power to make this world a more positive place by putting out more positive thoughts and energy into the world, and kindness is one of the best means for doing so. The kindnesses do not have to be huge—we can show great kindness by helping someone with a task, by allowing someone into the flow of traffic, by complimenting them on something that we know they're proud of, by telling them that we're glad we know them. We don't have to pay off their student loans or their cars, and we don't have to lie to them to make them feel better about something. But the positive that we put into the world does work on other people's thoughts and hearts, as Albert says, and if we choose not to contribute to that part of the world, we choose not to add to the positive part of the world.

But since kindness is free and it doesn't force us to make any obligations, why would we hesitate to show it?

Our conduct, the way we act, may be similar to a boomerang — especially loving acts of kindness. For kindness has a way of returning to those who express it to others. . . . It is the truly brave, the truly great, the truly unafraid who often exhibit the greatest kindness in their activities.

John Marks Templeton

Many people have written about the reciprocal nature of kindness, too, the way that things that we put into the world tend to come back to us. Some call it Karma, but no matter what you call it, don't you think it would be a good idea to be sending kindness into the world so that kindness will come back to you? Now, there are those people who think that for every act of kindness they show, they should see an immediate and obvious return to them. Those people lead frustrating lives, though, for they're really not going to see immediately the kindness that comes back to them. I've done kind things and I haven't seen any sort of return on my act for weeks on end, but that's okay—I look at it as kind of a bank account, and even if the next six weeks are filled with negative things, I *know for sure* that eventually, the kindness and positive energy will make its way back to me, and the more I've put out there, the more will come back to me.

Heck, sometimes it takes years, but those years of problems are simply years of building character, and when the kindness does work back to you, it truly is beautiful to witness and experience.

A single act of kindness may have a long trajectory and touch those we will never meet or see. Something that we casually offer may move through a web of connection far beyond ourselves to have effects that we may have never imagined. And so each of us may have left far more behind us than we may ever know.

Rachel Naomi Remen

When I was in driver's education classes, we were taught regularly that "courtesy is contagious," in an effort to turn us into courteous—and thus safe—

drivers. Kindness, too, can be very contagious, and there usually is no way of knowing whether or not a kindness that we've shown has been passed on. If I help you carry something to your car, you may be more inclined to leave a more generous tip when you stop for lunch. That's okay, though—we don't need to know what someone else does after we show kindness. We need to know only that we're capable of showing even more kindness. One thing that we can be sure of is that if we don't show kindness, there's absolutely no chance for us to leave behind anything positive with others, and thus there's no chance of it being passed on.

One day, when we're closer to death than we are now, how many of us will look back on our lives and say, "I could have been kinder—I had so many opportunities to show kindness that I never took advantage of." And won't that be a shame if we end up that way?

There really is only one way to allow kindness to have a positive effect on our lives, and to allow kindness to be a part of our efforts to live our lives fully. And that way is, of course, to be kind. To show kindness whenever and wherever we can, and not to care at all if people reciprocate in a like manner. We have no control over their actions, only ours—and we can make sure that ours are kind.

Questions to Consider

1. Just how important is kindness in our contemporary society? Is it something that we actively teach our young people?

2. How might you go about improving your kindness?

3. How do you feel when someone shows you kindness?

One Stanza on Kindness

Do you wish the world were happy?
Then remember day by day
Just to scatter seeds of kindness
As you pass along the way,
For the pleasures of the many
May be ofttimes traced to one,
As the hand that plants an acorn
Shelters armies from the sun.

Ella Wheeler Wilcox

Journal Entries

Day One: "A single act of kindness may have a long trajectory," says Rachel Remen. Think of a time when you've seen an act of kindness be passed on, and how it felt to witness it.

Day Two: Write down five acts of kindness that you can share with someone tomorrow. Make sure that they cost nothing and are easy to do.

Day Three: Why do you believe that so many people choose not to be kind when they have the chance? For example, in our society we seem to value making a joke about somebody over saying a kind word to someone—why might that be?

Day Four: Why do you think that we see so little kindness on our television shows and in our movies? Think of a movie that shows a great deal of kindness—was it successful?

Day Five: How would you be changing the world if you committed yourself to showing kindness to all other people you encounter during each day?

Thirty

Community

As I see the term "community," it's not limited to just the small geographic area where plenty of people live and feel a sense of belonging. In my mind, all the world is community, and it's only our unwillingness to see the world as such that keeps us from seeing it this way. After all, if we see the whole world as community, then aren't we responsible for the well-being of everyone in it? It's somehow a bit too daunting for us to widen our horizons quite that far.

But having lived in several different countries and in many different states in the U.S., I've come to learn that there really are no significant differences between us in this world. We all long for acceptance and companionship to varying degrees, we all want a sense of accomplishment, we all want to be taken seriously at what we do, we all want to feel as if we belong somewhere, somehow. There are many more similarities than there are differences, yet we tend to focus on those differences in order to justify our more limiting thoughts. Because frankly, letting go of those limiting thoughts is a pretty frightening prospect.

But "com" is "a *prefix* meaning 'with,' 'together,' 'in association,' and (with intensive force) 'completely.'" And we all know what "unity" means. There is nothing at all exclusionary in this term—yet we tend to focus on the limits of geography and space, thinking that community can't extend past certain boundaries. We now have online communities, but those tend not to extend past the boundaries of certain interests.

But what would this world be like if we ALL saw the world as one large community, and treated it as such?

If civilization is to survive, we must cultivate the science
of human relationships—the ability of all peoples,
of all kinds, to live together, in the same world at peace.

Franklin D. Roosevelt

We can make the argument that no one in China is part of our community, but then when we look at many of the items in our homes, we realize that they were made by people in that country. Some 19-year-old Chinese girl who is from a small town and living in the big city now and who is scared and doing her best to get by and make friends put together that clock on your mantel, while another person in Bangladesh sewed together the pieces of the shirt that you're wearing—evidence of our connections with people from almost everywhere surrounds us all the time.

But why is it important that we see others as part of the community of life? Quite simply because everything that we do and everything that we eat and all of the infrastructures that support all that we do come from other people. Yes, some of us grow most of our own food, but how do we get the water that allows the plants to grow? The electricity that allows us to light our homes and do so much more? The roads that allow us to travel to buy all we need? Only when we see the world as part of ourselves, and when we see ourselves as an integral part of the world, will we truly start to live fully, for then we're not excluding anyone from our love and compassion.

When we stop limiting our love and compassion, then we actually start living the lives we were meant to live. Jesus said "Love one another," and he wasn't talking about just our immediate family. It's only when we're able to love all the other people in the world without judging them or expecting them to live up to our expectations and beliefs that we can live our lives fully and completely.

We cannot live only for ourselves. A thousand fibers connect
us with our fellow men and women; and among those fibers,
as sympathetic threads, our actions run as causes,
and they come back to us as effects.

Herman Melville

Of course, there is the more immediate side of community, too—that geographically-based idea that the people who live in the same area that we live in are part of our communities. We have ample opportunities to contribute to those communities, yet we have to choose to do so. We can't simply expect our communities to continue to provide for us without giving something back to them, even if it's just in the form of a little time or money. Sometimes, the best thing that we can do in a community is simply to be a good neighbor to those who live very close to us, someone who's considerate and thoughtful.

In our age, though, one of the most disastrous effects of the technology that we've embraced is that it has pushed us further into our own little worlds, and further from the type of lifestyle that embraces and celebrates community. We can go days without seeing other people from our communities, and often we do. And while we can justify this truth by saying how busy we are or how inconvenient it is to try to find the time to see others, the truth is that we have lost a great deal when we lose our connections with other human beings. When we spend all our time with the television instead of neighbors, we lose connections that could help us in times of need or stress. We don't build support systems, and we don't become someone that others can trust in their times of need. We become isolated and cut off, and this very isolation causes us to feel much less happy with our lives, for we know that there's something missing, even if we can't put a finger on it.

We do have to keep in mind that once we become involved with community, we face a number of demands that we didn't face before, and the most important of these is time. People will want our time, and many people face the problem of committing too much of their time to outside groups and not enough to their own families or to themselves. We do have to maintain a balance between our giving to community and our giving to ourselves. As a teacher, for example, I know that I contribute directly to the community every single day by working with the children of that community, so I don't feel any pressure to spend more time contributing in other ways.

When a mentally retarded child is born, the religious question
we often ask is, "Why does God let this happen?" The better
question to pose is to ask, "What kind of community should
we be so that mental retardation isn't a barrier to
the enjoyment of one's full humanity?"

Rabbi Harold Kushner
(Though I'm fully aware that "retarded" is no longer an
acceptable term, it was used widely when Kushner wrote
these words, and I feel that his message is important
enough to let it stand as written.)

Other people make up most of the world—all of the world, actually, except for one tiny, tiny speck of a person. And while that one speck of a person is immensely important, so are all the other people here. We do have to ask ourselves regularly, am I contributing to the communities of which I'm a part? And if not, how might I do so in ways that aren't going to overwhelm me?

Community is one of the most important concepts in life, and the more unified we can help the world to become, the stronger the world is, and the stronger we are ourselves.

Questions to Consider

1. Is our focus in our society more on community or on individual achievement and action?

2. What are some of the benefits of being a part of a strong community?

3. Is our current level of technology use helping us to create stronger communities, or causing our communities to grow weaker?

More Thoughts on Community

I've always had major problems with the concept of community, for I've never felt a part of one. Even when I've had great opportunities to meet people, to develop friendships, to become a part of something bigger than myself, I've pulled back, never feeling that I belonged. The source of this feeling is very simple—since my father was in the military, we moved around constantly. I went to four grade schools, two junior high schools, and three high schools. We never got the chance to be included, and my father's desire to live off base affected us, too, for we weren't even able to be a part of the military community, and we didn't live in one place long enough to be a part of any civilian community. I don't say these things as a complaint, but as an observation—because it's taken me many years to become comfortable with the concept of belonging, to allow myself to belong in spite of my fear of things coming to an end, community is now extremely important to me. The people I meet who have always been a part of something often take community for granted, or even disdain the "boredom" of being involved with the same people for so long.

But our culture values independence and isolation far too much, it seems to me—we have a hard time making ourselves part of things, of making ourselves responsible to others, and trusting others to be there for us. Sure, there's pain involved if we get hurt, but there's far more pain in isolation. I love community because God gave us other people to live with, not to pull away from, and I learn so much from others that I can't imagine my life without the learning I've gained from getting to know other people. But community doesn't work without commitment—not the lukewarm type of commitment that many see as the ideal, but a strong commitment that lets others know they can count on you.

In retrospect, I see one of the greatest problems of my own shying away from community as the fact that I didn't allow people to get to know me—I kept myself hidden, isolated, and alone, and all that I had to teach was useless, for no one ever heard it. I've spent many years trying to develop the kind of confidence and strong self-image that would allow me to share what I have to share, and I'm glad to say that I'm much better at it now than I was just a few years ago, but I do still have quite a ways to go.

We lose our ability to live fully if we neglect or ignore our responsibility to the other people who share this planet with us. We simply cannot reach our full potential without the insights and observations that other people—our teachers—have to give us. We cannot feel whole until we are helping other people to reach for their potential and to grow as strong as they can grow. We do need down time, and we do need time to ourselves, but we very much need to acknowledge our ties to our fellow human beings and act as if those people meant more to us than our jobs or pets or cars do. They are much more important than anything material that we ever can get our hands on or strive for.

Journal Entries

Day One: Think of several communities that you belong to. What is your role in each one? Do they overlap? Is your role the same in more than one? (My community at school, my community at church; they're very different and they don't overlap.)

Day Two: Do you see community differently now than you did when you were younger? What has changed? What has stayed the same?

Day Three: If you could create your own community, what would be the most important elements of it? Why? Is there anything you would forbid?

Day Four: If a young person were to ask you what responsibilities a person has in his or her community, how would you respond?

Day Five: What are some of the things that keep us from being more active in our communities? What are some challenges to balancing personal lives with community activities?

Thirty-One

Self

What do we really mean when we talk about "self"? How much of it has to do with body? With spirit? With intellect? Of course, our selves must have something to do with all of these things, but just how do we define it? This is an important question because the ways that we define our selves have much to do with the way that we treat our selves. And much of the misery in the world has more to do with the ways in which people treat themselves than it does with the ways in which other people treat us.

It's a widely accepted fact that we really can't take care of others well until we take care of ourselves first. If we don't get to know our selves, if we don't feed our selves with love and acceptance and caring, it we don't show compassion to our selves, then it's pretty much impossible to take care of others. We see the results of people who never have taken care of their selves in the children that they raise—these are kids who have a strong need for attention and acceptance, and who very often act out those needs in inappropriate ways because they've found no other ways that are effective.

The older I get, the more I realize the importance of exercising
the various dimensions of my body, soul, mind, and heart. Taken
together, these aspects give me a sense of wholeness. I want to
be a whole human being rather than one who limps on one leg
because I don't know how to use all of my parts. Intellectual,
emotional, and physical activity are not separate entities.
Rather, they are dimensions of the same human being.

Robert Fulghum

When we consider our selves, the most important part of that consideration, it seems to me, is simple awareness of the many different elements that make up that self. Robert talks of "body, soul, mind, and heart," but that short list also includes elements of those parts, such as feelings, biases, fears, ambitions, hopes, dreams, beliefs, and the like. We are a combination of many, many different elements, and unless and until we're able to be aware of what they are and how they affect us, we simply won't be able to make any significant changes in order to improve our lives. If we don't see ourselves as a composite of our different factors, it's easy to become frustrated and confused as we try to figure out just how we might better ourselves.

On the other hand, awareness of our own diversity can help us to focus on just those things that need our attention. I might feel that I'm terrible with relationships, for example, and feel at a loss when I try to improve them. If I'm aware of what I do and how I do it, though, I might realize that my biggest problem is listening—I'm not necessarily bad at relationships, just bad at listening, and that one factor sabotages my attempts at developing relationships. If I can focus on my listening skills, then, I can improve my relationships as a matter of course.

I was always looking outside myself for strength and confidence, but it comes from within. It is there all the time.

Anna Freud

Our selves really are magnificent—unfortunately, though, we learn mostly how to limit them as we grow up, and then it's very difficult to learn how to cast away those limitations so that our magnificence can shine through. But when we can act as we truly are, and when we can show others our best attributes all the time, then we can allow our magnificence to shine through. It's been pushed down by insecure people who have wanted to keep us "in line" or "under control"—even the people we love the most and who love us the most do this—but it's still there, just waiting for us to dust it off and put it on display.

One of the major obstacles that we have to overcome, though, is the fact that we find it very hard to believe in our own magnificence. We find it hard to conceive of our selves as fantastic and beautiful—instead, we focus on what we perceive as our faults and our limitations. So I can't paint well—so what? That's a club that has a few billion members, and each of us has our own amazing skills and talents to tap into when we want and need to. But if I feel inadequate in one area, it's easy for me to convince myself that I'm inadequate in other areas as well. And thus the destructive cycle perpetuates itself: we convince ourselves that our selves are nothing special, and we act as if this were true.

But it's not true.

It is healthy to accept myself as I am, to like myself, and to love myself. It is okay for me to accept a compliment or praise. Because I am just as deserving and worthy as anyone else, I may treat myself as well as I treat others, live my own life, and enjoy my life. There is a difference between being unselfish and being a martyr or a victim. There is a time for putting myself first so that I may take care of myself and my needs.

Jill Wolf

You are just as magnificent as anyone and everyone else on this planet. You are a completely unique blend of spirit and body that has gifts that were given to you in combinations that no one else shares. You may not be acting as if you were magnificent; if that's the case, then you probably don't believe that you are. But your self has just as much value as any other that's ever walked this world of ours, and when you do see your own worthiness, you'll begin to act as a worthy person, and the world will then treat you as you act.

When we see the true value of our selves—the incredibly valuable people that we are—then we can start giving to the world from a position of worth and strength, and the world will benefit much, much more from our gifts.

Give your self a break. Trust your self, accept your self, allow your self to guide you, love your self. And the love that you give to your self will most definitely work its way out into the world in very positive ways.

Questions to Ponder

1. What do you consider to be your "self"? Is it the thoughts that you have? The feelings that you have? The body? The spirit?

2. Why is it sometimes more difficult to give our selves a break than it is to give a break to others?

3. What does it mean to you to be a "whole human being"? Is it easy to be one?

Thoughts on the Self

This self should never be lost sight of. It is the one thing of supreme importance, the greatest factor even in the life of the greatest service. Being always and necessarily precedes doing; having always and necessarily precedes giving. But this law also holds: That when there is the being, it is all the more increased by the doing; when there is the having, it is all the more increased by the giving. Keeping to oneself dwarfs and stultifies. Hoarding brings loss: using brings even greater gain. In brief, the more we are, the more we can do; the more we have, the more we can give. The most truly successful, the most powerful and valuable life, then, is the life that is first founded upon this great, immutable law of love and service, and that then becomes supremely self-centred—supremely self-centred that it may become all the more supremely unself-centred; in other words, the life that looks well to self, that there may be the ever greater self, in order that there may be the ever greater service.

Ralph Waldo Trine

Journal Entries

Day One: Write a letter to your ten-year-old self giving encouragement and hope. Doing this can help us to feel the dynamics of just what the self is and how it changes over time.

Day Two: Make a list of all the things that you can think of that comprise the self. (Likes, dislikes, strengths, talents, etc.)

Day Three: Do you appreciate your self? Respect it? How do you show it your appreciation and respect?

Day Four: Think of things that other people have tried to teach you about yourself, both positive and negative ("You're great!" or "You're not good enough!") Write down two lists, then cross out or throw away the list of the negative messages.

Day Five: How aware are you of your self? Do you feel that you can easily explain why you like what you do, why you do what you do, what kinds of changes you'd like to make, etc.?

Thirty-Two

Change

It's been rightly said (in an ironic way) that change is the only constant in life. We all face changes every day in every realm of our lives—changes in beliefs, in preferences, in knowledge, in our physical bodies, in relationships, in jobs. You name it, and you can be sure that there's a change in it, or in the ways that we relate to it.

In living our lives fully, it's important that we recognize our own attitudes towards change. Many of us fear change and do everything we can to prevent it, thus involving ourselves in a truly useless battle that leads us inevitably to frustration and even possibly anger as the changes we've battled come to be even though we've fought against them. Because things will change in life— kids grow up, jobs change to fit the business environment, people grow and learn and develop and see the world differently, people quit their jobs, prices rise—heck, even our climate is changing these days, and there's no way to put any of these things back where they were, so it's important to deal with them as they are, not how we wish that they were.

Those persons are happiest in this restless and mutable world
who are in love with change, who delight in what is new
simply because it differs from what is old; who rejoice
in every innovation, and find a strange alert pleasure
in all that is, and that has never been before.

Agnes Repplier

We can be happy with any change only if we accept it and react to how things are now. Of course, not all changes are positive—we're going through some very negative changes in our school these days—but that doesn't mean that we shouldn't accept those changes. Only when we completely accept the fact that something has changed can we work to fight that change, if not to put things back as they were, then to put things onto a more positive track for the future.

Change can be exhilarating, as Agnes points out, for when change happens, we're forced to learn new things and to grow ourselves. It becomes necessary for us to adapt and to approach life from a new perspective, to see things in new and different ways, and to re-create ourselves so that we can deal with new situations. Sometimes, if we're becoming bored and uninspired, we can decide to make changes that will force us out of our safety zones, out of our zones of little conflict into entirely new worlds in new cities, new jobs, and new environments. And when we do that, we're saying to life, "Yes, life, I trust you to make sure that things will turn out well, even if they appear to be going poorly for a while."

Some people, unfortunately, tend to rush into changes out of fear, and fear is a motivating factor that we usually shouldn't allow to determine our actions (unless our fear is for our life or of physical harm). Or they look for change simply for the sake of change, and they often don't learn much of anything at all from their current situations before they're looking for something new already. They jump from place to place or job to job without ever learning the important lessons that each place or job can teach them.

Others don't spend the time making sure the change that they seek is the most appropriate one. How many people seek divorce without ever considering counseling? How many quit their jobs without seeking to improve their performance or to deal with problems they have on their jobs?

Nearly all great civilizations that perished did so because
they had crystallized, because they were incapable of adapting
themselves to new conditions, new methods, new points of view.
It is as though people would literally rather die than change.

Eleanor Roosevelt

Fear is also a motivator that can make people avoid change. They may be offered a new job that pays better and has better working conditions, yet turn it down because they're afraid they won't do well in it, or because it involves changing residences, or because they're afraid of working with new people. How many people don't buy the new computer—even though they need it— because they're intimidated by having to learn an entirely new operating system? How many people won't leave destructive relationships because they're afraid that they won't meet someone else, and that they'll be alone?

But change is a universal—there is literally nothing on this planet that is exactly the same as it was two months ago. Even stones and mountains wear away little by little, whether we see the changes or not. Things simply have to change if they're to stay living and dynamic—so why do we spend so much time and effort trying to make things stay the same in our lives? Why do we decide that everything should be exactly the same as it was one year ago, or two? That kind of attitude forces us into stagnation, and stagnant water is unhealthy water that cannot support healthy forms of life—just unhealthy forms, and just for a short while until the stagnant water itself dries up and is no more.

Why should anyone be afraid of change? What can take place without it?

What can be more pleasing or more suitable to universal nature?

Can you take your bath without the firewood undergoing a change? Can you eat without the food undergoing a change? And can anything useful be done without change?

Don't you see that for you to change is just the same, and is equally necessary for universal nature?

Marcus Aurelius

Your change is necessary for your development, and it's necessary for the development of the other people in your life, and it's necessary for the world as a whole, too, just as Marcus Aurelius says. For you not to change is for you to defy life and its natural course, and we should not be defying life—we should be flowing with it and trusting it to take us where we need to go. So look for the places in your life in which you're stagnating, and begin the process of change. Read different books, or more books. Fight your addictions that keep you locked in certain behaviors. Ask for help from others who have been there. Pray—not for change, but for the strength to make the changes, and for the discernment necessary to know which changes really are important.

When you can start to see change as an ally that will help you to grow and learn and develop, rather than a threat to the status quo that keeps you safe and stagnant, then you can start to live your life as fully as your life was meant to be lived. You were created to be a dynamic, thriving being, and not a static, stagnant one.

Questions to Consider

1. Why are so many people uncomfortable with change? Why do they fight it?

2. What kinds of changes have you gone through in life? Which have been the most memorable?

3. Why does some change take forever to happen, while other changes happen very quickly and easily?

Thoughts on Change from Ralph Waldo Trine

Our complex modern life, especially in our larger centers, gets us running so many times into grooves that we are prone to miss, and sometimes for long periods, the all-around, completer life. We are led at times almost to forget that the stars come nightly to the sky, or even that there is a sky; that there are hedgerows and groves where the birds are always singing and where we can lie on our backs and watch the treetops swaying above us and the clouds floating by an hour or hours at a time; where one can live with his or her soul or, as Whitman has put it, where one can loaf and invite one's soul.

We need changes from the duties and the cares of our accustomed everyday life. They are necessary for healthy, normal living. We need occasionally to be away from our friends, our relatives, from the members of our immediate households. Such changes are good for us; they are good for them. We appreciate them better, they us, when we are away from them for a period, or they from us.

We need these changes occasionally in order to find new relations—this is a twofold sense. By such changes there come to our minds more clearly the better qualities of those with whom we are in constant association; we lose sight of the little frictions and irritations that arise; we see how we can be more considerate, appreciative, kind.

In one of those valuable essays of Prentice Mulford entitled "Who Are Our Relations?" he points us to the fact, and with so much insight and common sense, that our relations are not always or necessarily those related to us by blood ties, those of our immediate households, but those most nearly allied to us in mind and in spirit, many times those we have never seen, but that we shall sometime, somewhere be drawn to through ceaselessly working Law of Attraction, whose basis is *like attracts like*.

And so in staying too closely with the accustomed relations we may miss the knowledge and the companionship of those equally or even more closely related.

We need these changes to get the kinks out of our minds, our nerves, our muscles—the cobwebs off our faces. We need them to whet again the edge of appetite. We need them to invite the mind and the soul to new possibilities and powers. We need them in order to come back with new implements, or with implements redressed, sharpened, for the daily duties. It is like the chopper working too long with axe underground. There comes the time when an hour at the stone will give it such persuasive power that he can chop and cord in the day what he otherwise would in two or more, and with far greater ease and satisfaction.

We need periods of being by ourselves—*alone*. Sometimes a fortnight or even a week will do wonders for one, unless he or she has drawn too heavily upon the account. The simple custom, moreover, of taking an hour, or even a half hour, *alone in the quiet*, in the midst of the daily routine of life, would be the source of *inestimable gain* for countless numbers.

If such changes can be in closer contact with the fields and with the flowers that are in them, the stars and the sea that lies open beneath them, the woods and the wild things that are of them, one cannot help but find oneself growing in love for and an ever fuller appreciation of these, and being at the same time so remade and unfolded that one's love, one's care, and one's consideration for all mankind and for every living creature, will be the greater.

Journal Entries

Day One: Marcus Aurelius asks, what can take place without change? Can you think of anything that can? Why do you think that change is so necessary in life?

Day Two: Becoming comfortable with change is one of the most important things we can do if we don't want life's changes to overwhelm us. Discuss some strategies that people can use to make themselves more comfortable with change.

Day Three: Someone you know is dealing with significant changes in their life. Give them advice on how to view the changes that are happening.

Day Four: Write down what you think life would be like if nothing were ever to change.

Day Five: How can you become a change agent, actually embracing, causing and looking forward to change in your life? What would some of the advantages of this kind of approach be?

Thirty-Three

Adversity

Adversity is an absolutely necessary part of life, a part of our lives that if we can reframe it in a healthy way, can help us to live in much happier and much more fulfilling ways. When we're young, we learn from watching others that adversity is negative and frightening, that we should fear it and avoid it at all costs. But without adversity, much learning can ever take place, little growth can happen, few positive changes can occur. Adversity is what causes us to step up and be more than we were before the adversity appeared in our lives, and because it's such a valuable tool for us, it seems that we should view it in a much more positive light.

Once we accept that adversity is going to happen, we take away much of its power over us. There will be storms and floods and high winds and layoffs and accidents and conflicts and deaths, and sometimes they will affect us. There really isn't much we can do about that fact. What we can do something about is the ways that we look at adversity and the ways in which we respond to it. Do we withdraw back into our safety zones each time an adverse situation arises? Do we try to avoid dealing with it out of fear that we'll fail or prove woefully inadequate in our response? Or do we view them as challenges and push ourselves to deal with them effectively and positively, doing our best to make something less terrible out of what may be an awful situation?

Adversity, if for no other reason, is of benefit, since it is sure
to bring a season of sober reflection. People see clearer
at such times. Storms purify the atmosphere.

Henry Ward Beecher

Adversity forces us to look at our lives, look at our preferences, look at our actions, and look at our thoughts and feelings. It forces us to come up with a response, and the nature of our response depends on who we are, what we value, and what's going on in our lives. I know people who are kind and considerate people, but who turn into monsters, swearing and lashing out at others, when something goes wrong and they suddenly fear losing their control over their lives or their situations. I know others who aren't necessarily that kind to other people, but who don't allow adversity to bother them much at all. And because they don't allow it to do so, their lives are much more peaceful and much less stressful.

What it seems to come down to is not whether we're able to avoid adversity, but how we look at it when it hits us. Our perception of our lives' happenings are the most important element of our ways of dealing with them, and dealing with adversity is no exception. We will face adversity—but is it a terrible monster that threatens to destroy us, or a difficulty that challenges us to come up with new and creative ways to deal with it?

It is in the whole process of meeting and
solving problems that life has meaning.
Problems are the cutting edge that distinguishes
between success and failure. Problems call
forth our courage and our wisdom; indeed, they
create our courage and our wisdom. It is only because
of problems that we grow mentally and spiritually. It
is through the pain of confronting and
resolving problems that we learn.

M. Scott Peck

Seeing adversity in this latter manner can be one of the most effective ways of dealing with life that we can develop. If we can do this, then we can rid our lives of much of the fear and stress that often drags us down into sour moods and fearful ways of seeing things—and we will start to use our creative and artistic energies in ways that help them grow and develop. We will become more creative as a matter of course, no matter how we feel about our creativity now. And that's one of the most beautiful parts of adversity of all: when we deal with it, we're making ourselves stronger and more creative people as a result of the adversity.

And the other element of adversity that is positive is the gifts that it brings us, as Robert mentions below. When we do meet adversity head-on and deal with it effectively, it always brings some sort of gift to us, whether that be in the form of something new and important that we learn about ourselves, some new technique or strategy that we learn, or some insight about life that is revealed to us. Most people, though, never find these gifts when they hide away or avoid facing the adversity that comes their way. In my life, every time I've faced adversity I've come out of the experience a bit stronger and a bit wiser, even if I haven't always "defeated" the adversity. For example, when I was laid off several years ago, we ended up losing our house to foreclosure despite all of our efforts, but we came through that experience with a lot of new learning, no resentment, and a bit more wisdom in our lives.

In every adversity there lies the
seed of an equivalent advantage.
In every defeat is a lesson showing

you how to win the victory next time.

Robert Collier

We all face adversity. There's nothing saying that we're going to "overcome" adversity every time we face it, but if we do face it with a realistic sense of just what it is, we have a very good chance of gaining a great deal from our experience. And with what we learn and with the growing that we do, we eventually can get better at helping people to make their ways through the adversity that they're facing, and help them to see the positive sides of life even in the midst of their trials. There are few counselors better than someone who has been through the same thing, and who can lend a compassionate, caring ear to a person who is going through trials of their own.

Questions about Adversity

1. Why are so many people unable to see the positive elements of adverse situations?

2. Why do some people dread adversity, while others seem to welcome it?

3. Are there positive ways of seeking out adversity in our lives?

I Stood Yesterday. I Can Stand Today
by Dorothy Dix

I have been through the depths of poverty and sickness. When people ask me what has kept me going through the troubles that come to all of us, I always reply, "I stood yesterday. I can stand today. And I will not permit myself to think about what might happen tomorrow."

I have known want and struggle and anxiety and despair. I have always had to work beyond the limit of my strength. As I look back upon my life, I see it as a battlefield strewn with the wrecks of dead dreams and broken hopes and shattered illusions—a battle in which I always fought with the odds tremendously against me, and which has left me scarred and bruised and maimed and old before my time.

Yet I have no pity for myself; no tears to shed over the past and gone shadows; no envy for the women who have been spared all I have gone through. For I have lived. They only existed. I have drunk the cup of life down to its very dregs. They have only sipped the bubbles on top of it. I know things they will never know. I see things to which they are blind. It is only the women whose eyes have been washed clear with tears who get the broad vision that makes them little sisters to all the world.

I have learned in the great University of Hard Knocks a philosophy that no woman who has had an easy life ever acquires. I have learned to live each day as it comes and not to borrow trouble by dreading the morrow. It is the dark menace of the picture that makes cowards of us. I put that dread from me because experience has taught me that when the time comes that I so fear, the strength and wisdom to meet it will be given me. Little annoyances no longer have the power to affect me. After you have seen your whole edifice of happiness topple and crash in ruins about you, it never matters to you again that a servant forgets to put doilies under the finger bowls, or the cook spills the soup.

I have learned not to expect too much of people, and so I can still get happiness out of the friend who isn't quite true to me or the acquaintance who gossips. Above all, I have acquired a sense of humor, because there were so many things over which I had either to cry or laugh. And when a woman can joke over her troubles instead of having hysterics, nothing can ever hurt her much again. I do not regret the hardships I have known, because through them I have touched life at every point I have lived. And it was worth the price I had to pay.

Journal Entries

Day One: Think about when someone you love is going through adversity. Do you want to fix their problems for them, or help them to work through the problems? Why do you want to do this particular thing?

Day Two: Describe the relationship between adversity and acceptance. Must we accept adverse situations? Can acceptance help us to deal with them?

Day Three: Write about a time when you went through adversity only to have everything turn out better than you ever thought it would at the time.

Day Four: Robert Collier said, "In every adversity there lies the seed of an equivalent advantage." Do you find this to be true? Describe an experience in which this has been the case.

Day Five: How much of the way you view adversity have you learned from others, and how much is your own genuine perspective? What part is healthier and more effective?

Thirty-Four

Play

I am constantly astonished to see the number of adults who feel that play is a waste of time, that people who play are irresponsible or somehow not "acting their age." These are people who have come to believe that play is somehow just for children, and because they no longer practice the art, they never experience any of the benefits that play can bring to them.

Play, though, could be one of the most important elements of anyone's life. If we allow ourselves—and even push ourselves—to play, then we open up doors of our imagination and creativity that otherwise would lay dormant, undiscovered and undeveloped as we continue to do the same old things all the time, thinking about the same issues and the same ideas. When we play, though, we immerse ourselves in the present moment and we focus wholly on what we're doing, whether that's throwing or catching a Frisbee or a ball, climbing a tree, creating a fort, playing tag or laser tag, spraying each other with water guns, shooting baskets, or whatever else qualifies as "play" in our lives.

It is paradoxical that many educators and parents still differentiate between a time for learning and a time for play without seeing the vital connection between them.

Leo Buscaglia

In many ways, play is very similar to meditation, and it brings us many of the same benefits. When we involve ourselves fully in the play of the moment, our minds are free to focus on right here and right now, and for that period of time our cares and worries are not the main focus of our thinking. This happens, of course, if we allow ourselves to be completely at play, and not make a half-baked effort at it. If we start playing tag with the kids, then we need to be playing tag, and not thinking about the bills or the work that we have to do tomorrow. If we're playing Scrabble, then our minds should be on the letters we have and the words we can make, and not on something that someone said yesterday that's still bothering us.

Whenever I go to picnics or other similar activities, you won't find me with the adults, most of whom sit around on blankets or at picnic tables talking about the same things that they talked about yesterday and last week, talking about work and problems and things that are everywhere but where they are in the present moment—they're usually not talking about what a nice park they're in or how pretty the trees are. Yesterday's problems belong to a different time and place, but they bring them to the park anyway.

The kids, on the other hand, are involving themselves in the moment with their play, and that's where you'll find me. I have fun playing, mostly just because it's fun to play. But I also get many other benefits from it—I get a decent workout, I get to clear my mind of a lot of the junk that accumulates there (and believe me, my mind knows how to pick up junk), and I get to share time with kids and learn how they see the world and how they react to it. And the play is usually quite simple—it doesn't need to be complex for us to be involved in it.

The real joy of life is in its play. Play is anything we do for the
joy and love of doing it, apart from any profit, compulsion,
or sense of duty. It is the real living of life with the feeling
of freedom and self-expression. Play is the business of childhood,
and its continuation in later years is the prolongation of youth.

Walter Rauschenbusch

I think that Leslie is quite right when she says (below) that many adults avoid play because it seems like a waste of time—work is a much better way to spend our time, we believe. After all, we have to accomplish something with our time, and have something to show for it, don't we? That's what we've learned so far in our lives, but it that true? Not enough of us ever take the time that's necessary to sit down and ask ourselves honestly if that idea actually is true, or if it's a belief that we've developed that actually is harming us. Very few people who do take the time to do so reach the conclusion that work and accomplishment are the most important aspects of our lives, yet because very few people even think about it, guess where most of our beliefs are still centered?

Another problem with play these days is that too many people consider play to be something that must involve a computer or other technology. The "games" on computers, though, are developed with an eye towards addiction, and many people spend many hours in front of computer and television screens getting no benefits out of the time at all—they're just being controlled by their addiction. The games are designed to be addictive because someone somewhere makes more money if people are actually addicted to the games instead of just playing them casually now and then. The vast majority of such games ask for no creativity at all, either—they simply ask the player to react to things while sitting in a chair or on a couch.

Play can be stimulating and creative; it can be fun and rejuvenating. Play is a gift that has been given to us that we've put up on a shelf as we've gotten older, and we keep it there, waiting for that perfect day when we'll allow ourselves to play once more. It's like a starving person leaving a loaf of bread and a jar of peanut butter in the pantry, just waiting for the day when he or she needs them. But guess what? If you're starving, you need that food! And if you're human, you need that play if you're to live your life fully and completely, for the benefits of play are necessary, and play is one of the most precious gifts that we've been given.

Why is play so elusive for some grown-ups? Because we are so strongly attracted and attached to a profoundly goal-oriented, work-ethic-driven society. Like other forms of non-work, play connotes wastefulness, a stoppage in the way of what needs to get done. Yet often what really needs to get done has more to do with our hearts and spirits and less to do with a deadline or longstanding project. Play beckons to us, urging us to live in the present moment, a moment that becomes more luminous when we disallow interruptions like work and worry.

Leslie Levine

How can you play today? What can you do—even if just for ten or twenty minutes—that qualifies as play, that's fun to you, that brings your mind to a clear focus on the present moment and its activities, and that doesn't involve a computer, cell phone, or other technology? If you give it a chance, you'll find that it's fairly easy to reclaim the ability to play that you left behind as you grew to be an adult. And once you do that, you'll learn that you actually can learn more while you're playing than you can while you're working, as long as you allow yourself to be fully involved in the play. And once we learn that, imagine how our perspectives on life will grow into something much more than they are now?

Questions to Consider

1. What do you think about play now that you're an adult?

2. What are some possible benefits of play in your particular life situations?

3. Why do you think so many people "look down" on playing as if it were a complete waste of time and energy?

Possible Benefits of Play

Lower stress levels
Lower blood pressure
Better fitness
Having fun
Enjoying the company of others
Good exercise
Blowing off steam
Lots of fresh air
A free shower if it's raining
People may look at you like you're weird (which is a good thing!)
Something to talk about later
Memories of fun times as a kid
Learning new rules and strategies
You'll have more in common with kids you know
Spending time with like-minded people
A temporary escape from reality
Meditation break—focusing solely on your activity
Stimulating tons of brain activity
Develop eye/hand and eye/foot coordination
Etc., etc., etc.

Journal Entries

Day One: Think back on a time when you used to play when you were younger. Describe what playing felt like. Were you focused on what you were doing? Were you thinking about other things?

Day Two: How might you make more room for play in your life? Is it a question of time, or of making decisions to do it?

Day Three: Which friends do I have who might want to play with me? What would that be like? Write an invitation to an adult friend for a play date.

Day Four: You've heard another adult say that play is silly and a waste of time. Write a note to that person with your reaction to their words.

Day Five: Think about some of the important things you've learned from playing. How have they helped you in life?

Thirty-Five

Acceptance

Things are as they are. Right here and right now, that is a very simple truth, and there's absolutely no way to change that truth. If we want to change things, we change them for the future, and when moments of the future become the present, then things will be as they will be. But in this moment, they are as they are. We really have no choice at all but to accept them as they are, and to work from that reality if we want to make changes in our lives.

We sabotage our own efforts when we're unable to accept things and people as they are. We can make our lives miserable when we fight against things that are unchangeable, when we reject the truths of any given moment, when we refuse to believe that situations are what they are. A person who is lonely must accept that loneliness and allow it to be a part of his or her life instead of denying it and thus never being able to deal with it. And that's the problem with not accepting things as they are—we don't deal with our issues clearly; rather, we deal with what we think we want things to be, and the results of our efforts are thus skewed rather ineffectively.

*Some people confuse acceptance with apathy but there's
all the difference in the world. Apathy fails to distinguish
what can and cannot be helped; acceptance makes the
distinction. Apathy paralyzes the will-to-action;
acceptance frees it by relieving it of impossible burdens.*

Arthur Gordon

If a relationship is going poorly, it's important that I accept the problems of that relationship if I'm going to be able to do anything to deal with the problems in it. Many people, though, lie to themselves with the thought that there are no problems in the relationship—or that the problems are much less severe than they really are—and they actually act surprised when it suddenly ends. Or they try to make the relationship what they think it should be, rather than learning from the problems and trying to allow the relationship to develop on its own terms. A strong relationship, after all, also involves accepting the other person as he or she is, and accepting the development of the interactions of both people. Accepting the problems allows us to learn what those problems really are so that we can effectively deal with them head-on.

There is a tendency among people to think that when we accept things, we're being weak and allowing life to "have its way" with us, that we're relinquishing control over our lives. Nothing, though, could be further from the truth. Acceptance simply shows a great sense of awareness, and it allows us to be fully present in each moment as we make our ways through life.

Sometimes we get so caught up in seeing life as we want it to be that we're completely unable to see life as it is. When that happens, we're unable to deal with our situations as they are because we still see them as we want them to be. I might be somewhat less than adequate on my job, due to a lack of training or other factors, but until I accept the fact that I need to improve my performance, I never shall. And if I'm unable to see that I truly need to improve my performance, I never shall accept that fact, and I will continue to work at levels far lower than my potential.

Acceptance of one's life has nothing to do with
resignation; it does not mean running away from
the struggle. On the contrary it means accepting
it as it comes. . . . To accept is to say yes
to life in its entirety.

Paul Tournier

Learning to accept life as it is has been one of the most liberating perspectives that I've ever experienced. In the classroom, when I'm able to accept each student where they are right now, I give them the chance to grow from that point and improve in ways that are realistic to them. I don't expect everyone to be at the same levels—I accept them as they are, and we work from there. That means, of course, that not everyone's at the same level when we end a course, but that's okay, too—they don't need to be.

When I accept my wife as she is, then there's much less stress in both of our lives, for I'm not trying to change her to fit some image I have of what she should be like. I'm allowing her to be who she is, to think how she thinks, to do as she will—and we're both better off for it. And when she does the same for me, then we're simply able to spend time together and enjoy each other's company rather than trying to change each other because we refuse to accept some aspect of who that person is.

On a hot day, we have the choice between accepting the weather for what it is and making the best of it, or resenting it and wishing it were some other type of weather. If it's raining we may have to change plans, but the weather is what it is, and we must accept it if we want to keep our peace of mind. When we're stuck in traffic, things are as they are—and we can't do anything about it. So it's better to accept where we are and accept the fact that we can't move any faster so that we can at least try to enjoy the ride. If we're in debt, then we won't be able to do anything about it until we accept our debt so that we can start working towards paying it off.

The curious paradox is that when I accept
myself just as I am, then I can change.

Carl Rogers

Very often, our need to accept ourselves is our strongest need of all. We are who we are, and no amount of wishful thinking will make us someone else, will make us different. We are the product of our environments, the product of our genetic material, and the product of the choices and decisions that we've made and the thoughts that we have. We may be able to start right now to become someone different for tomorrow, but there really is no way of changing who we are at this moment. It's important to realize that we've done the best that we've can, we've made mistakes, and we've had our triumphs, and we are who we are. Accept that, and move on with your life, or deny it, and remain unable to make positive changes because you're not in touch with what really needs to be changed.

Acceptance is not giving up, and it's not being fatalistic, and it's not resignation. Rather, it's the healthy recognition of things as they are, a recognition that can help us to move on with our lives and improve them, and improve ourselves. Without acceptance, we continue to fight against forces that we deny even exist; with acceptance, we're able to work with life in order to make our lives and our experiences more positive and more fulfilling.

Questions about Acceptance

1. Is acceptance the same thing as resignation or giving up? What are some important differences between the meanings of the terms?

2. What kinds of things do you find to be easier to accept than others? More difficult?

3. Does our society encourage acceptance of things as they are, or modifying them or fighting them until they are what we want them to be? Why do you give the answer you do?

Thoughts about Acceptance

One of the main dangers of not accepting situations is that we will never be able to improve things if we don't accept the facts that the situation exists and that something needs to be done. If I don't accept the fact that I weigh more than is healthy, I'll never be able to work towards reaching a healthy weight. If I don't accept the fact that this person is lying to me, then I'll never be able to take steps to make sure that it doesn't continue to happen.

An important strategy for developing an accepting attitude towards the world is questioning our own perception. There are always clues to tell us when things aren't going extremely well in a certain area, and it's important that we pay attention to those clues. If this is the fourth time that what this person has told me has turned out not to be true, perhaps it's time for me to accept the fact that this person lies to me consistently.

This is especially important of our perceptions of things that are unpleasant to us. It's easy to accept things that we like. It's difficult to accept things that we don't like. We must ask ourselves questions about how we see the problems: Is this really going to go away by itself soon? Is this really not as bad as it seems, or is it as bad as it seems? Or worse? Could the problem in this situation be me, or my behaviors, rather than others?

Think of the words, "this is what it is." Have you lost your job? The situation is what it is, and we cannot change the past—so we have to accept the fact that we are now job seekers. And it's important that we not attach negative words to the statement—no "This is terrible" or "There's no way I can get past this." Those types of words only hinder our attempts to accept something. Has a loved one left you (or have you left someone)? The situation is what it is, and while it may change in the future, right here and right now, we must accept it. Telling ourselves "this is what it is" without adding judgmental words to the statement can help us to accept it for what it is and move forward.
(from the upcoming book, *Strategies for Living Life Fully*)

Journal Entries

Day One: Think of a situation that may be difficult to accept, such as a loved one telling you about an important decision that you don't think is a good one.

Day Two: "To accept is to say yes to life in its entirety," says Paul Tournier. If that's the case, then not accepting things is saying no to life. Do you feel this is true? What does it mean to you to say no to life?

Day Three: If someone you love is doing something destructive (like taking drugs, for example), does accepting this fact mean the same thing as approving of it? Can you accept a fact without approving of it?

Day Four: Explain the relationship between judgment and acceptance. Does judgment get in the way of acceptance? And if it does, then does it also get in the way of resolution of problems and situations?

Day Five: You have a friend who is having difficulty accepting an unpleasant fact about someone else. What advice would you give to this friend?

Thirty-Six

Forgiveness

It's sometimes amazing just how difficult it can be to forgive people. It's also sometimes amazing to see just how thoughtless and inconsiderate and even hurtful other people can be, and how much damage they can do to us emotionally, financially, spiritually, and physically. There are many people in this world who are so focused on their own wants, needs, and fears that they do whatever they feel is necessary to take care of themselves, and in the process they harm others. Needless to say, when they do this, they often harm us, and then we have to decide whether or not we're going to forgive them.

This isn't necessarily easy to do. When someone hurts me, for example, I know that every time I see that person in the future, that hurt is brought to mind. In a very real way, I re-experience that hurt. And though I may want to forgive that person completely, that new feeling of hurt is sometimes just as difficult to deal with as the original hurt was. In addition to this problem, the chances are that I've learned that I now can't trust this person, so even if I do fully forgive him or her, can I still work with this person as if nothing has happened? Can I spend time with this person even though doing so brings to the surface very negative and painful emotions?

If we can forgive everyone, regardless of what he or she may have done, we nourish the soul and allow our whole being to feel good. To hold a grudge against anyone is like carrying the devil on your shoulders. It is our willingness to forgive and forget that casts away such a burden and brings light into our hearts, freeing us from many ill feelings against our fellow human beings.

Sydney Banks

There are those people who make it sound as if forgiveness were simple, as if it's just a question of making a decision to forgive, and suddenly life is fine. If that were true, then life would be much easier, and we wouldn't face so many dilemmas about whom to trust and how to treat others. Forgiveness, though, is not simple at all, and it needs to be given its due as one of the more difficult acts that we will perform while we're alive. That definitely doesn't mean that it's impossible, but unless we recognize it for the difficult act that it is, we can't give forgiveness the respect that it deserves.

Forgiveness, after all, usually isn't something that benefits the other person as much as it benefits us, ourselves. When we're holding a grudge, after all, our minds are constantly focused on the hurt and the pain that we've experienced because of someone else's actions. It's even worse when the hurt was completely undeserved, for our minds are then focused on seeing ourselves as victims, too—we're not only focused on resentment and anger, but we're also focused on self-pity. Forgiveness is about allowing ourselves to leave these feelings behind and move on, thus making our own lives more positive and our own days brighter. Forgiving allows us to put all of our energy and focus into positive pursuits rather than splitting our focus between what we want to do and feel today and what has happened to us in the past.

While it is important to acknowledge that something wrong has happened and that we have every right to hold a grudge if we wish to, we also have to keep in mind that we also have a right to hold a lit match up to our arm for twenty seconds. The only difference between the two is that with the match, we actually see and feel the damage that we're doing to ourselves—there's no chance of us thinking that the burn is hurting someone else. With our grudges and resentment, though, we're also damaging ourselves—it's just that when we hurt ourselves that way, we don't necessarily see and feel or recognize the hurt that we're doing ourselves and our spirits. But the damage is real, and we don't actually see it or feel it until we do forgive, and we realize what a tremendous weight on our spirits we're leaving behind.

Forgiveness gives us the capacity to make a new start. . . And
forgiveness is the grace by which you enable the other person to
get up, and get up with dignity, to begin anew. . . In the act of
forgiveness we are declaring our faith in the future of a relationship
and in the capacity of the wrongdoer to change.

Desmond Tutu

There are a few very important aspects of forgiveness that are important to keep in mind if we truly want to free ourselves of our burdens. First of all, forgiveness can't be conditional. We can't say, "I'll forgive you if you change your ways." If we do this, then we're not really forgiving at all—and we keep our burdens with us as we watch to make sure that this person actually "deserves" our forgiveness. But we're the ones who deserve that forgiveness more than the other person, and expecting that person to change is keeping ourselves from experiencing the positive effects of forgiveness. Besides, it's not up to us to control anyone else's life, and we're bound to experience frustration if we do try. Also, forgiveness must be complete, but it must also be given in awareness that the person may hurt us again, and that we may end up having to forgive again.

That said, it's also important to keep in mind that the fact that we've forgiven someone doesn't mean that we now have to hand around that person as if nothing ever happened. With most family members, we do want to be with them still, but that's not true of everyone. If someone has violated our trust in a significant way and we think it's possible that it will happen again, then it's important that we make an intelligent decision and not deal with that person in the same ways again. Forgiveness does not necessarily lead to reconciliation.

Finally, forgiveness doesn't always have to be expressed to the person we're forgiving. If someone made a hurtful comment about us but is completely oblivious to that fact, it may or may not be useful to tell him or her that we forgive them. Sometimes it's important that we free our hearts and spirits of the burden, but keep the fact that we've done so to ourselves. If it won't help the other person at all, perhaps it's better that we don't share with that person.

Forgiveness of self is where all forgiveness starts. If I am unable
to forgive myself, it is impossible for me to truly forgive others.
And I must forgive others. What I give out is what I receive.
If I want forgiveness, I have to give forgiveness.

Betty Eadie

Betty also brings up a very important point about forgiveness—sometimes the most difficult person of all to forgive is one's self, for we know our own motivations and we're intimately familiar with our acts and the words we say. Forgiveness does have to begin with ourselves, for if we don't forgive ourselves, we're not in a position to forgive anyone else—or at least, our efforts to do so most definitely will not have the positive effects that they should have. We will also need to be forgiven by others for our own misdeeds and mistakes, so withholding forgiveness—of ourselves and others—most definitely will come back to affect us strongly at some point in our futures.

Forgive yourself. Forgive others. Live your life without resentment and anger and repressed hostility, and you'll find that your mind and spirit feel freer, lighter, healthier. If we are going to live our lives fully, we can't spend them being dragged down by negative feelings. And the release of those feelings lies within us, and in the decisions we make—even if the decisions are among the most difficult we'll make in our lives.

Questions to Consider

1. Is forgiving someone the same thing as approving of what they've done?

2. Is it necessary to "forgive and forget"? Is there a danger in doing so? But if you don't forget and you still hold something against a person, have you forgiven?

3. How strongly are judgment and forgiveness related? Judgment and the lack of forgiveness?

To Know All Is to Forgive All

Nixon Waterman

If I knew you and you knew me—
If both of us could clearly see,
And with an inner sight divine
The meaning of your heart and mine—
I'm sure that we would differ less
And clasp our hands in friendliness;
Our thoughts would pleasantly agree
If I knew you and you knew me.

If I knew you and you knew me,
As each one knows his own self, we
Could look each other in the face
And see therein a truer grace.
Life has so many hidden woes,
So many thorns for every rose;
The "why" of things our hearts would see,
If I knew you and you knew me.

Journal Entries

Day One: If someone you know is having a hard time forgiving another person in their life, write a note to them telling why it's important to forgive.

Day Two: It's a common truism that the person who does the forgiving benefits possibly even more than the person being forgiven. Do you think this is true? Why or why not?

Day Three: Can there be conditions attached to forgiveness? If there are, is it true forgiveness?

Day Four: Is it easier for you to forgive someone else, or yourself? What are some of the obstacles that make it difficult for us to forgive ourselves? What are some strategies for moving past those obstacles?

Day Five: You know a young person who did something wrong and who refuses to forgive him- or herself. Write him or her a note telling why it's important that they forgive themselves.

Thirty-Seven

Gratitude

There is much to be thankful for in life. This is an indisputable fact. The difficult part, though, is in our own individual attitudes and perspectives—after all, it's extremely simple to be caught up in the problems of our lives, the difficulties, the unfair situations, the potential disasters. And when I'm worried about paying bills or about a loved one's health, it can be easy to stay focused on those things and not on the other things for which I can feel a sense of gratitude.

From the fact that I woke up for another day on this planet this morning to the fact that I have a car that works and roads that are safe to the job I have, the money I earn, the food I eat, and the shelter I have, the list of things for which I can and should be grateful is extensive. There are people somewhere out there who are working every day to make sure that I have electricity and telephone service and running water, and I live in an era when I don't have to worry about many illnesses that would have killed me just 50 or 100 years ago. By my calculations, I probably would have died three or four times so far had I lived in an era without the medicines and medical technology that we have today.

In ordinary life we hardly realize that we receive a great deal more than we give, and that it is only with gratitude that life becomes rich. It is very easy to overestimate the importance of our own achievements in comparison with what we owe others.

Dietrich Bonhoeffer

If our lives are lacking anything, it very well could be a result of us not looking at it properly. I've been one of the worst of all at this over the course of my life—I've wasted much time being focused on what I thought was lacking in my life instead of focusing on what I had to be grateful for. For the most part, I'm over that, and even when things go badly I'm able to see the silver linings and I'm able to keep my mind on other things that are just fine (such as my health when I have troubles at work, for example).

The result of my somewhat skewed view of the world was that I often made myself miserable because I chose to put more of my attention on what I wished would change than I did on the things I should have been very grateful for. In my case, I know that more gratitude would not only would have been completely justified, but it would have made me a happier person and would have allowed me to enjoy all that I had much more than I actually did. It was all my choice, really, and I certainly often made the choice that hurt me rather than helped me.

I want my life to be rich, though, and I want to live it as fully and completely as I possibly can. One of the keys of accomplishing this goal is to keep in mind just how much other people have done for me, just how much the world offers me, and just how rich my life actually is already. I may not have tons of money in the bank, and I may not have a great deal of material goods, but there is plenty that I can be grateful for. There are times when I sit down and write lists of things for which I'm thankful, and that easy exercise helps me to realize the richness of my life as it is.

Whatever we are waiting for—peace of mind, contentment,
grace, the inner awareness of simple abundance—it will surely
come to us, but only when we are ready to receive it
with an open and grateful heart.

Sarah Ban Breathnach

Gratitude also, though, is a force in life. Our gratitude can help us to attract more positive things and events in our lives. If we think of it in the simplest of terms, it's obvious that someone would be more likely to do us another favor if we simply say "thank you" for the first favor. In a like manner, life itself will prove to be more generous if we feel and show gratitude for the wonderful things that life gives us to begin with. But if we're not careful, we can cut off the world's generosity by being ungrateful, by taking for granted the things that we have that are positive in our lives.

It is within our power to be grateful and to show gratitude. As Pam points out below, there are many wonderful things to be thankful for in life that are very simple and very important. If we can teach ourselves to be satisfied enough with the simple things that we can be grateful for them, then we will find ourselves being much, much happier—and nothing needs to change for this to occur except for our perspective and our attitude. Our society tries to tell us that things have to be exceptional for us to be thankful, and that we'll really be grateful when we have more of everything. Sometimes our dissatisfaction is present because advertisers have convinced us that we should be dissatisfied if we don't have their products. The reality is, though, that life is rather simple. When we learn this rule and understand it completely, we'll realize that things like a good cup of coffee, a piece of chocolate when we really crave it, a hug, a good umbrella when it's raining, and many, many more simple things are definitely worthy of our gratitude.

A bag of apples, a pot of homemade jam, a scribbled note,
a bunch of golden flowers, a coloured pebble, a box of seedlings,
an empty scent bottle for the children. . . . Who needs
diamonds and van-delivered bouquets?

Pam Brown

A sense of gratitude is within our grasp all the time, though we often get distracted from it and lose sight of it. It always is our choice, though, to be grateful or not. When we are, we do ourselves and other people in our lives a great favor, for we're spreading positive energy and helping ourselves and others to see the world more brightly. Feeling and showing our gratitude really is a simple way to give back to this world that has given so much to us, to contribute to the life that has provided us with all that we have and all that we are.

Questions to Ponder

1. Why do we tend to take many things for granted instead of feeling gratitude for them?

2. Do you have a lot to be grateful for? Do your problems outweigh your blessings?

3. Does our culture value gratitude for the things we have, or the effort to acquire more things, no matter how much we already have? Do we have to buy into our society's focus?

Creative Gratitude (an excerpt)
Wilferd A. Peterson

Creative gratitude is an attitude. It is magnetic and will draw good to you. It is good therapy, a road to happiness.

Thankfulness is a way of living more fully. Be thankful for your health and you will have health in more abundance. Be thankful for the love you receive and it will be increased. Be thankful for your success and you'll open doors to further achievement. Be thankful for your friends and more friends will come to you. Be thankful for beauty and you'll experience it more deeply.

Thankfulness is a way of enhancing relationships. Expressions of gratitude create in others an eagerness to reciprocate. When we become more fully aware that our success is due in large measure to the loyalty, helpfulness, and encouragement we have received from others, our desire grows to pass on similar gifts. Gratitude spurs us on to prove ourselves worthy of what others have done for us. The spirit of gratitude is a powerful energizer.

Thankfulness is a way of worshiping. All through the Psalms the emphasis is on thankfulness: "Sing to the Lord with thanksgiving". . . "Let us come before His presence with thanksgiving". . . "O give thanks unto the Lord, for He is good; for His steadfast love endures forever". . . "I will give thanks to the Lord with my whole heart."

When Jesus healed the ten lepers only one returned to fall at the feet of the Master and give thanks to God. With this in mind someone has written that nine were healed, while the one who gave thanks was made whole. The expression of gratitude made the big difference.

Creative gratitude is a force for harmony and goodwill. It brings people together in love and understanding. It is high on the scale of creative qualities to be practiced day in and day out in our moment-to-moment contacts.

Journal Entries

Day One: We all have things in our lives that we take for granted, be they people, computers, refrigerators, or any of a huge number of other things. Choose one person or thing that you take for granted and write down why you no longer feel gratitude for that person or thing.

Day Two: Can you make a decision to be grateful for something, or is it something that should happen naturally?

Day Three: Some countries have set aside a special day as a day of Thanksgiving. How do we feel on that day compared to other days? Is one day enough?

Day Four: Many people say that if we don't feel gratitude, we keep away from us more things for which we would or should be thankful. Is it true that a grateful heart and a grateful attitude can attract to us more for which we can be thankful?

Day Five: Write a short letter of thanks to God or life (depending on your beliefs, of course) saying thank you for what you have, and telling why you're thankful.

Thirty-Eight

Humility

I want always to be humble, but it's a very difficult road that arrives at humility. It's too easy to want to be right, to want to be recognized as having been right, or powerful, or kind, or particularly insightful. We like to be recognized by other people, and our egos like it even more than our spirits or our minds do. The struggle to remain humble really comes down to a conflict with our own egos—and if we're unable to put our egos in their right place, we'll continue to seek the approval and admiration of others instead of doing things because we know that they're right and proper.

As much as I wish to be humble, there's that other part of me that wants people to recognized all of the work that I've put in, getting to where I've gotten. That part of me wants the respect that comes with accomplishment, and it really is not at peace with being treated just like everyone else, even people who haven't put in nearly as much work or who haven't accomplished nearly as much. It's a part of me that I'm not too fond of, but a very real part nonetheless.

I remind that part of myself that all that I've accomplished, I've accomplished because other people have paved the way before me. I also tell it constantly that I'm very fortunate to have the skills and abilities that I do have, and that I did nothing at all to earn them. I might have worked to develop them, but that effort was mostly for self-gratification rather than for other motives that might have been more altruistic. It's important that I stay aware of my motives if I'm to be realistic about what I've done and why I've done it.

True humility is intelligent self-respect which keeps us
from thinking too highly or too meanly of ourselves.
It makes us mindful of the nobility God meant us
to have. Yet it makes us modest by reminding us
how far we have come short of what we can be.

Ralph W. Sockman

The desire to be recognized for what we've accomplished is a very important motivator for many of us, and we learn to expect recognition—even demand it, in some cases—as we grow up. The major problem with this approach, though, is that we learn to be motivated extrinsically rather than intrinsically, which means that all we do is motivated by others—either their advice, their directions, or their praise. Humility, though, is a state that allows us to be motivated simply by the act of doing, with no thought at all about how others are going to react. This isn't a form of arrogance or of being inconsiderate, though—rather, it's a way to approach life that allows us to see what needs to be done and then doing it, without being concerned about whether others praise us for having done it or not.

Humility is also a question of perspective, for how we see the world shapes how we are, just as how we are shapes how we see the world. This world is a beautiful, marvelous place—that would do just fine without us. The fact that we're here is a fantastic gift that we've been given, not a license to exert our will over creation. When we realize that we're here to help to contribute to the well-being of the world, we can see our place in this world more clearly. Realizing that we are but tiny specks in the vast realm of creation should not make us feel weak and insignificant, for we are neither. Humility allows us to realize just how small we really are, but just how much potential we have to contribute to our world at the same time. After all, a beautiful puzzle is the result of many small pieces working together to create a whole; likewise, our worlds would be incomplete without our personal contribution, but the contributions of others is just as significant and just as important as ours.

Being humble reminds me that I know very little about this world of ours. I know very little of other people's motivations and reasons. I know very little of the long-term effects of actions. My perspective, my knowledge, and my intuition are limited. That doesn't make me less worthwhile as a person, but it does remind me that there is much, much more to this life than I'm able to take in with my senses—so why should I spend so much time trying to control things?

Humility is the highest of all virtues. You can destroy your egotism
by developing this virtue alone. You can influence people.
You can become a magnet to attract the world.
It must be genuine. Feigned humility is hypocrisy.

Robert Collier

If I'm humble, I do not put unrealistic expectations upon others, and therefore I don't set myself up for the disappointment that doing so causes. If I'm humble, I don't place myself above others, and thus I don't set myself up for the fall that doing so sets us up for. If I live a humble life, I don't build a shelter of material goods that really does nothing to help to make me happy or content with life. My humility helps me to see the needs in other people, for it allows me to listen to them and to do my best to understand them. And other people do respond well to this trait of mine—they like being around other people who don't try to put them down to make themselves look better, and who aren't always involved in subtle games of one-upmanship that the humble person simply doesn't need to play.

Humility has suffered from the unfortunate tendency of some people to characterize it as weakness. Since the humble person doesn't feel a need to exalt him- or herself or to force others to submit to his or her will, that person sometimes seems to be more passive and less effective in life. The lack of aggression or even assertiveness, though, should by no means be seen as a lack of strength. In fact, it takes the greatest strength we have to go against the grain of our self-indulgent societies, to march to our own drummers when the whole world is telling us that we should—that we must—march to theirs. Finding our own fulfillment in a world that wants us to buy its fulfillment is a huge challenge, one that humility can help us to meet because we're not constantly involved in dealing with the conflicts that so many lifestyles constantly create.

We experience humility not because we have fought and lost but
because humility is the only lens through which great things can be
seen—and once we have seen them, humility
is the only posture possible.

Parker J. Palmer

Practicing humility demands that develop a healthy perspective on life, and that we allow ourselves to practice acceptance of life as it is. Yes, there are things in life that need to be changed, and we can even be the bringers of change, but causing change through humble means is much different than trying to exert our wills on others. A humble change-maker helps others to see the need for change instead of telling others what needs to be changed and how it needs to change. But acceptance of the world allows us to focus on our own spheres of influence, and allows us to give to the world the best we have, without feeling disappointment when we're not rewarded for our giving.

I want to be a humble person, and the fact that I've wanted this for a long time but still have made but modest inroads into being truly humble is an indication of the difficulty involved in living a humble life. I'm still caught up in possessions and asserting my will in many situations in which I later realize my will wasn't necessary—though not nearly to the extent that I used to be. Humility is a way of being that allows life to be life, and that permits us to enjoy it just as it is, without feeling that we have to modify it in order to make it more enjoyable. From a humble place, I can give more to others and they can find it easier to accept what I have to give, for there will be no demands on them for return. Humility is a difficult goal to strive for, but a truly worthy one.

Questions to Think about

1. What are some of the more attractive features of a humble person?

2. What are some of the social attitudes and expectations that tend to keep people from practicing true humility?

3. Is humility weakness? Why is it sometimes mistaken as such?

Thoughts on Humility

Humility is the highest of all virtues. You can destroy your egotism by developing this virtue alone. You can influence people. You can become a magnet to attract the world. It must be genuine. Feigned humility is hypocrisy. -Robert Collier

Humility must always be doing its work like a bee making its honey in the hive: without humility all will be lost.   -Teresa of Avila

Those who humble themselves shall be saved; those who bend shall be made straight; those who empty themselves shall be filled.   -Lao-Tzu

We experience humility not because we have fought and lost but because humility is the only lens through which great things can be seen—and once we have seen them, humility is the only posture possible.   -Parker J. Palmer

Journal Entries

Day One: Pretend that you're a kind or a queen, and you've been challenged to humble yourself. What are some of the difficulties you would face in being humble if you were king or queen?

Day Two: Think of someone in our world who doesn't seem to be humble at all, be it a friend or family member, an entertainer, or an athlete. Write this person a short letter telling them how their lives would improve if they were to show a little humility.

Day Three: Do people want to spend time with other people who aren't humble? What do we lose if other people don't want to spend time with us?

Day Four: Parker J. Palmer says that "humility is the only lens through which great things can be seen." What does he mean by that? Do you agree with him? Why or why not?

Day Five: Write down a list of benefits that living a humble life would bring you.

Thirty-Nine

Mindfulness

One of the most difficult skills that I've been working on for the past couple of decades has been that of mindfulness, the ability to look around myself at the world and notice all that is happening, all that is around me, without judging it or wishing it were different. It's just too easy to see things and not accept them as they are, but wish that they were somehow different.

We often spend our lives in a kind of a state that keeps us thinking, "What do I have to do about that?" We get so used to having to fix things and take care of things that we sometimes can't even look at a beautiful scene without thinking that someone needs to mow that grass or rake those leaves. We can't look at a tree without thinking that it would be prettier if (fill in the blank). Or, worse still, we can walk by absolutely beautiful scenes without even noticing them, or pass by situations that we should contribute to, oblivious to the fact that we could make a significant difference in something because our minds are too caught up in our thoughts to allow us to see what's all around us, right here and right now.

It's easy to get lost in our own heads. It's easy to allow the thoughts and worries and plans and hopes to take on their own lives and control our minds in such a way that we lose sight of all that's around us in any given moment. It's difficult to allow those thoughts and problems to take a back seat in our lives in order to be completely aware of what's right here, right now. Perhaps there's a person who really could use you to take a couple of moments to pay attention to him or her; perhaps there's a cool autumn breeze that's going to calm your spirit with its amazing touch—but only if you actually notice it.

Cultivating a generous spirit starts with
mindfulness. Mindfulness, simply stated,
means paying attention to what is actually
happening; it's about what is really going on.

Nell Newman

You're surrounded at the moment by beautiful and special things. The chances are, though, if you're like most of us, that you don't even see some of those things anymore because you've grown so used to them that your eyes just skip right over them when they're in your field of vision. After all, you can't spend a couple of moments admiring the beauty of that picture or that small sculpture on your desk because there's something much, much more important that you have to think about.

The truth is, though, that there really is nothing more important in this world than slowing down and taking the time—even if it's just thirty or sixty seconds—to appreciate something special in our lives. And even if we appreciate the same thing day after day, so what? If it's beautiful and we like it and/or it reminds us of someone or someplace special, then it's worth that small investment in time that it takes to be mindful of it.

But mindfulness obviously isn't just about appreciation and noticing things. While being appreciative and seeing things definitely can make our lives richer, they aren't the only reasons for which mindfulness is important. When we are mindful, we see things that can be or must be done. We notice the words of someone else that tell us "I'm saying that I'm okay, but I'm really not." We can see things that we missed and that are too important to be missed. In some professions, mindfulness is absolutely necessary—someone who makes a living cooking, for example, needs to pay close attention to all that's going on with the food, but also needs to be aware of his or her surroundings. A doctor needs to pay attention to the symptoms, but also has to listen to what the patient tells him or her. It's very easy to get hyper-focused on a task at hand—and there's nothing wrong with that in small doses—and then lose sight of everything else that makes our lives so rich and full. How many parents do you know who are not mindful of their children because they have so much else to do that's somehow more "important"?

I don't know if you can live inside each and
every moment. But when you can, try
to stop, look, and listen long enough to be
right where you are, not in your past,
not in your future. Just right in the middle
of a split second in time.

Leslie Levine

In his book *Island*, Aldous Huxley writes of a community of people who have trained birds all around who constantly repeat the words "Here and now" and "Attention." They serve as a constant reminder to those people of what's really important—who is here and what I can do, right here and right now. So when their inner monologues start in their minds and pull them away from the present and cause them to regret the past of worry about the future, a bird comes along and tells them exactly what's important in life: here and now. Because here and now are the only places, in space and time, in which we can actually have some sort of influence; the only places in which we can actually act. Huxley writes, "That's what you always forget, isn't it? I mean, you forget to pay attention to what's happening. And that's the same as not being here and now."

My mindfulness can be a blessing to others, as well. As a teacher, I'm pretty constantly thinking about what we're going to do tomorrow and next week, and it's very easy for me to get caught up in the subject. But in my entire teaching career, which now spans over twenty years, the moments that I remember as being the most important are those in which I've noticed something about particular students and I've commented on them. "You do a great job with the short stories." "Are you okay today? You look a bit down." "I noticed you carrying that book—do you like that author?" These have been the times when I've made true connections with my students, and they are times that have allowed the students to realize that I do pay attention to them, and that I do care. And they've come about because I've been able to step away from the stress and strain of teaching in order to pay attention to the human beings who are in my classes.

Mindfulness is simply being aware of what is happening right now without wishing it were different; enjoying the pleasant without holding on when it changes (which it will); being with the unpleasant without fearing it will always be this way (which it won't).

James Baraz

Mindfulness can be simple, as James points out. But "simple," alas, doesn't always mean "easy." Mindfulness allows us to listen to someone share an opinion that we see as silly or even harmful, and not try to change that person's opinion, but to try to understand it. Mindfulness allows us to recognize and accept something negative in our lives, even as we do what we can to deal with it.

Most importantly, mindfulness helps us to learn about life, to witness and appreciate all that is around us, and a truly mindful person is one whose wisdom grows steadily because he or she is much less likely to try to impose his or her will onto the world, being satisfied instead to learn and to grow. When we learn like this, we also learn to discern between situations that truly need our input or effort and those situations that are best left alone to be resolved by others. When we're mindful of the world, we see the causes and effects without necessarily putting ourselves in the situations, and we gain knowledge that can be very important to share with others, later.

One of my most important goals is to be more mindful. There are many strategies that I can take to do this, from putting up little notes to remind me of the present moment to emailing myself reminders to pay attention to electronic alarms on my watches and clocks that bring me back to the present moment. With so many different methods available to me to remind myself to be "here and now," there really is no reason not to be more present in my life, is there?

Questions to Consider

1. Why are we taught so little about mindfulness as we grow up?

2. Are mindfulness and awareness the same thing?

3. What are some of the benefits of being mindful in life?

I'd Pick More Daisies (an excerpt)
Don Herold

If I had my life to live over, I would pay less attention to people who teach tension. In a world of specialization we naturally have a superabundance of individuals who cry at us to be serious about their individual specialty. They tell us we must learn Latin or History; otherwise we will be disgraced and ruined and flunked and failed. After a dozen or so of these protagonists have worked on a young mind, they are apt to leave it in hard knots for life. I wish they had sold me Latin and History as a lark.

I would seek out more teachers who inspire relaxation and fun. I had a few of them, fortunately, and I figure it was they who kept me from going entirely to the dogs. From them I learned how to gather what few scraggly daisies I have gathered along life's cindery pathway.

If I had my life to live over, I would start barefooted a little earlier in the spring and stay that way a little later in the fall. I would play hooky more. I would shoot more paper wads at my teachers. I would have more dogs. I would keep later hours. I'd have more sweethearts. I would fish more. I would go to more circuses. I would go to more dances. I would ride on more merry-go-rounds. I would be carefree as long as I could, or at least until I got some care—instead of having my cares in advance.

Journal Entries

Day One: "Mindfulness is simply being aware of what's happening right now without wishing it were different." How easy is this to do? What are some of the reasons we so constantly wish things were different? How does this wish affect us?

Day Two: Right now, look around and find three things that are happening around you that you hadn't noticed before. (Birds feeding outside, snow falling, flame on the candle flickering.) What kept you from noticing these things earlier?

Day Three: Think about a time in your past when you haven't noticed something that turned out to be important. How would things have been different if you had noticed? (I didn't notice that a friend of mine wasn't doing well, and I made a comment that made things worse.)

Day Four: Think of three practical strategies that you can use to become more mindful. (I often decide to wear something like a bracelet or a ring to remind me to pay attention to life.) What benefits might come from putting these strategies into practice.

Day Five: Who would benefit from you *not* being more mindful? Who in our society would be better off if people didn't pay attention to what's going on in the world?

Forty

Patience

I've definitely learned patience the hard way. I grew up as a person who was probably more patient than his peers, but still quite impatient. I wanted things now, and I wanted to finish things as soon as I started them. If something needed to be done, I often didn't respect the process necessary to do it well; rather, I tried to get it done as quickly as I could, and that tendency often resulted in rather mediocre results.

I remember one incident that was rather representative of the way that I did things: when I was in my last year in college, I needed a bike and I didn't have much money, so I figured that I needed to get a used bike. Unfortunately, there weren't many being offered in my price range, so I bought the first one that I found within my price range, even though I had misgivings about doing so even while I was making the purchase. And the misgivings should have guided me, but I needed the bike now, I thought.

It turned out to be a horrible bike, and one that I couldn't really ride comfortably. A few days later, I saw some very affordable new bikes in a store, and I felt like an idiot because I had to buy one if I was going to have a bike that I could use. In that case, my only loss was some money, but as tight as money was then, it also caused me a great deal of stress and anxiety to lose even that relatively small amount of money.

One who is master of patience
is master of everything else.

Edward Lindley

That's a relatively minor incident that involves money and material goods, but it does illustrate an important point: sometimes in our minds, we *believe* that something has to happen quickly if it's going to happen at all, or if other people aren't going to be disappointed in us. The truth is, though, that you can't eat an apple until it ripens, and it will do so when it's ready. If you eat it too early, you will pay a heavy price in stomach pains (and I can vouch for this, too), just as trying to get a job done quickly often results in a very poor job—so the praise that you expect for finishing quickly is replaced by the criticism you receive for shoddy work.

I know where much of my impatience comes from. As I studied about being an ACOA, I learned that the instability of my younger years caused me to get used to broken promises—and to think that if something didn't happen now, it wasn't going to happen at all. The outing that was promised this weekend never happened because of someone else's actions, yet if that same someone came home and said "Let's do this now," it did come to pass.

As the years have gone by and I've learned to become more patient, I have seen an amazing transformation in how I see the world and how I feel about the world. As I practice patience, I see that other people—especially my students— very much appreciate the fact that I'm not being impatient with them. And they tend to learn more when they can learn in their time. My patience allows me not to expect too much too soon, for I've learned that not everyone can grasp everything immediately in every subject. Yes, my students have to learn certain skills and concepts, but some of them will get them immediately, and others won't get them until we've repeated them for several weeks. That's just life, and the timing I want isn't necessarily the timing that my students are able to meet.

Patience is power. Patience is not an absence
of action; rather, it is "timing"; it waits on
the right time to act, for the right
principles and in the right way.

Fulton J. Sheen

Developing patience, in my experience, requires a lot of self-talk—the positive kind. When I need to be more patient, I need to remind myself, "it doesn't matter if it's done in ten minutes or in twenty"; "It's not that important if we leave at this moment or if we leave in fifteen minutes"; "I want the job to be done now, but I also want it to be done well, and I still have four more steps that I have to do well, or the finished product won't be as good as I want it."

It also requires us first of all to be patient with ourselves. We often have such high expectations of ourselves that we tend to be very impatient with our mistakes or our own lack of sufficient speed. Our own impatience with ourselves, in fact, often leads to lower self-esteem and lessened self-respect. And as Brian Adams says below, impatience breeds a lot of very negative feelings, and they can be disastrous when they're directed at ourselves. When we learn to be more patient with ourselves, there are many more positive feelings that result, and we become much more capable and much more effective in all that we do.

Learn the art of patience. Apply discipline to
your thoughts when they become anxious over the
outcome of a goal. Impatience breeds anxiety,

fear, discouragement and failure. Patience creates
confidence, decisiveness, and a rational outlook,
which eventually leads to success.

Brian Adams

Sometimes we mistake patience for weakness, but the patient person often realizes that it's much more important for another person to discover his or her own gifts and shortcomings—the patient person doesn't feel a need to "fix" other people, and sometimes will let certain things slide until the other person recognizes the problems. Patient parents often let their kids make the same mistake two or three times because they know that a lesson learned oneself is almost always preferable to a lesson given to us by an authority figure like a parent.

Our patience can be a very important boon to ourselves, but it also can be a very welcome and very helpful gift to other people in our lives. The cashier who makes a mistake can stand to be shown a bit of patience. The co-worker who's overwhelmed with work and who hasn't been able to get to our project yet. The child who's still learning how to do something and is taking a very long time at it still. So many people can use our patience, and their lives will be made much, much easier when we share it with them.

And our lives, too, will become much easier, much more effective, and much more pleasant when we develop our patience and we become patient people.

Questions to Think about

1. Is our society a patient one in general? Are we becoming more or less patient as time goes on?

2. What are some of the benefits that you've experienced from being patient? Do they help you to be more patient more often?

3. What are some of the reasons for which we tend not to be patient sometimes? What makes us want to have things done more quickly?

Ralph Waldo Emerson on Patience
from his essay "Education"

Leave this military hurry and adopt the pace of Nature. Her secret is patience.

Do you know how the naturalist learns all the secrets of the forest, of plants, of birds, of beasts, of reptiles, of fishes, of the rivers and the sea? When he goes into the woods the birds fly before him and he finds none; when he goes to the river bank, the fish and the reptile swim away and leave him alone. His secret is patience; he sits down, and sits still; he is a statue; he is a log. These creatures have no value for their time, and he must put as low a rate on his.

By dint of obstinate sitting still, reptile, fish, bird and beast, which all wish to return to their haunts, begin to return. He sits still; if they approach, he remains passive as the stone he sits upon. They lose their fear. They have curiosity too about him. By and by the curiosity masters the fear, and they come swimming, creeping and dying towards him; and as he is still immovable, they not only resume their haunts and their ordinary labors and manners, show themselves to him in their work-day trim, but also volunteer some degree of advances towards fellowship and good understanding with a biped who behaves so civilly and well.

Can you not baffle the impatience and passion of the child by your tranquility? Can you not wait for him, as Nature and Providence do? Can you not keep for his mind and ways, for his secret, the same curiosity you give to the squirrel, snake, rabbit, and the sheldrake and the deer? He has a secret; wonderful methods in him; he is—every child—a new style of man; give him time and opportunity.

Journal Entries

Day One: Someone has just asked you how they can become more patient. Write them a letter telling them how they can do so.

Day Two: Brian Adams says that "patience creates confidence, decisiveness, and a rational outlook." Why are these three things important in our lives?

Day Three: Think of a very patient person whom you've known. What do you most admire about that person? What about their patience did you notice most strongly?

Day Four: What, to you, are some of the greatest causes of impatience? How do you deal with them?

Day Five: Why is patience considered to be power?

Forty-One

Rest

I'm a very strong proponent of rest, and it scares me quite a bit when I see just how few people seem to value the concept enough to make it an integral part of their lives. It frightens me because I know that many of the people around me are doing mediocre jobs and pushing themselves to unhealthy limits simply because they refuse to take the time to recharge, reinvigorate, and rejuvenate themselves. They're hurting themselves and others by not taking the time to do something that's absolutely necessary, and they're justifying their actions by claiming that they have no choice, that life demands that they be so busy.

But rest is not a luxury. Rest is a necessity. Study after study shows that people who are well rested are more efficient, more accurate, and more satisfied at their jobs and in life in general. A well rested parent isn't going to snap at his or her kids like a tired parent will; a well rested police officer is going to make better decisions and be able to deal with conflict better; a well rested doctor will be less likely to make mistakes that can harm and possible even kill a patient.

When I'm rested, I'm less likely to see the world darkly, for my mind is more alert and I'm much more aware of my surroundings and my life in general. I can see and notice the positive in situations even when bad ones come up, whereas when I'm tired and drained, anything negative gets amplified greatly in my mind so that it's easy for me to become depressed, anxious, and nervous.

Rest is not idleness, and to lie sometimes on the grass
on a summer day listening to the murmur of water,
or watching the clouds float across the sky,
is hardly a waste of time.

John Lubbock

Rest is also, of course, good for the body. When you're hiking up a mountainside, it's important to stop now and then and allow your body to recover from the effort. One of my favorite short stories is that of two men who were in a competition to harvest the wheat from a field, an all-day effort. One man, the physically stronger one, started out quickly and kept going, impressing everyone with his speed and strength. The other man started out at a decent speed, but it was obvious that he was conserving his strength. And then, after a few hours, he actually stopped and rested and had something to eat! In the morning, the stronger man built a significant lead, but by the time the afternoon came, he completely burned himself out and couldn't keep on. The other man took a lunch break and then kept working at his steady pace, eventually accomplishing far, far more than the stronger man.

This is why substitutes are so necessary in sports such as basketball and football, and why lunch hours and breaks are built into work days. Our bodies need breaks from what we're doing; otherwise, we'll burn ourselves out and not be able to work nearly as effectively as we could if we took a break now and then. I used to watch college students sit for five or six hours straight, trying to get all their work done in one marathon session. Their last couple of hours, though, were usually wasted time because they were so exhausted, mentally and physically. I would tell them that they'd be much better off working for two and a half hours, taking a twenty-minute walk, and then finishing up with the last two hours of their study sessions, for both the brain and the body need time to be focused on something else. We need our rests.

The most valuable thing we can do for the psyche, occasionally,
is to let it rest, wander, live in the changing light of room,
not try to be or do anything whatever.

May Sarton

One of the most insidious aspects of our society is the mistaken—and even cruel—belief that wanting to rest is a sign of weakness, and that it shows that we're somehow lazy. Personally, I'm a person who likes to be busy: I did two MA's simultaneously for two years, and I consistently take on extra work or classes. But I also make sure that I'm well rested when I'm doing such work. I make sure that rest is planned into my schedule, for if it weren't, the amount of work would be more than overwhelming, and the results would be mediocre at best. I also have run many very long distances, and when I do, I make sure to build in rests while I go. If I'm running 100 miles, it's important that I build in rests as early as the ten- or fifteen-mile marks so that I can be sure to have something left twenty hours later.

I even build short breaks into classes I teach, when I ask students to write a 10-minute reflective essay or to work on some sort of exercises to practice something we've been discussing. Mental strain builds up rather quickly when trying to teach concepts to others, and such short breaks are very helpful. I use the time to help the students individually, but it is a break from the normal classroom routine.

If you feel a need to rest, that's not laziness—that's your mind and/or body telling you that it's important for you to take some sort of break. There's absolutely nothing wrong with taking that break, either, for the work that you do later will be of higher quality if you do make sure to take care of yourself now. While we don't want to let things go too far and end up being slackers, we do want to take care of ourselves so that we don't wind ourselves up so tightly that we eventually reach some sort of breaking point—that would be the worst thing that we could do to ourselves. Our newspapers are full of stories of people who do reach that breaking point, and it's not pretty when it happens.

Activity and rest are two vital aspects of life. To find a balance in them is a skill in itself. Wisdom is knowing when to have rest, when to have activity, and how much of each to have. Finding them in each other— activity in rest and rest in activity— is the ultimate freedom.

Sri Sri Ravi Shankar

I like the idea of balance between rest and activity. To me, 15-20% of our work time should be rest (that's about ten minutes an hour), and I do try to reach that balance regularly. I know, though, that there are often times when I'm going to go three or four hours with no break at all, but that's okay as long as I balance that sort of effort with sufficient rest afterwards. I also know that something that's effort for someone else—a long walk, for example—is actually rest for me. We should make the effort to know ourselves well enough to recognize the signs that tell us that we do need to rest, signs such as crankiness or a lack of ability to focus or simple physical tiredness. The rest that we take is important not just to us, but to the quality of the work that we're doing and to the quality of the relationships with the people with whom we work.

If we do want to live our lives fully, we need to take rests from our work, from our computers, from our cell phones, from our relationships, from our stressors, from our worries, from our television sets. Too much of anything becomes harmful, and rest is one of our most important—and most often undervalued— methods of dealing with many of the things that ail us. Do yourself and the others in your life a huge favor and make sure that you're well rested, for it truly is up to you whether you are or not.

Questions to Ponder

1. Do you get enough rest? Why does our society often seem to frown upon rest?

2. How do we decide how to balance rest and work and activity in our lives?

3. What are some of the most important benefits of rest?

from *On the Open Road*
Ralph Waldo Trine

Our complex modern life, especially in our larger centers, gets us running so many times into grooves that we are prone to miss, and sometimes for long periods, the all-around, completer life. We are led at times almost to forget that the stars come nightly to the sky, or even that there is a sky; that there are hedgerows and groves where the birds are always singing and where we can lie on our backs and watch the treetops swaying above us and the clouds floating by an hour or hours at a time; where one can live with his or her soul or, as Whitman has put it, where one can loaf and invite one's soul.

We need changes from the duties and the cares of our accustomed everyday life. They are necessary for healthy, normal living. We need occasionally to be away from our friends, our relatives, from the members of our immediate households. Such changes are good for us; they are good for them. We appreciate them better, they us, when we are away from them for a period, or they from us.

We need these changes occasionally in order to find new relations—this is a twofold sense. By such changes there come to our minds more clearly the better qualities of those with whom we are in constant association; we lose sight of the little frictions and irritations that arise; we see how we can be more considerate, appreciative, kind.

In one of those valuable essays of Prentice Mulford entitled "Who Are Our Relations?" he points us to the fact, and with so much insight and common sense, that our relations are not always or necessarily those related to us by blood ties, those of our immediate households, but those most nearly allied to us in mind and in spirit, many times those we have never seen, but that we shall sometime, somewhere be drawn to through ceaselessly working Law of Attraction, whose basis is *like attracts like*.

And so in staying too closely with the accustomed relations we may miss the knowledge and the companionship of those equally or even more closely related.

We need these changes to get the kinks out of our minds, our nerves, our muscles—the cobwebs off our faces. We need them to whet again the edge of appetite. We need them to invite the mind and the soul to new possibilities and powers. We need them in order to come back with new implements, or with implements redressed, sharpened, for the daily duties. It is like the chopper working too long with axe underground. There comes the time when an hour at the stone will give it such persuasive power that he can chop and cord in the day what he otherwise would in two or more, and with far greater ease and satisfaction.

We need periods of being by ourselves—*alone*. Sometimes a fortnight or even a week will do wonders for one, unless he or she has drawn too heavily upon the account. The simple custom, moreover, of taking an hour, or even a half hour, *alone in the quiet*, in the midst of the daily routine of life, would be the source of *inestimable gain* for countless numbers.

If such changes can be in closer contact with the fields and with the flowers that are in them, the stars and the sea that lies open beneath them, the woods and the wild things that are of them, one cannot help but find oneself growing in love for and an ever fuller appreciation of these, and being at the same time so remade and unfolded that one's love, one's care, and one's consideration for all mankind and for every living creature, will be the greater.

Journal Entries

Day One: How do you tend to feel when you don't have enough rest? How often is a lack of rest due to your decisions rather than due to circumstances outside of your control?

Day Two: Why do so many people feel that they're able to function properly without rest? What does our society tell us about taking rest and taking care of ourselves?

Day Three: Think of someone you know who doesn't ever get enough rest. Write a letter to that person telling them why they should change their habits and start getting enough rest.

Day Four: Make a list of the benefits you get when you rest an adequate amount. How do those benefits add to your overall well-being?

Day Five: Write down three strategies for working more rest into your schedule.

Forty-Two

Solitude

There is a certain peace in being alone that we simply never shall find if we're always surrounded by other people. Why, then, are we so often afraid of being alone? Solitude is really the only state in which we can accomplish the reflection that we need to understand our lives and our selves, and it's in solitude that we're able to develop the strength that allows us to deal with many of life's setbacks and obstacles. When we're alone we can tap the creative depths of our minds and hearts without the distractions and tangents that are introduced to us by others. Our aloneness is a healthy, marvelous place, yet we somehow learn to fear it—we somehow learn that if we spend time alone, there's something "wrong" with us.

In my life, solitude has been an extremely valuable asset, though for many years I saw it as a curse. I simply didn't want to be alone, and I wanted to be with other people. My very nature, though, was geared towards solitude, for I never really enjoyed many of the things that other people do to avoid being alone; especially difficult for me was the way that alcohol was so often a major part of most "social" gatherings. Having grown up in a family with an alcoholic parent, I simply didn't want to be around people who were drinking. Even as a child, I spent a lot of time alone, reading or drawing or writing, while the rest of my family watched TV (another activity I'm not particularly fond of). When I was alone as a grown-up, though, I spent most of my time wishing I were with other people rather than taking advantage of my alone time.

There are many things that we can do when we're alone that we simply can't do when we're with other people. In solitude, we have time for more reading, more reflection, more walks alone, more hiking and camping in places that other people probably wouldn't want to go. Yes, it is great to share experiences, and the company of our fellow human beings can be one of the most important elements of life, but it's also important that we accept our solitude when we've been gifted with it and use it to fulfill some of our deep needs that can't be filled when we're in groups or even part of a couple.

Deliberately seeking solitude—quality time spent away
from family and friends—may seem selfish. It is not.
Solitude is as necessary for our creative spirits to develop
and flourish as are sleep and food for our bodies to survive.

Sarah Ban Breathnach

Some people view other people's solitude as selfishness, as Sarah points out. But just as rest and relaxation are necessary to keep ourselves strong and able to deal with our lives, solitude can provide us with a spiritual and emotional rejuvenation that can make us stronger and more resilient in the face of life's challenges.

Not all of us can find the means to spend two weeks alone whenever we feel like it, of course, but solitude doesn't necessarily need to be extravagant or extreme. Sometimes it's as simple as going into another room with a book and closing the door behind us. Sometimes, the long walk in the morning can be a balm that soothes our nerves and allows us to ponder life and consider the challenges we're facing.

For me, the solitude is a beautiful experience in itself, but it also helps to strengthen other experiences. Just as the best meals I've ever had have come after times of having very little to eat, some of the best times I've spent with others have come after time that I've spent alone. When I've spent time in solitude, I tend to listen more when I'm with others, and I tend to appreciate their presence more. I don't feel a need to talk as much, and I'm able to just be with the other people without having any expectations or preconceived ideas of how people should act or what they should say. And I know, when this happens, that it's one of the many benefits of having spent time alone and learning even more how to value myself and be comfortable with myself just as I am.

It is a difficult lesson to learn today—to leave one's
friends and family and deliberately practice the art
of solitude for an hour or a day or a week. And yet,
once it is done, I find there is a quality to being
alone that is incredibly precious. Life rushes back
into the void, richer, more vivid, fuller than before.

Anne Morrow Lindbergh

Why does our society value keeping people in groups as much as possible? In part, it's because when we're in groups, we spend more money. But also, being with other people helps us to deal with many of our fears of being alone in life, our fears that we're somehow not good enough, somehow rejected by our fellow human beings. Many years ago, Blaise Pascal said that all of our miseries result from not being able to sit in a quiet room alone, which implies that we do not feel comfortable being alone with our own thoughts.

Being with a group—or even with just one other person—means that we never have to experience our thoughts as deeply as we can, or as fully as we can. Our thoughts frighten us, because when we do sit alone in a quiet room, we sometimes find ourselves thinking things that we don't necessarily want to think—but that we need to think if we're ever going to work our ways past the fears and insecurities that those thoughts imply. Being alone allows us time to work our ways through our thoughts and feelings, and we can come out of our aloneness with a new resolve, with a new sense of strength that can come only from knowing ourselves a bit better and feeling more confident of what we want and our ability to fulfill our own wishes.

The awareness we experience in solitude is priceless for the peace it can give. It is also the key to true loving in our relationships. When we have a part of ourselves that is firm, confident, and alone, we don't need another person to fill us. We know that we have private spaces full of goodness and self-worth, and we grant the same to those we love. We do not try to pry into every corner of their lives or to fill the emptiness inside us with their presence.

Kent Nerburn

Solitude is within our reach almost all the time. Of course, I'm not going to find a lot of solitude when I'm in my classroom with 25 students, or if I'm working in a store serving customers constantly. But if we consciously search out the moments of solitude that can help to rejuvenate us—those few minutes that we can spend completely with ourselves and our own thoughts—then we can use solitude to make our lives richer and fuller. And even in the crowds, according to Emerson, solitude is within our reach: the great person, he says, is the one "who in the midst of the crowd keeps with perfect sweetness the independence of solitude." It's a matter of perspective, and a matter of effort, but the solitude we crave and need is always available to us.

Questions to Consider

1. Why is it sometimes difficult to spend time alone? Why do people avoid it so often?

2. What are some of the good sides of being on our own? How can it help us to live our lives more fully?

3. Why do most of the religious traditions teach the importance of solitude? Why do people who are "enlightened" tend to spend much time alone?

Solitude and Seclusion

Khalil Gibran

Life is an island in an ocean of solitude and seclusion.

Life is an island, rocks are its desires, trees its dreams, and flowers its loneliness, and it is in the middle of an ocean of solitude and seclusion.

Your life, my friend, is an island separated from all other islands and continents. Regardless of how many boats you send to other shores or how many ships arrive upon your shores, you yourself are an island separated by its own pains, secluded in its happiness and far away in its compassion and hidden in its secrets and mysteries.

I saw you, my friend, sitting upon a mound of gold, happy in your wealth and great in your riches and believing that a handful of gold is the secret chain that links the thoughts of the people with your own thoughts and links their feelings with your own.

I saw you as a great conqueror leading a conquering army toward the fortress, then destroying and capturing it.

On second glance I found beyond the wall of your treasures a heart trembling in its solitude and seclusion like the trembling of a thirsty man within a cage of gold and jewels, but without water.

I saw you, my friend, sitting on a throne of glory, surrounded by people extolling your charity, enumerating your gifts, gazing upon you as if they were in the presence of a prophet lifting their souls up into the planets and stars. I saw you looking at them, contentment and strength upon your face, as if you were to them as the soul is to the body.

On the second look I saw your secluded self standing beside your throne, suffering in its seclusion and quaking in its loneliness.

I saw that self stretching its hands as if begging from unseen ghosts. I saw it looking above the shoulders of the people to a far horizon, empty of everything except its solitude and seclusion.

I saw you, my friend, passionately in love with a beautiful woman, filling her palms with your kisses as she looked at you with sympathy and affection in her eyes and the sweetness of motherhood on her lips; I said, secretly, that love has erased his solitude and removed his seclusion and he is now within the eternal soul which draws toward itself, with love, those who were separated by solitude and seclusion.

On the second look I saw behind your soul another lonely soul, like a fog, trying in vain to become a drop of tears in the palm of that woman.

Your life, my friend, is a residence far away from other homes named after you. If this residence is dark, you cannot light it with your neighbor's lamp; if it is empty you cannot fill it with the riches of your neighbor; were it in the middle of the desert, you could not move it to a garden planted by someone else.

Your inner soul, my friend, is surrounded with solitude and seclusion. Were it not for this solitude and this seclusion you would not be you and I would not be

I. If it were not for that solitude and seclusion, I would, if I heard your voice, think myself to be speaking; yet, if I saw your face, I would imagine that I were looking into a mirror.

Journal Entries

Day One: Many people have a hard time being alone. Why do you think this is?

Day Two: Make a list of things that you'd like to do and that you can do all on your own. Would these things be possible with someone else around?

Day Three: Kent Nerburn said, "The awareness we experience in solitude is priceless for the peace it can give." How can being alone bring peace? Why does it bring awareness?

Day Four: Think about times when you haven't wanted to be alone—why haven't you at those times? Has fear been part of the picture?

Day Five: Write a letter to yourself encouraging yourself to spend time in solitude, including benefits of and reasons for doing so.

Forty-Three

Awe and Wonder

I sincerely hope that I never lose the sense of awe and wonder that I've been able to carry with me so far in my life. I want never to lose the perspective that makes me stop and gaze in wonder at the beauty of a sunrise or a sunset, that makes me smile when I see the amazing face of a very young child, or that makes me choke up when I stand before a mountain range or a Grand Canyon or a seemingly endless ocean. This sense of wonder helps me to appreciate the depth and breadth of this amazing planet upon which we pass these lives, and it allows me to recognize the unbelievable vastness of the universe in which this planet continues to spin and fly its circular path day after day, year after year. And that vastness helps me to stay humble and to keep a realistic sense of perspective on life.

When we're children, awe and wonder are such a natural part of who we are that they are effortless elements of our lives. Almost everything that we see is new and wonderful and exciting to us, and we want to see more of it, to get to know it better. Our sense of wonder causes us to explore and to enjoy our explorations, no matter what we find out. But as we grow older, more and more things become things that we already know, so they aren't new any more; there's no need to explore them and try to get to know more about them. We don't wonder anymore about most of the elements of our lives, because we start to learn about routine, and about doing the same things and seeing the same things each day.

Think of how amazing our computers were when we first got them, and how wonderless they are now. They're now tools that we use to take care of tasks and to fulfill obligations, and it didn't take long to lose the sense of wonder that they inspired in us. And this has happened even though the computers now have amazing processing speeds, huge hard drives that we couldn't even imagine twenty years ago, and display screens that even on the cheapest computers give us a better picture than any of the affordable television sets that even existed just thirty years ago. They truly are amazing machines in very small packages, and the cell phones that we have now are even more amazing—but they've become simply something else that we take for granted and fail to wonder at.

I was struck by the fact that I hadn't been awed in a while.
Did that mean awesome things had disappeared from my life?
No. What it did mean was that I'd gotten too caught up in
distractions and mind mucking to recognize anything as

awe-inspiring. . . . I hadn't been paying attention
to the beauty around me.

Sue Patton Thoele

This lack of wonder and awe, though, is not a natural part of life—it's something that we choose to adopt as we grow older and supposedly wiser. Sometimes we even choose not to feel wonder or to pretend that we don't, simply to impress others with our worldliness. "That's a nice rainbow, but I've seen so many that are nicer." "That's a nice rainbow, but I really do have to text my sister right now." "That's a nice rainbow, but I don't have the time to stop and stare at the sky right now."

We choose not to allow ourselves to feel awe, and thus we lose a very important part of who we are as human beings—the ability to appreciate the magic and wonder that surrounds us all day, every day.

But are the things that we do focus on really worth the loss? Have we sacrificed something truly important for something truly trivial? My hunch is that we have, and I also believe that we have paid an extremely high price because of this sacrifice. As Sue says above, awesome things hadn't disappeared from her life, but she had gotten "caught up in distractions and mind mucking," so an important part of her life simply wasn't available to her, even though it was still there all the time. In this way, our sense of awe is directly connected to our awareness and to our mindfulness, and a loss of wonder is a direct result of our loss or our lack of use of our mindfulness. And we have to ask ourselves: Is not being mindful and aware of wonder any way to go through life? And if it's not, why do so many of us go through life thus?

I am mentally preparing myself for the five-year-old mind.
I want to come down to their physical limitations
and up to their sense of wonder and awe.

Shinichi Suzuki

The good news is that our connection with awesome and wonderful things is easy to reestablish, because they really never did go away. They always are a part of the world, and they're just waiting for us to notice them and allow the natural feelings that arise within us to be accepted and actually felt. As I look from where I sit now, I see a clock that keeps the time faithfully, and has for many years—it's amazing to think of the mechanisms that continue to function properly so long after it was made. And it works because of a battery, a small object that actually holds an electrical charge, and continues to provide that charge to the clock's mechanisms for more than a year! How do they make these things? How do these things work for so long? It truly does amaze me. And let's not even start with the television set that gives us a beautiful image that's provided many miles away and comes to us via a cable or—even more amazing—via satellite or via a plastic disc with an aluminum coating that holds a series of 1's and 0's that the computer decodes and transmits as a series of pictures and sounds. It truly is wonderful, yet it's so easy to take no notice of it at all until the battery goes out in the remote or it somehow stops working.

If you stop right now and look around yourself, you'll see plenty of things that can truly inspire a sense of awe and wonder. They're around you right now, waiting patiently for you to pay a bit of attention to them and to allow yourself to feel the natural feelings of awe that are within us all, also waiting patiently for us to allow ourselves to feel them.

They're also going to be around you all day, wherever you go, and allowing yourself to be awed by them is going to be a very important part of your day. I want to stay able to be awed by a rain- or snowstorm; I want to feel wonder when I see the sunrise and sunset; I still want to be awed by skyscrapers and jets and ships and cars and books pieces of furniture that were made half a world away, yet found their way to our home.

True and lasting wonder needs to be renewed regularly, even daily. Otherwise, life's inevitable formula will be: Wonderful is followed by wonder-half-full, which is followed by wonder-quarter-full, which quickly becomes wonder-less. If you want to make your capacity for awe as wide as the sky, you must take preventative action. Otherwise, you'll end up as a wonderless wanderer and life will cease to be a joyful adventure.

Edward Hays

Feeling awe and wonder may be something that we put aside as we aged, but it doesn't have to be something that we continue to neglect and ignore. And when we do feel that sense of wonder again, each time it's feels like a completely new feeling, one that helps us to recognize and appreciate our place in this world and the marvelous complexity of the world itself. I hope to continue to be awed until the day I die, for if I ever lose that ability, then things around me will seem normal and bland, and I'm sure that I'll take them for granted. And I have no right to take things for granted that truly do deserve my love, appreciation, and wonder.

Questions to Consider

1. How many people encourage you to search out awe and wonder in your life?

2. Why do people often think that awe and wonder are parts of our childhood and no more?

3. What would life be like without things that strike us with awe and wonder?

Thoughts about Awe and Wonder

If a child is to keep alive his or her inborn sense of wonder, he or she needs the companionship of at least one adult who can share it, rediscovering with the child the joy, excitement and mystery of the world we live in.   -Rachel Carson

The problem with our time, perhaps, is that we have been seduced by facts and data, at the same time, become bereft of wonder. We want to know it all rather than to understand the meaning of it all for the good life here and now. The universe, however technological it may now be, is still the ultimate mystery, the essential human question, the greatest spiritual revelation. Everything else is distraction. To know all the elements, all the chemistry of life, is one thing; to know what it means to live a good life in the midst of the knowledge of what humans can do with them to destroy it is entirely another.   -Joan Chittister

We teach children how to measure and how to weigh. We fail to teach them how to revere, how to sense wonder and awe.   -Harold Kushner

Journal Entries

Day One: Do you regularly experience awe and wonder in your life? Write down some of the things that give you a sense of awe when you experience them.

Day Two: Why do young children seem to be more capable of feeling awe and wonder than we adults are? Is it a result of our education, or simply a side effect of growing up?

Day Three: What kinds of strengths do we have in our lives if we maintain a sense of awe?

Day Four: Think of some place that you want to visit that you know will inspire a sense of awe within you. What about that place will cause the awe?

Day Five: Think of a movie or a book that inspires a sense of wonder for you. Write a book or movie review that explains just how that work inspires you so.

Forty-Four

Simplicity

There have been times in my life when I've been forced into very simple lifestyles, in which material items hardly entered the picture because of circumstances—my four years in the Army and the three years I lived in Europe with just the possessions I could carry with me leap to mind. And as I think of those times in retrospect, I realize that they were very good times—the fewer possessions I had to worry about, the fewer obligations that I had outside of home, even the less money that I had, all combined to make my life much simpler than it has been at other times, when I've owned homes and had many outside obligations.

That doesn't mean, of course, that I would advocate that everyone sell off their houses and live in one-room shacks for the rest of their lives. While such a strategy has proved to be effective for some people, it definitely wouldn't work for us all. Rather, what I do know to be true is that the simpler we're able to make our lives within the frameworks that make up our reality, the easier it is for us to focus on what's truly essential in our lives—our relationships with the people we love, excellence in our work, creating a comfortable and inviting home that we enjoy returning to each evening.

The more we complicate our lives, the less room we leave in our lives for those things that distract us, that keep us from our essential and authentic selves. It seems to be natural for us to want to complicate our lives, for we do like having the bigger or the nicer house, the more expensive car, the more complex computer system, more friends and acquaintances. But the more we complicate our lives, the more responsibilities and obligations we end up having, and the more can go wrong. And these days, the more that can go wrong, the more time we end up devoting to fixing things that we may not necessarily need, and the more money we end up spending on them.

*Do you know the more I look into life, the more things it seems
to me I can successfully lack—and continue to grow happier.
How many kinds of food I do not need, or cooks to cook them,
how much curious clothing or tailors to make it, how many
books I have never read, and pictures that are not worthwhile!
The farther I run, the more I feel like casting aside all such
impediments—lest I fail to arrive at the far goal of my endeavor.*

David Grayson

A perfect example happened last week with an mp3 player that I had just bought. When I plugged it into the computer to sync it, I was expecting a ten-minute process that I wouldn't have to pay much attention to. Four hours later, after several failed syncs and converting it back to factory condition twice, the job was finally finished. While I enjoy listening to the music on it, I have to think about how nice it would have been spending those four Saturday hours sitting down and reading a good book instead of struggling with the computer to fix something that needed to be fixed if I didn't want to have wasted money on it.

Sometimes, complications in life just seem to be necessary. At the moment, I'm working full time and taking two college courses, as well as working some twenty hours a week on other tasks. My life is not simple, but I know that this is only for a short season—I had the chance to do the two courses for free (and actually get paid for one of them), so it was worth my while to commit myself to a more complicated lifestyle for four months to be able to achieve something that's necessary for me. That said, though, once the courses are over, I definitely will not commit myself to such a schedule for a very long time.

Our tendency to over commit ourselves and reject simplicity keeps us stressed out and unbalanced. Simplicity, on the other hand, allows us to balance our lives rather easily, for there's less to balance. Choosing a simpler lifestyle also allows us to focus more strongly and more clearly on those things that are truly important to us. Because my life is very complicated at the moment, for example, there are activities that I love doing that I've had to give up completely until the college courses are done. I could still try to fit them in, but I know that I would do them poorly because I would have to rush through them, and I'm not willing to do that. By putting them aside instead of trying to do everything, I'm at least simplifying my complicated life as much as I can.

The ability to simplify means to eliminate the unnecessary
so that the necessary may speak.

Hans Hofmann

Simple lives allow us to do well all that we do instead of doing things quickly at lower levels of quality. When our lives are simple, we can find the time for the rest that we need to be functioning always at high levels of effectiveness. In a simple life, problems are easier to recognize and deal with, so they don't tend to hang on and keep us stressed out for long periods of time. Simplicity allows us to breathe, to relax, to enjoy fully—that cup of hot cocoa tastes so much better when we can drink it at our leisure, not having to hurry through it to get to our next task.

It's not as difficult as it may seem to simplify our lives. There are quite a few good books out there with many good tips, but we can start just by stopping for once, looking around ourselves, and asking ourselves, "what is truly necessary here?" When we can identify different aspects of our lives as "needs, wants, or neither," we can make it easier to recognize the things that pull us from simplicity and start to work them out of our lives—either immediately by getting rid of them, or slowly by phasing them out.

Leading a simple life does not mean living a Spartan life. There's no need to get rid of everything you own and sleep on a mat on the floor, eating just rice and noodles. We can still own things—we just have to make sure that we own them, and that they don't own us. One simple question to ask ourselves is whether a certain object makes us spend time doing things we don't want to do or otherwise wouldn't need to do. Adding a pond to the garden would be nice, but it's going to take a lot of time from us in maintenance and upkeep. That complicate home theater system may be nice, but do we really need it and do we really want to spend the time necessary to learn all of its functions and settings? And when there's a problem with it, how do we get it repaired? We don't own the cheapest Blu-ray player on the market, but the one we have is fine for us—and if it goes out, we'll just replace it without having lost any money. I've spent far too much time in the past trying to get electronics fixed, only to have to take them back after I got them home and they still didn't work. The simpler the things I own, the less stress they cause me when they stop working properly.

If one's life is simple, contentment has to come. Simplicity is extremely important for happiness. Having few desires, feeling satisfied with what you have, is very vital: satisfaction with just enough food, clothing, and shelter to protect yourself from the elements.

the Dalai Lama

Most of us couldn't say with any degree of truth that we know what it's like to go through an entire day without any real responsibilities. We don't know what it's like to be able to sit quietly and enjoy the peace and quiet—we have to fill the air with sound and fill our time with accomplishments.

Simplicity, though, is a choice that we all can make. It would require getting rid of some things, and minimizing the numbers of other things. Living simply requires constantly asking ourselves questions such as "Do I really need this?" "Will this add quality to my life, or stress?" "Do I truly have time to take on this new hobby or responsibility?" And then we have to answer the questions with complete honesty, and make our decisions based on those answers. After all, there is nothing inherently wrong with accomplishment or even being busy—

but until we actually experience the peace of simplicity, it's very difficult to imagine what it's like.

Questions to Consider

1. Why do we spend so much time thinking that we have to complicate our lives in order to make them richer?

2. Why is simplicity as a life strategy not something that we teach our children?

3. How can a simpler lifestyle be more fulfilling without all the trappings of the more complicated life?

Henry David Thoreau on Simplicity

Our life is frittered away by detail. An honest man has hardly need to count more than his ten fingers, or in extreme cases he may add his ten toes, and lump the rest. Simplicity, simplicity, simplicity! I say, let your affairs be as two or three, and not a hundred or a thousand; instead of a million count half a dozen, and keep your accounts on your thumb nail. In the midst of this chopping sea of civilized life, such are the clouds and storms and quicksands and thousand-and-one items to be allowed for, that a man has to live, if he would not founder and go to the bottom and not make his port at all, by dead reckoning, and he must be a great calculator indeed who succeeds. Simplify, simplify. Instead of three meals a day, if it be necessary eat but one; instead of a hundred dishes, five; and reduce other things in proportion.   -from *Walden*

I do believe in simplicity. It is astonishing as well as sad, how many trivial affairs even the wisest thinks he must attend to in a day; how singular an affair he thinks he must omit. When the mathematician would solve a difficult problem, he first frees the equation of all incumbrances, and reduces it to its simplest terms. So simplify the problem of life, distinguish the necessary and the real. Probe the earth to see where your main roots run.   -from a letter, 1848

What you call bareness and poverty is to me simplicity. God could not be unkind to me if he should try. I love the winter, with its imprisonment and its cold, for it compels the prisoner to try new fields and resources. I love to have the river closed up for a season and a pause put to my boating, to be obliged to get my boat in. I shall launch it again in the spring with so much more pleasure. This is an advantage in point of abstinence and moderation compared with the seaside boating, where the boat ever lies on the shore. I love best to have each thing in its season only, and enjoy doing without it at all other times. It is the greatest of all advantages to enjoy no advantage at all. I find it invariably true, the poorer I am, the richer I am. What you consider my disadvantage, I consider my advantage. While you are pleased to get knowledge and culture in many ways, I am delighted to think that I am getting rid of them.   -*Journal*, 1856

Journal Entries

Day One: How do you view the concept of simplifying your life, as a positive thing, or a negative one? Does simplicity represent loss or gain to you?

Day Two: Does our culture value simplicity? Do people who want to sell us material goods want us to adopt simplicity as a way of life?

Day Three: Why do so many people actively attempt to complicate their lives by taking on more tasks and buying ever more material objects?

Day Four: Imagine that someone is trying to convince you to take on more tasks that you know would make your life much more stressful. Write a note to this person telling him or her why you want to maintain a more simple lifestyle.

Day Five: Write a list of simple pleasures that you can enjoy, such as a walk in the woods or a cup of coffee at home, and compare them to more complicated pleasures, such as going out to a movie or going out somewhere for a fancy outing.

Forty-Five

Thanksgiving

There have been times in my life when it's been very difficult for me even to consider giving thanks for anything. Not impossible, mind you, but very, very difficult. After all, in my mind it was much easier to focus on those things that were not going well for me than the things that were going well—it was much easier to dwell on the negative than to allow the positive to sweep me up in all that it offered me. While I did try my best to be positive and to be thankful, giving thanks was not something that I did constantly.

Even when things have been going well for me, it's been very easy to take them for granted and to neglect the giving of thanks in my life. In fact, I think that the biggest obstacle that I face when it comes to giving thanks is not the lack of thankful feelings or things for which to be thankful, but simply neglect due to the fact that my mind gets caught up in so many different things. How can I stop to give thanks for my health if I have so much work that has to be done tomorrow? How can I be thankful for my job when I have so many papers to grade by next week? Life does make it difficult at times to stay focused on what's going right in our lives, doesn't it?

That said, though, once we realize that we do have such difficulties, we should be able to shift our focus consciously; we should be able to give ourselves some cues that help us to remember just how important it is to be thankful. After all, it's the thankful heart and spirit that draw to it more for which to be thankful; it's when we regularly give thanks for our blessings that we attract more and more similar elements into our lives—more and more blessings.

Thanksgiving for me really was a time of being thankful.
I think it is great for people of all ages to celebrate
the day with good people, good food, and football, but I
hope in the midst of our busy lives we have not forgotten the
importance of observing the real reason for
the holiday: to give thanks.

Matthias Reightman

I find it a very positive sign that in our society, we have set up a day that is dedicated to giving thanks for all that we have, and that this day has become one of the most important holidays of our year. It has become a time when families come together to spend time and break bread, to share traditions and love and hope, to recognize the abundance in their lives and give thanks for that abundance. As time goes on, however, we face a very real risk from the people who want to turn the day into a day of profit, a day of commercial excess in preparation for the even stronger commercial excess of Christmas, and it's important that if this holiday is going to maintain its integrity, we stay focused on its original intent and purpose.

Because unfortunately, that's what tends to happen to gratitude in our lives: it becomes taking things for granted. And very often we start to set up a sort of hierarchy—this is something for which I'm very grateful, but this over here doesn't deserve as much gratitude, so I'm not quite as thankful for it. Or we have thoughts such as, "I'd be much more thankful for my home if I had someone to share it with," or "I'd have much more gratitude for my job if it were more fulfilling."

But gratitude is like love—the more of it we feel, the more capacity we cultivate in our hearts and spirits to feel even more. And gratitude becomes even stronger when we focus ourselves on it—when we decide to become even better at our jobs, or when we decide to make our homes the most comfortable places they possibly can be—without focusing on what we perceive as lack.

We remember the Pilgrims on Thanksgiving Day, not so much
for their turkey dinner, but for the sheer faith that inspired them
to give thanks in a year that saw nearly half their number die
of sickness. Yet they prayed with thanksgiving.

Ralph F. Wilson

This Thanksgiving, I want to stay focused on the good things in my life. I want to add to those good things by keeping my mind on them, and continually reminding myself of just how fortunate I am to have them as part of my life. In this moment, for example, it's 20 degrees outside, yet our home is heated. I just ate breakfast, and I have light to work with even though the sun hasn't yet risen. I have a good computer to work on, I have comfortable clothing, running water, a decent job, chocolate, plenty of food to eat, music to listen to, books to read, pretty things to look at and to spark memories—in short, I have an awful lot to be thankful for, and while I could do without some of them more easily than others, this fact does not mean that I should feel less thankful for those things.

This Thanksgiving Day, make it a point to stop what you're doing every now and then and take a quick inventory. Look around yourself and bring into your conscious mind the things that you have to be thankful for, even the little things, and perhaps even the people who in some ways make your life difficult—even those people contribute something to who we are, even if it's more patience or tolerance.

When you stop like this, though, you stop taking for granted. You cease to be an unthinking member of the flock who's flying along just because everyone else is flying along, and you become an individual who is reflecting on life and living, who is recognizing and appreciating the blessings that truly are a part of all of our lives.

I am grateful for what I am and have. My thanksgiving is perpetual. . .
O how I laugh when I think of my vague indefinite riches. No run on
my bank can drain it, for my wealth is not possession but enjoyment.

Henry David Thoreau

Thanksgiving is too important a day to allow ourselves to go through it by rote. It's important because it serves as a reminder to us that we do have much for which to be thankful, and that gratitude for the things we have and love brings even more of those things into our lives—more love, more relationships, more abundance—perhaps even more chocolate. If we simply walk through the day without feeling, though—without reminding ourselves of just how much we need to feel thankful for elements of our lives that make our lives special—then we're losing a wonderful opportunity not just to feel those feelings, but to share them and to help others recognize their blessings, too.

Questions to Consider

1. How can giving thanks on a regular basis make our lives healthier?

2. Why is Thanksgiving a holiday on which we traditionally bring our families together?

3. How might we express our Thanksgiving in common, ordinary ways on common, ordinary days?

Thoughts on Thanksgiving—Why Should We Be Grateful?

I've met people who don't consider gratitude to be an important part of their lives. After all, they've worked hard for everything that they have and they've received very little help from others, so what's to be thankful for? In their minds, all that they have for which they could be thankful is the result of their effort, so if they're going to be thankful, they have only themselves to thank.

Many of these people have a point, no matter how weak that point may be. Personally, I know what it's like to fight battles alone, with no help from anyone. Many times in my life I've found myself in situations in which nobody was there to offer encouragement or assistance. Sometimes those situations have been much more difficult because of that lack of support, but fortunately, I've been able to make it through most of those situations pretty well. There have even been times in my life when I've felt that everything I did, I did alone, and there was really nothing to be thankful for. Yes, I found a job that I liked, but that school needed a teacher anyway, and if it wasn't me, it would have been someone else. Sure, I accomplished that task, but it would have been much easier—and probably much more enjoyable—if someone had been there to help me.

This lack of gratitude, though, has been quite a hindrance to me. Not acknowledging the things that I have to be thankful for has kept me separated from life, pushed even further into isolation and separation. Gratitude is a force that allows us to feel the connectedness of life, the oneness with everything that surrounds us and helps us to get through life. When I don't feel gratitude, I don't realize that the trees around me are working hard to produce oxygen so that we can all breathe and live. Of course, there's a valid argument that the trees aren't doing this consciously, that they aren't working to give us anything, but I believe that argument to be more harmful than helpful.

You see, gratitude isn't something that we practice in order to show others how grateful we are. Gratitude is a force that we work on developing because it makes us stronger human beings. It gives us strength in our dealings with others, and it helps us to feel that we are part of something larger. It helps us to see the purpose behind things that we otherwise might view with despair or cynicism. Think about it—when you die, would you prefer that the people who are dear to you feel grateful that they had you in their lives while you were there, or would you prefer that they spend their days in despair because you're no longer there. I would love to think of the people I love having a big party after I die, glad to have known me and glad that I've gone to a better place.

Despair, anger, and frustration come when we aren't grateful for the simple things in life—the smile and greeting, the touch on the shoulder, the hug, the beautiful flowers, the cool breeze on a summer day or the warm breeze on a chilly spring day, the favorite songs we listen to when we're down. When we actively reflect on how grateful we are for these things in our lives, we connect ourselves to them, and we're part of a much larger whole. When we recognize this connectedness, the negatives don't seem so bad, for we see that there's usually a larger purpose behind them, a purpose that will help us to grow and develop as people.

Gratitude is a choice. Thanksgiving is something that we can work on and develop, and the stronger we develop our skills of giving thanks, the easier it is to see the purpose and the beauty of life. We can choose to be completely logical and realistic and view things as logical outcomes of certain actions and situations, but when we do so, we rob ourselves of the acknowledgement of our place in the world, and the many blessings that we all have through no effort of our own.

Journal Entries

Day One: Imagine you're starting your own country, and you need to come up with a calendar. When you decide on holidays, would you include a Thanksgiving Day? Why or why not?

Day Two: Has Thanksgiving Day been a positive part of your life (assuming you live in a country that celebrates such a day!)? What could we do to make it more positive?

Day Three: List five things for which you're thankful. Why are you grateful for those five things? What positive contributions have they made to your life?

Day Four: What kinds of things have you taken for granted in life? Has taking them for granted ended up causing some sort of hardship or difficulties?

Day Five: Choose an inanimate object that you own and write a thank-you note to it for all that it's allowed you to do. (My car, a pair of skis, shoes, etc.)

Forty-Six

Sadness

Many of us seem to learn early in life that there are many things that we should avoid at all costs, for they seem to hurt us. This is especially true of feelings, and we spend much of our time trying to avoid certain feelings, or trying to deny that we have them in the first place. Some of these feelings may be ones that we do want to try to keep under control, such as anger or resentment, for they can truly harm us if we allow them to dominate our thoughts. Others, though, are simply normal parts of life, and are feelings that can help us to learn more about ourselves and living and life in general, and sadness is one of these.

Sadness is not a feeling that we should try to deny or suppress. It's a very natural feeling that arises from situations in our lives and from the workings of our minds, and it's strongly related to grief or even depression (which is where we want to start trying to reign it in). Most of us seem to think that sadness is negative because it puts us in a state in which we don't appear to be loving life, in which we seem to be "down," in which we aren't enjoying ourselves fully.

To me, though, it's important that we take a cue from nature when we think about sadness—is every day full of sunshine, bright blue skies, and perfect temperatures? We all know the answer to this question, and if we're able to apply the question to our lives, we ask, "Should we expect ourselves to be cheerful and joyful and full of energy every single day that we live?" The answer obviously is "no." And while we can't use this line of thinking to justify a constant focus on the harmful and the negative in our lives, we certainly can try to develop a more positive perspective on sadness and allow it to be a part of our experience as human beings instead of trying to fight it every time it shows up in our lives.

So you must not be frightened, dear Mr. Kappus, if a sadness rises up before you larger than any you have ever seen; if a restiveness, like light and cloud-shadows, passes over your hands and over all you do. You must think that something is happening with you, that life has not forgotten you, that it holds you in its hand; it will not let you fall. . . .

Rainer Maria Rilke
Letters to a Young Poet

I love Rilke's perspective on sadness: "You must think that something is happening with you." Not to you, but with you, and the sadness is here for a reason. Many people have used the analogy of tempering to explain the obstacles in our lives—many metal alloys and glass often put through a series of heat treatments that can be likened to many of our trials in life. And the interesting thing about tempering is that it's a process designed to increase the toughness of the alloy by decreasing its hardness.

Think about that and how we can apply it to ourselves: it increases the toughness by decreasing the hardness.

Sadness can do that with us, too. Sadness is one of those feelings that, if we allow it to do so, can help us to come into contact with deeper parts of ourselves so the we can understand ourselves better and reach conclusions and achieve a more expansive state of mindfulness in our lives. When we try to understand our sadness rather than rejecting it outright, we learn about different aspects of our psyches that can help us to make more sense out of life and living.

It's when we become too focused on the sadness and use it to start feeling sorry for ourselves that sadness becomes a truly negative force. When we wallow in it and spend our time brooding, even forcing ourselves sometimes into the depths of depression, then the sadness can become a destructive force. One of the most important things that we can do with sadness is to recognize it and accept it for what it is, without allowing it to become more than what it is or different from what it is by nature.

It is not ignoble to feel that the fuller life which a sad experience
has brought us is worth our personal share of pain. The growth of
higher feeling within us is like the growth of faculty, bringing
with it a sense of added strength. We can no more wish to return
to a narrower sympathy than painters or musicians can wish to return
to their cruder manner, or philosophers to their less complete formulas.

George Eliot

Our sadness can bring us many benefits. George Eliot tells us that it can bring us greater sensitivity and strength; Carl Jung tells us that our happiness would be diminished if it weren't balanced with times of sadness. When we accept our sadness and allow it to take its course, learning from it and moving through it, we create a richer and more fuller life. We allow ourselves to know that some days were made to be dreary (Longfellow—see below), and to keep in mind that even though we are feeling sad, there is still brightness and happiness in the world, and once we pass through the sadness, we'll be in the sunlight once more. It hasn't abandoned us, and it hasn't banished us—the light is still there, waiting patiently for us to pass through our difficult times.

And as hard as it may sound, it really is our decision whether we want to stay in the sadness or move out of it. Sometimes, when the sadness is very deep, it becomes comfortable and somehow safe—it's what we know best, and we don't want to risk leaving it behind, so we cling to it and keep it in our lives. When we do this, though, we're turning our backs on the rest of life in order to be somewhat self-indulgent and even selfish, for there are still people who need us, and we cannot serve their needs if we're allowing ourselves to stay tethered to our sadness for fear of leaving it. But life is about moving on and welcoming new changes in our lives, and just as there comes a time when a person must put an abusive relationship behind them and move on, so must we face our fear and put our sadness behind us at the proper time, and keep on keeping on with our lives.

There are as many nights as days, and the one is just as long as the other in the year's course. Even a happy life cannot be without a measure of darkness, and the word "happiness" would lose its meaning if it were not balanced by sadness. It is far better to take things as they come along with patience and equanimity.

Carl Gustav Jung

On a train ride through the mountains, you will see some amazing sights that take away your breath. You will also pass through some tunnels, and while you're in them, you won't see any of the magnificent sights that still are there, but not accessible to you while you're in the tunnel. Our sadness is much like the darkness of the tunnel, or the darkness of the night—it shall pass, and we shall move on to brighter and better things. It's inevitable, as long as we allow our sadness to take its course—and our lives can be much, much richer when we do face our sadness and learn from it.

Questions on Sadness

1. Why do we so often see sadness as something strictly negative?

2. What might we learn about life and living when we pass through our sad times?

3. Why do we automatically try to cheer people up when they're sad? Is there anything wrong with being sad, or does it just scare us?

The Rainy Day

Henry Wadsworth Longfellow

The day is cold, and dark, and dreary;
It rains, and the wind is never weary;
The vine still clings to the mouldering wall,
But at every gust the dead leaves fall,
And the day is dark and dreary.

My life is cold, and dark, and dreary;
It rains, and the wind is never weary;
My thoughts still cling to the mouldering Past,
But the hopes of youth fall thick in the blast,
And the days are dark and dreary.

Be still, sad heart! and cease repining;
Behind the clouds is the sun still shining;
Thy fate is the common fate of all,
Into each life some rain must fall,
Some days must be dark and dreary.

Journal Entries

Day One: What kinds of positive effects can sadness have on us? How might we try to allow those positive effects to work their ways into our lives even while we still feel sad?

Day Two: Do our sadnesses really help to balance our happiness, as Jung suggests?

Day Three: Why do so many people deny or avoid sadness?

Day Four: Are you comfortable just being with your sadness? What kinds of things might you be able to do to make yourself more comfortable with it?

Day Five: George Eliot implies that our sadness makes us stronger and wiser. Do you find that to be true?

Forty-Seven

Perseverance/Determination

Sometimes I want to give up. There are times in life when we all face moments that seem too difficult to bear, when we feel like giving up because our efforts seem fruitless, when we feel that we don't have enough strength left to persevere without wiping ourselves out completely. These are the times when it's difficult to keep our perspective, and when it's difficult to think clearly, for our fear or our pain are dominating our thoughts.

Sometimes we feel worn down, as if we've been fighting and struggling forever without seeing results, and we see other people work not nearly as hard as we're working, yet somehow they're seeing more results to their efforts. Our frustration level grows and grows, and we feel a lack of the hope that should be keeping us going.

These are just the times when, as some people put it, we find out "what we're made of." There are many people in this world who use such situations as a reason to stop trying, as grounds for giving up. They abandon their goals and dreams because they've proven to be too hard to reach, or because they don't feel that they're strong enough to keep on trying. They go back to what they were doing before because the new things aren't working out quickly enough or easily enough, so they retreat to safety in order to preserve themselves—or so they believe.

Nothing in the world can take the place of persistence. Talent will not; nothing is more common than unsuccessful people with talent. Genius will not; unrewarded genius is almost a proverb. Education will not; the world is filled with educated derelicts. Perseverance and determination alone are omnipotent.

Calvin Coolidge

Life, though, is not about safety, and it's not about being easy. We search for the easiest routes sometimes because we don't want to have to struggle, and we don't want to face the possibility of failure. Sometimes, of course, the easiest route can get us to where we need to go. Other times, though, the easier path will never allow us to reach our goals or our dreams, and then it's very easy to give up, to not strive to get further or to reach our desired destination. I may want to have a certain degree, but unless I'm willing to work hard for it—over the course of a lot of time—that degree won't be mine. If I want to be very, very good at my job, then I need to do the work necessary to get better, and not give up because it's "too hard."

We're tested as people not by doing the same things over and over again, but by pushing through obstacles and giving our best to go further in life, not to stay in the same place. The world is full of people who tried for a while, but then gave up—people who weren't willing to push themselves any harder. But what if I don't want to be one of those people who have given up?

Then it's very important that I keep telling myself that just because something is hard, it won't kill me or devastate me. I have to remind myself constantly that many other people have pushed on through hard times and down times to finally reach a point at which they succeed. I have to keep in mind that the difficulties and the anguish will pass eventually, and I'll be extremely glad when they do pass that I stuck with my original plans through thick and thin.

It is not so much brilliancy of intellect, or fertility of resource, as persistency of effort, constancy of purpose, that makes a great person. Persistency always gives confidence. Everybody believes in the people who persist. They may meet misfortunes, sorrows, and reverses, but everybody believes that they will ultimately triumph because they know there is no keeping them down. "Do they keep at it? Are they persistent?" are the questions which the world asks about us.
Even the person with small ability will often succeed if he or she has the quality of persistence, where a genius without persistence would fail.

Orison Swett Marden

There are, of course, situations in which perseverance isn't the best course of action. If I'm running a marathon and I start feeling severe pain in my knee at ten miles, then I'm not going to finish that marathon. Note, though, that I said "severe" pain—there are other types of pain that I've learned as a runner can simply be run through, and they'll go away after some time. If I've set my goal as reaching a certain position in my job, but in the meantime a new supervisor has been hired who treats people horribly, perhaps it's time to scrap that goal and make a new one—in a different workplace. Sometimes persistence is simply stubbornness disguised as something more positive, and it's important that we recognize things like stubbornness in the many masks that they wear.

All in all, though, persistence is one of the most important character traits that we can develop. No novel or book has been written without it; no important research can be developed and finished if those doing the work don't have the determination necessary to bring it to a close.

There are many lessons about perseverance all about us, every day, that we can learn if we just keep our eyes open for them. If we wait, the tide will come back in (or go back out); even the darkest night will eventually give way to day; the light will appear at the end of the tunnel; the water and wind eventually will wear down any stone; time and again teams win games in the very last moment possible. In each case, they have to keep on keeping on, doing what they're doing without giving up. Sometimes the results may not be exactly what we hoped for of planned, but determination can be one of the most important elements of any life.

No one ever did anything worth doing
unless they were prepared to go on with
it long after it became something of a bore.

Douglas V. Steere

I want to be a determined person. I want to pursue my goals without giving up, even when they may seem hopeless. I want to pursue my dreams no matter how many people tell me to be more realistic. I won't fool myself into thinking that perseverance alone will solve all the ills in my life, but I will keep in mind that without perseverance, I can pretty much guarantee that I will not be able to do many of the things that I dream of doing.

Questions to Think about

1. Why do we so often give up on things that we attempt?

2. What are some of the major obstacles that we face when we try to persevere?

3. Because it's not easy to persevere, few people do so. What strategies might help us to be the people who are able to persevere in adversity?

Thoughts on Perseverance

People who have attained things worth having in this world have worked while others idled, have persevered when others gave up in despair, have practiced early in life the valuable habits of self-denial, industry, and singleness of purpose. As a result, they enjoy in later life the success so often erroneously attributed to good luck.   -Grenville Kleiser

There are but two roads that lead to an important goal and to the doing of great things: strength and perseverance. Strength is the lot of but a few privileged people; but austere perseverance, harsh and continuous, may be employed by the least of us and rarely fails of its purpose, for its silent power grows irresistibly greater with time.   -Johann Wolfgang von Goethe

It is not so much brilliancy of intellect, or fertility of resource, as persistency of effort, constancy of purpose, that makes a great person. Persistency always gives confidence. Everybody believes in the people who persist. They may meet misfortunes, sorrows, and reverses, but everybody believes that they will ultimately triumph because they know there is no keeping them down. "Do they keep at it? are they persistent?" are the questions which the world asks about us. Even the person with small ability will often succeed if he or she has the quality of persistence, where a genius without persistence would fail.   - Orison Swett Marden

Journal Entries

Day One: In what kinds of situations do you tend to give up most easily? Why do you think that is? What could you do to change this tendency?

Day Two: How are faith and confidence and perseverance related? Or, What would a life without perseverance look like?

Day Three: Someone you know who is attempting something very difficult has written to you and said that they're giving up. In a letter, try to persuade them to persevere.

Day Four: Under what circumstances do you feel that it's okay not to persevere? In which kinds of situations would it not be the best idea to do so?

Day Five: Think of someone you know who has accomplished something very important simply by sticking to it and never giving up. What do you think about what this person has done? Could you do the same thing?

Forty-Eight

Moderation

While I truly love the holiday season, it's dismaying sometimes to see that it has become a season of excess—in the giving of gifts, in the amount of money spent on decorations, in the expectations that we have of one another, in the competitions that seem to exist to "out-do" one another in any of several categories. 'Tis not the season of moderation.

Moderation, though, is one of the keys to a balanced and healthy life. We live in a society that tells us that moderation is for fools, mainly because there are so many people trying to sell us goods that if we all practiced moderation in our lives, we would not be buying many of the almost-useless products that we currently buy. We run up excessive balances on our credit cards in order to maintain lifestyles that are dependent upon having, possessing, and consuming. We gain weight because we don't practice moderation in our eating habits, and because we neglect our exercise. When we live in extremes, though, we don't live in healthy ways; rather, we stagger from extreme to extreme—gorging to fasting, luxury to monastic simplicity—and the roller coaster ride never allows us to gain our equilibrium, and we can't simply stand in one place and relax.

It isn't usually a question of gluttony or greed that causes us to do such things. In my case for example, I learned rather late in life that my tendency to want to stockpile things comes from the fact that I grew up in a household with an alcoholic parent. When I would shop and I'd see something at a good price, I'd buy tons of it, for I couldn't trust that I would ever see it at that price again. My wife was constantly astonished at how full our pantry was—and it was full because I had grown up not trusting the future, not trusting that in the future, I would have enough money or enough food or enough of anything. I've had to literally train myself to trust life and to stop buying so much of everything when I shopped, but I have to admit that the urge to do so is still within me, and I'm sure it will be until the day I die.

Balance recognizes that many good things in life are good only
in moderation. There really can be too much of something wonderful.
Most virtues, taken to excess become vices. When an interest,
affection, or endeavor becomes utterly consuming, it doesn't
allow room for other kinds of goodness.

unattributed

I'm fortunate in that I learned early on just how unpleasant it is to eat too much. Excess in almost any form is unhealthy mostly because it robs us of perspective and causes us to lose sight of what the other side of the coin is like. If I don't practice moderation in my pleasure seeking, as Stephen mentions below, then I never allow myself to experience life without those pleasures—and I never allow myself to learn that life can be absolutely amazing in its pure, raw form. The person who gets pleasure from watching television, for example, and who watches it for untold hours each week, robs him- or herself of the chance to experience the outdoors in all its glory. There are those days that are simply too cold for going outdoors, for example, and then it can be nice to have an indoor movie day or two. In general, though, too much time in front of the television keeps us from practicing crafts, cleaning the house, spending time with friends, getting the exercise we need, and a huge number of other things.

Moderation can be a question of perspective, too. My wife and I, for example, have a very large collection of movies—and some might call it excessive. But we don't spend our money going to movies, we don't have a Netflix account, and we don't spend money on any movie channels. We also buy our movies at pawn shops and thrift stores, where we pay an average of about two dollars a movie. And once we watch them, we keep them, so over the course of quite a few years, the collection has built significantly, even though we watch only two movies a week at the most, on weekends. So by no measure can our film watching or our spending on films be considered excessive, even if the collection that you see seems to indicate otherwise. We are very moderate in our film-watching habits. We recently bought all nine seasons of a television show that my wife loves for three dollars a season, and I can guarantee you that those discs will last us at least two years before we finish watching them. But anyone walking into our house will think that we're definitely addicted to television shows.

Innocent pleasures in moderation can provide relaxation for the body and mind and can foster family and other relationships. But pleasure, per se, offers no deep, lasting satisfaction or sense of fulfillment. The pleasure-centered person, too soon bored with each succeeding level of "fun," constantly cries for more and more.

Stephen Covey

The danger with not practicing moderation is just what Stephen says it is: we become bored with the current excess, and it no longer is excessive, but not enough—and we need even more. This is how people become alcoholics, how people become addicts, how people lose control of their ability to judge properly when enough is enough. We build tolerances to substances and situations, and once that tolerance is built we need more of it to provide the stimulation that the lesser amount used to provide.

One of the reasons that I know that moderation is important in our lives is the way that I've felt when I've been around people who don't practice it. Whenever I'm around someone who does things to excess, I feel uncomfortable. Not judgmental and not critical, but uncomfortable. There's something inside of me that tells me that something's wrong, that excess is neither normal nor healthy, and I want to pay attention to that something, the instinct with which we all are born but that we spend so much time ignoring. When I see a table filled with much more food than is necessary, when I see people spending much more money than is necessary, or when I see people drinking to excess, I feel that something's wrong, and our feelings are very important indicators of what's right and what's wrong in life.

Practicing moderation has many very positive benefits. With a moderate diet, we avoid many weight and health issues. With moderate spending, we avoid problems that can come with running out of money or having to borrow to make ends meet. When we're satisfied with a really good car instead of a much more expensive model, we don't put ourselves into a deep hole of debt. There are many examples of how we can help ourselves with moderation, and it's important that we keep them in mind when we have decisions to make as to just how far we'll go or just how much we'll need.

To go beyond the bounds of moderation is to outrage humanity.

Blaise Pascal

Our planet does not have unlimited resources for us. Moderation also helps us to be responsible stewards of this amazing planet on which we live, for it will keep us using only what we need. Sometimes we may feel the desire to use or own more than our share, but if we keep in mind the responsibility we have to help to maintain our planet's ability to support us, we just may find that moderation is easier for us to practice. And even if advertisers and marketers continue to try to convince us to buy more and own more, we can rise above their influence by being true to ourselves and principles that we find to be important in our lives.

I firmly believe that one day when I'm on my deathbed, I'll be much more satisfied with having lived a life defined by moderation and responsibility than I would have been had I lived a life focused on excess and irresponsibility. And since I want my deathbed to be a peaceful place, I know that I'll want to have the peace of mind that will come from not having abused the resources available to me, and from having accepted the need to practice moderation out of respect to the world in which I've lived.

Questions to Ponder

1. Why do so many people seem to consider "moderation" to be a dirty word?

2. What are some of the benefits of moderation in our lives? In our eating? In our commitments? In our spending?

3. Why do so many advertisers try to convince us not to be moderate in our spending? What would happen to their profits if more people practiced moderation?

Thoughts on Moderation

Follow the wisdom provided by nature. Everything in moderation—sunlight, water, nutrients. Too much of a good thing will topple your structure. You can't harvest what you don't sow. So plant your desires, gently nurture them, and they will be rewarded with abundance.   -Vivian Elizabeth Glyck

Out of moderation a pure happiness springs.   -Johann Wolfgang von Goethe

Moderation is the inseparable companion of wisdom, but with it genius has not even a nodding acquaintance.   -Charles Caleb Colton

Journal Entries

Day One: Why do so many people find it easy to go to extremes and difficult to practice moderation?

Day Two: In which areas do you find it most difficult to be moderate? Why is it hard for you to limit yourself?

Day Three: What would you tell someone who has trouble being moderate in, for example, eating? What advice would you give, and what would you say the result of your advice would be?

Day Four: When have you seen concrete results of a lack of moderation? Were they positive results? How could they have been avoided? Why did the person(s) not avoid them?

Day Five: Imagine you were teaching a class on living a moderate lifestyle. What areas would you cover? Why? What strategies would you suggest?

Forty-Nine

Feelings

Why do we so often consider our feelings to be worthless or useless? Why do we see them as obstacles to our lives instead of wonderful sensors that help us to understand our world and what's happening in it? How often are we told not to let our feelings get in the way, or not to trust our feelings, especially when it comes to things like money and business? In our world, "feelings" has become almost a dirty word, for in competition, it's important to leave your feelings behind and focus on winning or doing better than everyone else.

Our feelings, though, are one of the most important elements of being human. Part of the definition of humanity has to include the feelings we have that separate us from other forms of life, as well as our ability to share and express those feelings. They're a part of ourselves that we should be celebrating, not hiding; sharing and not keeping to ourselves.

Of course, feelings can get away from us, and they can become destructive when people allow themselves to be controlled by their feelings and emotions. While our feelings can be very effective as a guide, they should not be in control of who we are. When our feelings are hurt, for example, we often say and do things that we later regret; when we're feeling down, we often follow that feeling into depression. It's very important that we get in touch with our feelings so that we can recognize them and understand them—we can't really control them (repressing them is not controlling them), but they can be an important part of our lives if we know how to deal with them.

Pay attention to your feelings. They are there to help
you; they are your friend. When you feel off, take notice.
Gently observe your thinking. Where is it? If your thoughts
aren't in the here and now, rather than being hard on yourself,
or getting too much into details of your thinking (analysis
paralysis!), simply direct your attention back to the moment.
Don't allow your thoughts to pull you away from happiness.

Richard Carlson

As Richard says above, taking notice of our feelings is a method that can help us to make our feelings useful. Our feelings are our first reaction to almost anything that happens to us—our intellect takes over only after whatever immediate reactions that we have. Sometimes, those feelings can be completely inaccurate—such as feeling fear when we see a person who is absolutely no threat at all, or feeling disgust when we see something that looks like something else that disgusts us. In these cases, our logical minds do come to our aid to help us find a balance between our feelings and our thoughts, as following that first response often would be inappropriate. Someone who is very good at manipulating others can get us to feel trust, and it may take our reason and logic to start to notice holes in whatever story we're being fed.

As a culture, though, we've put intellect and reason on a very high pedestal, and in doing so we've effectively disenfranchised our feelings, turning them into a part of ourselves that we no longer trust. We make our decisions based on rational thought, and we don't trust our gut instinct. We judge others highly when we see that they value reason above all else, and we judge others harshly when we see that they trust their feelings and make decisions based upon them.

This cultural tendency has turned us into a community of people who in many ways aren't able to feel any more. We say that we feel love, but then we offer logical reasons for which that love is justified. We say that we feel compassion, but we limit our compassion to situations that we can justify logically—how many people make donations to worthy causes only because of the tax breaks and positive public relations that they'll receive in return?

We should not pretend to understand the world only by the intellect;
we apprehend it just as much by feeling. Therefore, the judgment of
the intellect is, at best, only the half of truth, and must,
if it be honest, also come to an understanding of its inadequacy.

Carl Jung

When we suppress a gift as wonderful as our feelings, though, we truly limit ourselves in this world of ours, which is a world that seems to have been designed to maximize our feelings of awe, wonder, love, hope, compassion— and even supposedly "negative" feelings such as despair, longing, fear, or distrust. Our feelings are gifts to us, and we're making a huge mistake when we relegate them to second-class status in our own beings. They can make our lives much richer and fuller when we allow ourselves to feel them fully, and get to know the feelings that we're having. As Shakti says, they are an important part of who we are, and when we deny or suppress them, we cannot be at one with ourselves. That loss of unity can be a dreadful situation for us to experience.

One of my biggest problems early in life was that my feelings scared me—if they were positive I "knew" they wouldn't last, so I shouldn't trust them; if they were negative, they always had the chance to become far, far worse, and so I dwelled on them, and guess what? My focus on the negative feelings actually caused me to go deeper into them, to make them grow into something bigger than they actually were, to make me miserable and hopeless for many, many days of my life. Now, my relationship with my feelings was forged by having an alcoholic parent (read some of the traits of adult children of alcoholics), but other people have uneasy relationships with their feelings for different reasons. The most important thing that we can do, though, is to recognize our feelings, accept them for what they are, and learn not just to live with them, but to understand them and actually listen to the messages that they have to give us.

Notice what happens when you doubt, suppress, or act contrary to your feelings. You will observe decreased energy, powerless or helpless feelings, and physical or emotional pain. Now notice what happens when you follow your intuitive feelings. Usually the result is increased energy and power and a sense of natural flow. When you're at one with yourself, the world feels peaceful, exciting, and magical.

Shakti Gawain

Recognizing our feelings is a non-judgmental process. Just see what they are, and notice that, but don't judge your feelings ("it's ridiculous to feel that way") or yourself ("I'm an idiot to feel that way") for them. They are a part of who we are, so we should let them be what they are and acknowledge them ("I'm feeling confused right now"), and with that acknowledgement we can do something about them ("If I'm confused, I should seek clarification" or "If I'm angry, I should deal with the situation in a positive way or find out for sure if my anger is justified"). The messages that they give us are extremely important, and they can help us to make decisions about future actions that can actually contribute to our mental and emotional well-being. If we repress them and ignore their messages, then we will hurt ourselves, even if we don't recognize the harm that we're doing in the short run.

We have to listen to them carefully, though, for the messages can be mixed or misinterpreted. For example, I can't count how many times I've thought I was angry at a person when I was really extremely frustrated with a situation. Because I wasn't able to recognize what my feelings truly were, I wasn't able to deal with situations well, and I often made them worse by expressing my anger instead of facing the frustration.

Love your feelings. When you love them, you'll see them clearly and you'll allow them to speak to you—and you'll actually listen to their messages when they do so. They are a truly vital part of who we are, and it's a great tragedy that so many of us have learned to repress our feelings instead of learning from them. Make them an important part of your life, and your life will grow richer and fuller as you become a person who is more in tune with yourself.

Questions to Consider

1. Why do so many people so often encourage us not to show our feelings?

2. How do our feelings help us to cope with different situations in our lives?

3. Why do so many songs and films focus so strongly on our "negative" feelings (sadness, loss, etc.) and so little on our "positive" feelings (joy, happiness, etc.)?

Thoughts on Feelings

Life is an exercise in the development of feeling. When we repress feelings, we become sour and judgmental. When we live awash in great feeling over small things, we become jaded long before we have even begun to enjoy. When feelings are in balance they sweeten long days and great distances with gratitude and hope.   -Joan Chittister

Part of the problem with the word "disabilities" is that it immediately suggests an inability to see or hear or walk or do other things that many of us take for granted. But what of people who can't feel? Or talk about their feelings? Or manage their feelings in constructive ways? What of people who aren't able to form close and strong relationships? And people who cannot find fulfillment in their lives, or those who have lost hope, who live in disappointment and bitterness and find in life no joy, no love? These, it seems to me, are the real disabilities.   -Fred Rogers

Many of us have a tendency to deny any negative feelings. We judge them as "bad" or "unenlightened" when, in fact, they are our stepping stone to enlightenment. Our so-called negative feelings or attitudes are really parts of ourselves that need recognition, love, and healing. Not only is it safe and healthy to acknowledge and accept all of our feelings and beliefs, it is necessary, if we are to get in touch with the fears and pockets of blocked energy that are holding us back from what we want.   -Shakti Gawain

Journal Entries

Day One: What feelings are hard for you to share with others? Why do you think they're difficult to share?

Day Two: If someone asked you for advice, would you tell them to share their feelings or to keep them in? In which circumstances, and with which people?

Day Three: What types of feelings can be destructive to us? Which can be constructive and positive?

Day Four: Does our society value more the expression of feelings or hiding them?

Day Five: How can your feelings help you to experience and understand the world better?

Fifty

Diversity

We all have been given an amazing gift on this planet, and that gift lies in the differences between us. The perspectives that each person has are completely unique to each individual—even though we often decide to share certain things with others with whom we live—and if we truly respect those differences and try to learn what they are, they can teach us new and exciting ways of seeing our world. When we decide that someone else is simply "wrong" because they don't see the world as we see it, then we close off any chances that we have to learn from them, instead becoming victims of our own ignorance and judgment.

We have many, many lessons in nature and art that show us quite clearly that diversity is much more to be desired than conformity. What would a painting look like if every color were the same, if it weren't given the opportunity to work with the other colors to stand out next to this one, to complement this other one, to create its own message? One of the reasons that flowers are so beautiful is because they have subtle differences that distinguish them from each other, even when they look similar at first glance—and they always have the green of their leaves and stalks to complement the colors and shapes that they show the world. And what if all our foods tasted the same? We accept fully the fact that our foods should taste different, but somehow we find it disturbing or uncomfortable that other human beings should see the world differently from us.

Just as many threads work together to form a beautiful tapestry or the many blocks make up a quilt, it takes many individuals to make up a community. We've come to believe somehow that the fewer differences in opinion or perspective we have among members of communities, the fewer problems we'll have in those communities. Because of this mistaken belief, we've striven to keep our communities stable by keeping out people who might be "different" from us. We've even created myths or rumors to share with others so that the others also will believe that it would be bad to let these people into our communities.

If we are to achieve a richer culture, rich in contrasting values,
we must recognize the whole gamut of human potentialities, and
so weave a less arbitrary social fabric, one in which each
diverse human gift will find a fitting place.

Margaret Mead

And just what do we lose when we keep people out of our lives because of their skin color, religious beliefs, or ethnic heritage? Mostly, we lose the opportunity to learn from someone else who sees the world in different ways. We lose the chance to learn from rich cultural heritages that these people have spent their lives learning from, and that they can now pass on to us.

Think about it this way: If four people from completely different backgrounds were to get together for the very first time and have only twelve hours to spend together, what would be the best way for them to spend their time?

Should they spend those twelve hours discussing life and lessons that they have learned about it, learning from each other as they do so?

Or should they spend those twelve hours telling why what they think is right, and arguing that what the other three think is wrong?

When we're faced with diversity in thought and perspective, we often spend so much of our time trying to prove that our perspective is the "right" one that we don't take the chance to learn about other perspectives, and perhaps even modifying our own perspectives a bit based on what we learn.

One small example in my life was that as I grew up in America, I learned that it's perfectly fine to use the insult as humor, trying to make other people laugh by insulting someone. Five years in Europe, though, taught me that this kind of humor is really mean, not funny—and the laughter that comes from it is based more on fear and feelings of superiority than it is on humor. Because of what I learned by living in other cultures, I've been able to make important decisions about how I relate to other people, and that has made a huge difference in my life.

When you're finally up on the moon, looking back at the earth, all these differences and nationalistic traits are pretty well going to blend and you're going to get a concept that maybe this is really one world and why the hell can't we learn to live together like decent people?

Frank Borman

To me, diversity is not about race or ethnic origin—I believe that these are artificial distinctions that we make between human beings in order to differentiate ourselves from others based on the most superficial of criteria. Where humanity is concerned, skin color means nothing; country of origin means nothing, even gender means nothing. Yes, there are certain traits that we develop as Russians or Algerians or Australians, or as men or women, but the truth is that in each body of each human a heart is beating, lungs are functioning, and a brain is calculating and considering and dreaming.

Diversity, rather, is a question of the ways that we see and share the world, the ways that we react to stimuli and create the lives that we're living. Much of the way that we see the world has to do with traits that we've adopted from those people who live around us, and therein lies what we see as "cultural" differences. But those differences are not inborn in us—rather, they are adopted by us as we grow. They can be extremely valuable and helpful in understanding other people, but they truly don't define us as human beings. We tend to use them as our measure of diversity, though, because they're easy to see and to quantify and to understand.

True diversity lies in our uniqueness, the aspects of ourselves that are truly ours alone, the ways that we understand life and living and our relationships with other human beings. We see this true diversity not by looking at the skin, but by looking in the eyes and realizing that those eyes are the windows to a soul, an amazing being who is different than us, and who can teach us a great deal if we only take the chance to listen.

Some people do things completely differently from the way you would do them. It does not mean that they are right or that you are wrong. It means that people are different. There are things that people say which you would probably say in a different way, at a different time. It does not mean that people are wrong to speak up, to speak out, or to speak their minds. Nor does it mean that you are wrong for choosing not to do so. It means that people are different. Different is not right or wrong. It is a reality. Differences become problems only when we choose to measure ourselves by our difference in an effort to determine who is right and who is wrong.

Iyanla Vanzant

Our cultures and societies are richer and stronger for diversity, not weakened by it. We will truly benefit from that diversity, though, only when we completely accept the fact that other human beings see life in ways that are different from our ways. We aren't on this planet to make other people think and feel and act just like we do—we're here to work with others to help to make this world a more positive and more loving place.

We now spend a huge amount of time trying to convince others that our ways of seeing the world are right, and theirs are wrong. Think about how much we could get done together if we were to stop spending time this way, and instead spend time working together constructively to actually accomplish things that help other people to live their lives in more positive ways. The shame of not accepting others for who they are and what they believe is that we limit our own potential concerning what we can accomplish in the short time that we're here on this planet.

Questions to Ponder

1. Why is diversity such a potential strength in our lives and in our societies? Do we allow it to reach that potential?

2. What are some of the barriers that keep diversity from being seen as a strength?

3. How might we go about making use of the diversity that surrounds us constantly?

Thoughts on Diversity

There never were in the world two opinions alike, no more than two hairs or two grains; the most universal quality is diversity.   -Michel de Montaigne

We have become not a melting pot but a beautiful mosaic. Different people, different beliefs, different yearnings, different hopes, different dreams.   -Jimmy Carter

The splendor of the rose and the whiteness of the lily do not rob the little violet of its simple charm. If every tiny flower wanted to be a rose, spring would lose its loveliness.   -Therese of Lisieux

Journal Entries

Day One: Why do you think that so many people fear diversity rather than embrace it?

Day Two: Where in nature can we find any two things that are exactly alike? What does that tell us about diversity in the natural world?

Day Three: If a young person were to ask you why diversity is important in life, how would you respond?

Day Four: What would our world be like if everyone were the same?

Day Five: How have your ideas about diversity changed over the years? How did you see differences when you were a young child? When you were half your current age? Now?

Fifty-One

Creativity

I am a very creative person, and I'd be willing to bet that you are, too. I'd also be willing to bet, though, that you're much like I am in that you haven't learned to see yourself as a creative person first and foremost, and that you probably even would say that you're not very creative at all if someone were to ask you. When it comes to creativity, most of us tend to judge our own creativity against things that we see from other people, be it paintings or writing or crafts. "I could never do something like that," we say, thus lowering our perception of our own creativity.

Creativity, though, isn't limited to artistic endeavors. Almost everything that we do in life, from our jobs to cooking to doing the yardwork, can involve incredible amounts of creativity. Even our lives themselves can be full of creativity, depending on how we choose to live them and the decisions that we make while doing so. We can be creative in our relationships, creative in our hobbies, even creative in the ways that we try to be creative (if that makes sense). I once read about a man who raked leaves into piles that represented different armies in different situations, then raked them together as the armies met in battle, having fun and exercising his mind while he did a simple task. (Personally, I'd probably want to imagine that the piles were flocks of birds flying south, for example, than armies of people killing each other, but to each his or her own, right?)

Part of our problem is the way that our cultures define creativity, and celebrate it only when and if it becomes famous or earns a lot of money for the person who "created." Most of our creativity is private, and we can be creative in little ways that aren't going to make us famous at all. And much of what we see as "art" isn't actually very creative at all—it's simply product that's been carefully designed to appeal to people's wants so that they'll buy more of it. Many movies, for example, follow simple formulas of character, setting, and plot, with only slight differences between them—different actors or settings, for example. We think they're the result of creativity because they're supposedly entertaining, but the truth is that they're calculated products, not creative inventions. And if we start thinking that that is what creativity consists of, then we're making a big mistake.

Creativity is inventing, experimenting, growing, taking risks,
breaking rules, making mistakes, and having fun.

Mary Lou Cook

I can be creative by taking a different route to work, by figuring out new ways to do tasks, by finding new solutions to problems. We practice creativity when we find a way to make a vegetarian dish out of something we've always made with meat, or when we find a new way to cook that steak or make those cookies. Sometimes we don't even notice that we're being creative—we're just taking care of something that needs to be taken care of.

Fostering and developing our creativity can have extremely beneficial effects for us. When we work at being creative, we're using our minds in ways that are inspirational and uplifting, and we're finding new possibilities in a world in which it seems as if everything's been done already. We're reminding ourselves that our world is full of new things and new ways to do things, and we're giving ourselves a chance to look at the world in new ways, a fact that rejuvenates our perspective and helps us to become even more creative.

Have you ever noticed how when we're being creative, it becomes much easier to follow up a creative project with something else that's creative? It's like running or working out—when you're doing it regularly, a five-mile run is extremely easy, but when we neglect our running, the five-mile run becomes a five-mile ordeal. Our creativity thrives when it's being used, not when it's put into a jar and hidden in the pantry.

Creativity of all kinds focuses your mind, engages your imagination, and feeds your soul. Being creative can also facilitate understanding and encourage healing. Creativity is mindfulness in motion—intuitive, artistic motion. Creative moments and activities give you a boost and help you feel energized and good about yourself.

Sue Patton Thoele

Our creativity is one of the elements of our lives that make us feel truly alive. It can help us to stay truly focused on the moment as we work on a creative endeavor; it can help us to think abstractly as we envision the final project of what we're creating; it can help us to feel joy as we see something that we've made or finished that didn't exist one or two days ago; it can help us to feel extremely good about ourselves as we realize that yes, we do have skills and talents that are uniquely ours. Our creativity can be an amazing spark that sets us on fire—not the destructive type of fire that destroys everything in its path, but the constructive fire that sheds light and provides warmth.

Our creativity also, as Sue points out above, helps us to practice mindfulness and to be more aware of our surroundings than we usually are. When we're being creative, we see how things work—and how they don't work. We start to understand or strengthen our understanding of many principles, from learning how baking times differ depending on ingredients to how long paints need to dry before you can paint over them to what kinds of paper are stronger than others to which notes work well together, and which don't.

The bottom line is that we are creative creatures. We're born that way, and our spirits thrive when we practice the creativity that is innate in each one of us. It's important, though, that we keep in mind that we should not be comparing the results of our creative efforts with the creativity of other people—creativity is not a competition. It is an integral part of who we are, and we should view it as just that, without putting extra pressure on ourselves to "perform" for others by trying to impress them with our creativity. If we're just creative, if we just do what we do in order to spark and develop our own creativity, we'll be doing what we need to do in order to make our lives richer. The compliments and accolades from others may or may not come—and it's perfectly okay if they don't. We're not on this world to impress others. We're on it to develop ourselves to be the best people we can be, and our creativity is a huge part of who we are.

Creativity is a central source of meaning in our lives. . . most of the things that are interesting, important, and human are the results of creativity . . . when we are involved in it, we feel that we are living more fully than during the rest of life.

Mihaly Csikszentmihalyi

You can be creative today. You don't need to write the best poem or short story ever written to be creative, and you don't need to make the best egg dish ever or anything that will win prizes at county fairs. But you do need to be willing to take a chance or two, to think of things in slightly different ways, and to put yourself out there and risk that what you create won't be exactly what you envisioned. Creative people often find that their results don't match their plans at all. But if you take the time to do something creative on this day, you'll find that your creativity comes just a bit easier tomorrow, and easier still the day after, until your creativity is a major part of the life that you're living. And when that becomes the case, that life will be rich indeed—and you'll be able to help others tap into their creativity, too.

Questions to Consider

1. Why do most of us grow up seeing ourselves as being "not very creative"?

2. How can our creativity make our lives richer? Do we take advantage of that potential?

3. What can you do on this very day to spark your creativity?

Thoughts on Creativity

Creativity is woven into the fabric of simpler times. And there are as many paths to creativity as there are human beings on this planet. You can be a creative homemaker and mother (I am married to one.) You can also be a creative builder, a creative gardener, a creative hang glider. There is creativity in solving personal problems, in overcoming obstacles, in keeping relationships warm.

Creativity is not optional equipment. It is a built-in potential, a seedling planted deep in the human personality. And like any other human possibility, creativity can be helped to grow and flourish. Because both my happiness and my livelihood depend on maintaining my own creativity, I have a vested interest in understanding it. . . . Motivation needs to turn to ideas, and ideas need to be incubated. You need to move things around in your head and with your hands. You experiment. You move your mind around, allowing yourself to look at what you're doing from different angles. . . . To be creative, all you need is room to play, room to think, room to just be. -Thomas Kinkade, *Simpler Times*

Journal Entries

Day One: What are some of the aspects of your life that keep you from being as creative as you'd like to be? How might you work around the limitations in order to spark your creativity?

Day Two: You know some young people who are going to face the loss of their creativity as they grow up. Write them a note telling them how they might hold on to it.

Day Three: Write down ten creative things that you can do today, with materials that you already have on hand. Then do three of them.

Day Four: Mihaly says above that "Creativity is a central source of meaning in our lives." What does he mean by that? Do you agree? Is creativity a key element of your life?

Day Five: What do you think our world would be like if we were all encouraged more to be creative in all aspects of our lives?

Fifty-Two

Common Sense

In my experience, one of the most important parts of living life fully is using the common sense that we've been given to help us to make our decisions and set our courses. We all have within us a great deal of wisdom that tends to be obscured by the vast amounts of information and entertainment to which we subject ourselves, and often we feel desperate for answers when very simple answers are readily available to us all the time—as long as we access our common sense and trust it. Far too often we think far too much; I can't even begin to count the number of times I've told students that they're not able to find the answers they need because they're over-analyzing and thinking far too much. And I can tell them that because I recognize it, having done myself the exact same thing so often.

Because we think so much, the use of common sense is far less common than it should be. I don't think that we lose it, but I do believe that we too often decide to forego the common sense approach because it seems too simple or because we want to impress others with our ability to reason. But common sense can be one of the most valuable guides that we have, and it can help us through all sorts of problems and difficulties. Common sense sees simple solutions instead of complex ones; it see straightforward approaches rather than strategies that force us to work our through a difficult maze of steps and procedures.

The three great essentials to achieve anything
worthwhile are first, hard work; second,
stick-to-itiveness; third, common sense.

Thomas Alva Edison

Common sense has been called the combination of knowledge and experience, but that seems to be only the cover of the book. We also have to be able to make connections between what we know, what we've seen, and what we've done so that the next time a similar situation comes up, it will be easy for us to make a decision based on what we know may be the results of that decision.

What are some examples of common sense? For example, if you place a heavy plate full of food on the edge of a flimsy table, there's a good chance it's going to fall. If you're going very fast in your car and you need to stop, it's going to take you longer to do so. If you click on something and you don't know what it is, there's a good chance it's going to cause you problems. If you spend all your money today, then you probably won't be able to pay the bills that are due next week. Generally, we think of common sense as an "if. . . then" concept, and our problems arise when we ignore the facts that we really should know. After all, the very term "common sense" indicates that one doesn't need to be a genius in order to understand the concepts.

Our problems with common sense arise when we ignore it. If we put that plate full of food on the edge of a flimsy table, instead of having a nice relaxing meal, there's a good chance that we'll end up cleaning up a mess, losing some perfectly good food, and maybe even breaking a good plate. How many car collisions happen because people ignore common sense? After all, common sense does tell us that we shouldn't drive after drinking, doesn't it?

At school, I often see ridiculous things happen because administrators feel pressured to follow complicated procedures when there are simple, common-sense solutions to problems. I saw a school go into lockdown because a student had shot another student with a self-made bow and arrow—that he had made from toothpicks. I've seen students suspended for extremely minor offenses, while other students who have done far worse things have merely gotten a slap on the wrist and a warning because there were no rules written for their offenses. Common sense is often left outside the door when administrators walk into their offices because they're so afraid of making mistakes that they rely far too much on written rules to make their decisions for them.

A fifteen-year-old recently decided to streak across a football field, a pretty harmless stunt when all is said and done. School administrators, however, decided to threaten criminal charges which would have required the boy to register as a sex offender for the rest of his life if he were found guilty. Overwhelmed by the response to his silly prank, the boy hanged himself.

It is a thousand times better to have common sense without education than to have education without common sense.

Robert Green Ingersoll

The news is full of stories of people who have committed minor drug possession violations put in prison for years because of supposed "three strikes" laws, while people who commit far more serious crimes get far more lenient penalties. Alabama has a law, for example, that requires life imprisonment for a fourth felony conviction, even for something as minor as stealing a bike. Does it really help the state to be paying to support that person in prison for his or her entire life? Does it really help society to use public funds to pay for such a thing to keep minor thieves off the streets?

If we're to make this world a better place and make our lives richer, we really do need to pay closer attention to common sense. It's a gift that has been given to us that can help us to make the world and our lives much more enjoyable and much less stressful, but we choose so often to ignore it—or we get so caught up in thinking that we don't recognize it when we see it—that sometimes it's completely useless because we don't take advantage of it. Often, we get so caught up in how other people say things should be that we really don't consider how they really should be, and how they actually would be if we weren't so concerned about how those other people view us when we do allow common sense—instead of the expectations of others—to be our guiding principle.

Common sense is the knack of seeing things as they are,
and doing things as they ought to be done.

Harriet Beecher Stowe

We can find success in business, in relationships, in hobbies, in challenges that we undertake, if only we can tap into the common sense that we already possess. Perhaps we'll need to learn how to do so, and the common-sense approach to doing so simply says that we should spend more time with people who use their common sense regularly, as we learn from example far more effectively than we learn from theory. Perhaps our grandparents have much more to teach us than we give them credit for. And if we don't have many people like that in our lives, then reading books that focus on common sense (Dale Carnegie and Rachel Naomi Remen leap to mind) can help us by providing examples that we can emulate.

And it's important not to forget that we can be common sense role models, especially for our children, but also for our families, friends, and co-workers. When we value our common sense and make use of it consistently (and show positive results from it, of course), we can help others to see the value of tapping into their own common sense. And imagine what our world would be like if we all were to value common sense and use it regularly in our lives. It may not turn into heaven, of course, but it would become a place in which far more things made sense than they seem to do now.

Questions to Consider

1. Which do we value more in our lives of today: common sense, or statistics? Why?

2. What happens to a person's life when common sense is not present?

3. Can common sense be taught, or is it usually passed on from one person to another?

The Art of Common Sense (an excerpt)
Wilferd A. Peterson

Common sense is a personal compass for guidance around the rocks and shoals of life.

Common sense is not based on theory; it is not a hypothesis. It is life acted out, it is discoveries made in the crucible of existence. It is the tried and tested experiences of humankind.

Common sense sits in judgment on the centuries, on every science, every religion, every art, every government. It is based on what has been proved true, sound and practical.

Common sense is the voice of the ages. It is the distilled essence of what people have learned about life as expressed in the proverbs and maxims of all nations. "That person is happy who lives on his or her own labor," observed the Egyptian. "Just scale and full measure injure no person," recorded the Chinese. "Examine what is said and not who speaks," said the Arabian. "An idle brain is the devil's workshop," wrote the English. . . .

Common sense is pragmatic. It is what William James called "the cash value of an idea." It is a method that works, a truth that can be applied.

Journal Entries

Day One: Is common sense as common as it used to be? If not, what has happened to it?

Day Two: Do you trust your common sense more than you trust your reasoning based on things that you've learned and heard from others? Why or why not?

Day Three: What advantages does common sense have?

Day Four: Can education get in the way of common sense?

Day Five: Think of someone you know who uses common sense very well. What do you think of this person? What are his or her strengths? Would you trust him or her to take on a problem for you?

Fifty-Three

Authenticity

"Authenticity" is a word that I didn't hear regularly until I had been on this planet for quite a while already. But it has become one of the most important words of my life, a star to follow, an ideal to cherish, for it's a word that holds within its meaning a richness of being that is simply one of the most important things that we can strive for in our lives. If I strive to be my authentic self, I give myself permission to do the things that I know are right without worrying about what others think; I claim the right to reject what I know to be bad without fear of losing at something; I allow myself to treat people as I feel inside that they should be treated, without having concern about my standing in society or in my cultural groups.

I will still make mistakes—after all, that's part of being human—but those mistakes will come as I strive to be the best me that I can possibly be, and not to meet the expectations of others who want me to be what they think I should be.

My biggest problem with living authentically has always been caused by the fear of making other people mad at me, or facing their criticism for things that I do or say. We all have that fear to some extent or another, and it's important to learn just how that fear can affect our lives. When we make decisions because we're afraid of other people's responses, then we've lost much of what we call authenticity. We're then letting other people's possible responses cause us to do things—we're not doing them because our hearts, minds, and spirits tell us that they're truly the right things to do.

It is finally when you let go of what people expect you
to be and people's perceptions of you that you're able to be
the version of yourself that you're supposed to be— like in
God's eyes. It doesn't matter if you're half crazy, or eccentric,
or whatever it is— that you have to be true to who
you were born to be.

Gwyneth Paltrow

How many people have entered career fields because their parents have pushed them in that direction or because of potential financial benefits, not because they genuinely loved the work they were committing themselves to do? How many people have entered relationships because the other person has been more "acceptable" to their friends and families? How many of us have put aside hobbies or pastimes that have been considered a waste of time by others? And how often do we not say something because we feel that it will bring criticism or ridicule upon us?

When we live as our authentic selves, though, decisions become easier because we aren't concerned with what others think of us—rather, we're concerned that we're doing right or wrong, and we know in our spirits what the difference is. It doesn't mean that we judge ourselves or others; instead, it means that we follow that still voice within that guides us rather clearly if we allow it to do so. If I really need a quiet Friday night to myself in order to recover my energy after a hectic week, I can say no to that social engagement that someone else is trying to convince me to say yes to. If a friend is doing something that I'm not comfortable with, my heart will tell me to avoid this thing, and I can do so without feeling guilt or fearing ridicule or anger. If I'm living authentically, I recognize immediately that any ridicule or anger is a reflection of the other person who is not respecting my right to make my own decisions on my own terms.

Since I've begun to realize the importance of allowing my authentic self to shine through in my daily life, I've noticed a definite increase in the quality of my life. People almost always respect my decisions because I'm able to explain them in non-judgmental ways. I look forward to much more during each day because I know that I'm not going to face any real conflicts when I do things in the ways that I truly enjoy or feel are the best. I fill my life with activities that I truly enjoy, and I have fun doing them. I'm able to say no to many things that previously I probably would have agreed to.

Most of all, though, I get the feeling that other people feel better around me, for they're around someone who isn't constantly conflicted, who doesn't always worry about what I should do and what I shouldn't do. And most importantly, they can trust me to be honest about what I feel and about what I want to do in my life.

Also, I'm almost completely unaffected by advertising—no ad can make me want something I don't want, or do something that I don't wish to do.

We need to find the courage to say NO to the things and
people that are not serving us if we want to rediscover
ourselves and live our lives with authenticity.

Barbara De Angelis

We're taught from the time we're born to go along with the crowd. In our consumer society, we're often "taught" by ads just what's desirable and just what's not. We're taught not to rock the boat, but to go against the grain. To be a good boy or girl, but to see the allure of being "bad." Our lives are full of conflicting messages from a multitude of sources, almost none of which truly has our best interests in mind. Few people, though, want us to be honest and self-sufficient, to pursue our own lights and goals and dreams, for once we do so, they think that we're invalidating them and we don't spend enough money on consumer goods.

But how do we find out just where our authenticity lies? It can be difficult, but it isn't impossible. The secret is, though, that we don't have to wade through the zillions of conflicting messages in our lives in order to find our authenticity. Rather, we need to find time to be quiet, time to ourselves for reflection. And when we get by ourselves, we need to quiet our minds and our hearts and allow ourselves to feel. We need to ask ourselves what our dreams are, where our aspirations can carry us, what will give us that sense of satisfaction that we all seek in our lives.

But sometimes major change just isn't possible, at least in the short term. If that's the case, we need to reflect on how we can make our current situations better by ceasing to allow ourselves to get involved in things that don't make us feel good, and by acting in ways that are true to our consciences. That woman at work who talks so much about others makes it easy to become involved in gossiping, but that's not the person I want to be, so I won't listen to that talk any more, and I certainly won't participate in it. That other woman whom I appreciate so much—I've never told her how much her efforts mean to me. I need to tell her and thank her for what she does.

And this weekend, I need to take a walk in the woods, because that's something that I truly love to do. And while I know that I'm expected to give several hours a week volunteering at church, that time is making me stressed out and defeating the whole purpose of the weekend—I need to tell them that I can do that every other week, or even every third week.

Often misconstrued, authenticity is not about being an open book,
revealing every detail of yourself without rhyme or reason. It is simply
the act of openly and courageously seeing what needs to be seen,
saying what needs to be said, doing what needs to be done,
and becoming that which you are intent on being.

Scott Edmund Miller

My authentic self is not interested in public recognition or fame. It's not interested in being a part of the herd. It takes no joy in doing things that it knows it shouldn't be doing. My authentic self is peaceful, self-assured, and loving, and when I act from that self, my life becomes much more pleasant and fulfilling. It's quite ironic that our authentic selves are the most neglected parts of who we are, but once we realize that fact we can go about peeling off all those layers that we and society have covered us with so that we can go about living the lives that we were meant to live, in the ways that bring us the most fulfillment and love.

Questions to Think about

1. Are you in strong touch with your authentic self? Are you strongly aware of your specific needs, wants, and desires?

2. What kinds of influences try to keep you from being in touch with your authentic self?

3. What would our lives be like if we always lived from an authentic place, doing what we truly feel is right and avoiding what we truly feel isn't, without being influenced by outside forces?

Thoughts on Authenticity from Ralph Waldo Emerson
from "Self-Reliance"

I read the other day some verses written by an eminent painter which were original and not conventional. The soul always hears an admonition in such lines, let the subject be what it may. The sentiment they instill is of more value than any thought they may contain. To believe your own thought, to believe that what is true for you in your private heart is true for all men, that is genius. Speak your latent conviction, and it shall be the universal sense; for the inmost in due time becomes the outmost, and our first thought is rendered back to us by the trumpets of the Last Judgment. Familiar as the voice of the mind is to each, the highest merit we ascribe to Moses, Plato, and Milton is, that they set at naught books and traditions, and spoke not what men but what they thought.

A man should learn to detect and watch that gleam of light which flashes across his mind from within, more than the lustre of the firmament of bards and sages. Yet he dismisses without notice his thought, because it is his. In every work of genius we recognize our own rejected thoughts: they come back to us with a certain alienated majesty. Great works of art have no more affecting lesson for us than this. They teach us to abide by our spontaneous impression with good-humored inflexibility then most when the whole cry of voices is on the other side. Else, to-morrow a stranger will say with masterly good sense precisely what we have thought and felt all the time, and we shall be forced to take with shame our own opinion from another. . . .

Trust thyself: every heart vibrates to that iron string. Accept the place the divine providence has found for you, the society of your contemporaries, the connection of events. Great men have always done so, and confided themselves childlike to the genius of their age, betraying their perception that the absolutely trustworthy was seated at their heart, working through their hands, predominating in all their being. And we are now men, and must accept in the highest mind the same transcendent destiny; and not minors and invalids in a protected corner, not cowards fleeing before a revolution, but guides, redeemers, and benefactors, obeying the Almighty effort, and advancing on Chaos and the Dark.

Journal Entries

Day One: Do you generally speak and act as your authentic self, or do you think and act how you think other people want you to? What does it mean to you to be authentic?

Day Two: Does our culture value having people become their authentic selves, or does it tend to push us into conformity?

Day Three: What changes would you make in your life if you were to live completely authentically?

Day Four: What does "authentic" mean to you? How would you explain it to someone who asked you what it meant?

Day Five: How might you help others to live authentically? How might you help them to discover what their own authentic self is like?

Fifty-Four

Education

There is very little that we can do to improve our lives if we aren't first willing to do what it takes to educate ourselves. Education is not just what is supposed to be happening in our schools, either—education is constant learning, especially from the people who have faced situations that are similar to ours and who have come out of them not only having survived, but having grown and learned and improved themselves without having compromised their principles or ethics.

My best education has come from experience, of course, and not just my own. I've spent years reading material from people who have been through difficult times and who have faced challenges that most of us can hardly even imagine, and I've done my best to learn from these people strategies that can help me when I find myself in similar situations. The information is often contradictory and sometimes out of date, but all in all, I feel that my education has been extremely valuable because it has come from people who truly care about life and living and who have shared what they have learned with all of us.

Education is a choice. We don't become educated by watching television, and we don't learn a whole lot having similar conversations with the same, safe people day after day. Our education comes from pushing up against boundaries, from taking risks that may seem at first to be overwhelming, and by persevering past the first disappointments or shortfalls until we reach a point at which actual learning takes place. Determination and perseverance are absolutely vital to developing a true education—rarely, if ever, do we learn the most valuable lessons in the first few steps of the journey.

We get lots of information about
life but little education in life from parents, teachers,
and other authority figures who should know better from
their experience. Information is about facts. Education is about
wisdom and the knowledge of how to love and survive.

Bernie Siegel

Unfortunately, in our cultures we tend to believe that the passing on of information is actually education. While the memorization of information can be beneficial (I really would like police officers to know the laws they're enforcing), it's also something that's very limited and not very practical in life. In America at least, we've raised the memorization of information to almost a necessity, while true education is consistently lowered in value until it means almost nothing. How many fathers can tell us everything about his favorite football team, yet tell us nothing of his children's interests and desires in life, or of strategies for helping his kids to grow up as well adjusted individuals? How many people do we know who can function flawlessly on the computer or on their phones when they're on Facebook or streaming a movie, yet know nothing about how to maintain and strengthen friendships and other relationships?

Supposedly, our schools are designed in order to give our children strong educations, but the teachers in the classrooms rarely are given the ability to fulfill that task. Rather, they're told that children have to perform well on tests and that the children need to be exposed to the same information and processes that every other child is exposed to, with no regard whatsoever for their individual strengths and interests. The schools that are set up to provide educations, then, are helping to perpetuate the myth that information equals education, and our society does suffer from this tendency because we have fewer people coming out of our schools who are ready to face life head-on and who are able to help others to do so.

Education is not the piling on of learning, information, data, facts, skills, or abilities—that's training or instruction—but is rather a making visible what is hidden as a seed. . . To be educated, a person doesn't have to know much or be informed, but he or she does have to have been exposed vulnerably to the transformative events of an engaged human life. . . One of the greatest problems of our time is that many are schooled but few are educated.

Thomas Moore

The good news, though, is that we don't have to rely on our schools to give us the education that we need—it's up to us whether we become educated or not. Do you know someone who has come through a tremendous challenge with his or her head held high, regardless of the pain or grief that the challenge has caused? Then sit down and talk with that person, and really listen when he or she tells you just what it was that allowed them to keep going. Have you read about another person's courage? Then read more about that person—or other people who have shown great courage—and find out what factors gave them their courage? When we can learn what keeps other people going, we can incorporate those concepts into our own lives.

I've learned more about love from watching other people, talking to them, and reading their ideas than I ever could have learned through trial and error in my own life. I've learned about letting go through my reading, for I've had few good role models in my own life who have shown me what it means to let go. I've learned about compassion by watching compassionate people and reading about the effects of compassion. In short, I've taken an active approach to educating myself in the matters of life—while I do have a Ph.D. and several M.A.'s, they really would mean nothing to me if I didn't have a true education about life to complement them.

My academic training has been valuable, but I would hardly call it an education. My education involves how to be happy, how to be fulfilled, how to help others to make their lives better. My education involves learning the importance of caring for our planet and being good stewards of our resources—and actually putting into action what I've learned. My education is about learning how to listen to others, using my common sense, and showing love and compassion. It's about making good decisions that will have positive results, and avoiding those situations and decisions that are bound to have negative results.

Much education today is monumentally ineffective.
All too often we are giving young people cut flowers when we
should be teaching them to grow their own plants.

John W. Gardner

Education is not about getting the answers, as John mentions above. Education is about learning how to prepare the soil, plant seeds, cultivate seedlings, nourish the soil, water the plants regularly, and then watch the results. And if we have a drought, education helps us to see alternatives or even to deal with failure, for an educated person doesn't see failure as a final condition, but as a temporary setback that can be dealt with effectively if one chooses to do so.

An education comes from our friends and families, our co-workers and our bosses, our trials and tribulations, our successes and our failures—and sometimes even from our teachers! Our education is what helps us to make effective choices based on what we know to be good for us and for others. It's a mistake to think that our education has come from schools, for what we learned there is not what will make us happy and loving people—it's simply what may help us to get jobs so that we can support ourselves while we learn what's truly important in life—if we choose to learn rather than ignoring the lessons. And getting an education is always a choice, one that we have to renew constantly if we want to learn what's truly valuable in our lives.

Questions to Consider

1. What are some of the dangers and problems involved with trying to provide everyone with the same "universal" education?

2. What are some of the ways other than school that we are educated in life?

3. What are some of the things that you feel were lacking in your own education? How can you go about learning those things now?

Thoughts on Education

The most erroneous assumption is to the effect that the aim of public education is to fill the young of the species with knowledge and awaken their intelligence, and so make them fit to discharge the duties of citizenship in an enlightened and independent manner. Nothing could be further from the truth. The aim of public education is not to spread enlightenment at all; it is simply to reduce as many individuals as possible to the same safe level, to breed and train a standardized citizenry, to put down dissent and originality. That is its aim in the United States, whatever the pretensions of politicians, pedagogues and other such mountebanks, and that is its aim everywhere else.   -H.L. Mencken

The true end of education is not only to make the young learned,
but to make them love learning;
not only to make them industrious, but to make them love industry;
not only to make them virtuous, but to make them love virtue;
not only to make them just, but to make them hunger and thirst after justice.

John Ruskin

Education is not the piling on of learning, information, data, facts, skills, or abilities—that's training or instruction—but is rather a making visible what is hidden as a seed. . . To be educated, a person doesn't have to know much or be informed, but he or she does have to have been exposed vulnerably to the transformative events of an engaged human life. . . One of the greatest problems of our time is that many are schooled but few are educated.   - Thomas Moore

Journal Entries

1. Do you consider yourself to be educated? Where has the bulk of your

education come from?

2. Why might some people in a society not want others to be educated? If people are well educated, do they buy as much based solely on advertising? Do they believe everything a politician says based on personality?

3. Tell a young person why it's important to become educated. Then suggest different ways to actually do so, not limiting your ways to schools.

4. What benefits would a well-educated populace bring to a society?

5. Why in our country do we spend more money on prisons than we do on education? Does this make sense? Is it helping us?

Fifty-Five

Life

One of the most important lessons that I've learned over the many years that I've spent studying life and living has been a very simple one: Our lives are what we make them. Yes, there are outside factors to everything in life, and there are other people who do things that mess up our efforts, and there are earthquakes and fires and storms that can seem to destroy our efforts, but the fact remains the same: Our lives are what we make them. Within the limits that we currently face, we always have the choice to improve our lives, keep them the same, or make them worse. And we do these things with the choices that we make, the people with whom we choose to associate, the risks that we take or avoid, and the attitudes that we bring to the situations that we face.

Life is what it is, and we spend much of our time trying to mold it into what we think it should be. This is a strategy that's doomed to failure, and that failure causes huge amounts of frustration in all of us—we think things should be a certain way, so we put forth effort to make life conform to our beliefs. But it just doesn't work. Yes, there are certain things we can accomplish, such as getting better jobs or changing laws to protect certain things or starting organizations that work for social justice, but when we recognize that the world is full of billions of other people also trying to mold life to their beliefs, we start to see that our frustration isn't helping us a bit, and that life will be life and it will go on on its own terms, with or without us. And that's perfectly okay.

Life is brimming with things to be discovered and known,
skills to be mastered, challenges to be overcome. And when
you are discouraged, dig a hole in the earth and think of
the possibilities. So many things can be planted in your lifetime,
skills that once mastered will bear fruit forever. . . . Pluck
up some enthusiasm for the business of life, for the loamy
matter that supports us all. Become a handyman and spread
your skills wide, digging deeper into the earth's crust
to uncover its secrets.

Christopher Kimball

When we get it through our heads that life is a process of discovery and creation, then we can start to act in ways that bring us to higher levels of knowledge, empathy, compassion, and wisdom. And then we can start being much more content with life and what it throws our way—we can start living our lives fully instead of thinking that there must be something more that we're somehow missing. The lives that we lead are gifts that are beyond our comprehension, really, and it's important that we do our best to make the most of those gifts.

But would you tell a gift-giver, "Thanks for the gift, but it should have been something else?" We all know that saying such a thing would be a sign of ingratitude, a sign that we don't appreciate the gift at all. And without gratitude and appreciation, the gift will simply be a waste of everyone's time. If we accept it for what it is, though, and try to make the best of all of its qualities, we can make the most of the gift of life by turning the lives into works of art, creative wonders that honor the gift-giver and the gift itself.

Being able to do this, though, requires that we recognize that if we're to live our lives, we cannot be passive observers of life—we must be active participants. As Shakti Gawain says below, life doesn't just happen to us; rather we create the conditions that cause life to respond in the ways it does. True, that person did something very awful to you, but how did that person get into a position of influence over you in the first place? We allow people into our lives, and we have the power to put them out of our lives, too. Perhaps you don't have enough money at the moment to do what you dream of doing, but you do have enough money to do something. When we lose something dear to us, it often turns out to be very positive for us as we let go and move on—if we allow ourselves to let go in the first place.

Many of us have had the attitude that life is something that happens to us and that all we can do is make the best of it. It is basically a victim's position, giving power to people and things outside of ourselves. We are beginning to realize that the power rests in us, that we can choose to create our life the way we want it to be.

Shakti Gawain

There are so many amazing things that we can do with life, but most of us simply put ourselves into a little box that we think defines us and we allow ourselves to stay with the same patterns and actions for years and years. It isn't life that limits our possibilities—it's something that we do ourselves as we consider our choices. Life gives me the chance to explore new surroundings and new thoughts and ideas each day, but I generally choose to stick with what I know. That way, I don't allow my fear to grow too strong. But that way, I also don't allow my heart or my mind to grow too much, either.

Look at all that life offers. Some of it is out of reach at the moment, but if we really, truly want something, we can make it happen in our lives. It takes effort and perseverance and a bit of faith, but anything can be done that doesn't violate the known laws of physics, right? When we approach life with a positive attitude and an indomitable faith, there really are no limits as to what we can accomplish. Yet most of us approach life with hesitation and fear, and we come to see our lack of accomplishment as life's fault, not our own.

Life is about love, and about becoming the people we were meant to be. And there's a good chance that that person isn't rich or famous or even well-known; some of the most important contributions in life have come from people of humble means who have taught very valuable lessons to others who have gone on to spread those lessons throughout the world.

I love life. Life allows me to walk in the snow, to hear children's laughter, to run marathons, to taste chocolate and wine (not together, though), to read good books, to enjoy good movies, to experience other people's smiles, to help people who are in need, to be helped by others when I'm in need, to see the stars and hear the wind and stand in awe at the sunset. Life allows me to learn, to know more today than I knew yesterday, or to be better at something today than I was yesterday. Life is the tenderness of a loving touch, the beauty of a bird's song, the fantastic feel of rain on my skin and in my hair, the joy of waking up after a good sleep.

Yes, life does offer me challenges and obstacles, but these are the things that teach me, that help me grow, and that make me appreciate the times when I'm not facing any particular challenges.

The great affair, the love affair with life, is to live as variously as possible, to groom one's curiosity like a high-spirited thoroughbred, climb aboard, and gallop over the thick, sun-struck hills every day. Where there is no risk, the emotional terrain is flat and unyielding, and, despite all its dimensions, valleys, pinnacles, and detours, life will seem to have none of its magnificent geography, only a length. It began in mystery, and it will end in mystery, but what a savage and beautiful country lies in between.

Diane Ackerman

How is your relationship with life? Is it a love affair, or is it antagonistic? Is it full of appreciation and wonder, or full of blame and accusations? It may be confusing and even frightening at times, but life definitely gives us gift after gift, and it's completely up to us what we do with those amazing blessings—we can accept them and put them in their best light, or we can let our fears control us and see those gifts as nothing at all special. No matter what we choose to do, though, life will keep giving us gifts. Eventually we're going to have to make those gifts important parts of our lives and make our lives the special, marvelous experiences that they always were meant to be.

Questions to Think about

1. How often do we think about life and what it's all about? Are we sometimes too busy to ponder just what our lives may be all about?

2. How do we go about making sure that we love life and living? How do we not get caught up in the negative things that happen so that we can keep our focus on the good sides of life?

3. How do we learn about life? Other people? Do we know where their perspectives come from?

A Psalm of Life

What the heart of the young man
said to the psalmist
Henry Wadsworth Longfellow

Tell me not, in mournful numbers,
Life is but an empty dream!
For the soul is dead that slumbers,
And things are not what they seem.

Life is real! Life is earnest!
And the grave is not its goal;
Dust thou art, to dust returnest,
Was not spoken of the soul.

Not enjoyment, and not sorrow,
Is our destined end or way;
But to act, that each to-morrow
Find us farther than to-day.

Art is long, and Time is fleeting,
And our hearts, though stout and brave,
Still, like muffled drums, are beating
Funeral marches to the grave.

In the world's broad field of battle,
In the bivouac of Life,
Be not like dumb, driven cattle!
Be a hero in the strife!

Trust no Future, howe'er pleasant!
Let the dead Past bury its dead!
Act,— act in the living Present!
Heart within, and God o'erhead!

Lives of great men all remind us
We can make our lives sublime,
And, departing, leave behind us
Footprints on the sands of time;

Footprints, that perhaps another,
Sailing o'er life's solemn main,
A forlorn and shipwrecked brother,
Seeing, shall take heart again.

Let us, then, be up and doing,
With a heart for any fate;
Still achieving, still pursuing,
Learn to labor and to wait.

Journal Entries

Day One: How do you see life? Is it something you're participating in, like a softball game; something that challenges you, like a maze; something that's negotiated, like a business; or something that offers you wonderful things, like stopping by a generous person's house for pie and coffee? Or something completely different?

Day Two: If you could dispense just two pieces of advice for dealing with life and have everyone in the world hear them, what would they be?

Day Three: Do you love life? If not, what would it take to get you to do so?

Day Four: Why does life seem so different to everyone, and seem to treat everyone so differently? Is life fair, or is it beyond fairness?

Day Five: What do you expect from life? Do you often get it?

Fifty-Six

Recreation

I've known many, many people who truly have had no idea what recreation means. They might have had an idea of what it's supposed to be in the backs of their minds, but they never truly engaged in any sort of recreation themselves, and without exception, they paid very heavy prices for this neglect in their lives. There are few things as important to us as true recreation, putting ourselves in situations in which we are able to put aside the day-to-day stresses and anxieties and focus fully on the present moment—in which we're doing something completely different than we normally do.

In my own life, there are few things that are more important than recreation. I don't focus on recreation to the extent at which I neglect my responsibilities, but I do make sure that I set aside time in order to do things that are fun, that get me out into nature, and that keep me focused on something different from the things that I normally focus on, whether that be paying attention to a hiking trail and my surroundings, walking through a town or a park where I've never been before, or even playing tag or throwing a frisbee around with a kid who doesn't have any desire at all to talk about my job or my family or my bills.

Recreation is about using our bodies in different ways and keeping our minds focused on something different—in this latter way, it's definitely a form of meditation when it can keep our thoughts occupied with thoughts that push out those thoughts that cause us stress and keep us worried. And when our recreation keeps us focused on an activity for an extended period of time, we can return to our thoughts about work or family problems almost with a new mind, and certainly with a refreshed mind, which can help us to gain new insights and to tackle problems without also having to deal with exhaustion.

The word "recreation" is really a very beautiful word. It is defined in the dictionary as "the process of giving new life to something, of refreshing something, of restoring something." This something, of course, is the whole person.

Bruno Hans Geba

Few of us would be cruel enough to run a horse to exhaustion. But many of us are cruel enough to run ourselves to exhaustion, especially mental exhaustion. The symptoms of mental exhaustion generally aren't visible enough for us to take them for the very real warning signs that they are, so we allow ourselves to pass through them, telling ourselves that we're just tired or cranky or wimpy, and that we should just drive on and get things done. This is a very destructive pattern of behavior, though.

When I teach writing, I tell my students that if they have a five-hour block set aside to write a paper or to study a unit, it's much better to work for two hours, then take a twenty- or thirty-minute walk, and then come back to the work. This short recreation break can make the difference between work well done and work finished in a state of exhaustion—which probably won't be the best work they can do. The recreation allows them to shift their thinking to something else so that when they come back to the subject of their work or study, their minds are fresher and much more able to make important connections.

Our age has become so mechanical that this has also affected our recreation. People have gotten used to sitting down and watching a movie, a ball game, a television set. It may be good once in a while, but it certainly is not good all the time. Our own faculties, our imagination, our memory, the ability to do things with our mind and our hands—they need to be exercised. If we become too passive, we get dissatisfied.

Maria von Trapp

And I have to agree with Maria—sitting down and watching something is not a true form of recreation, for it's completely passive in nature. Recreation needs to be active so that our minds can be focused on something other than a screen—we focus on catching or hitting a ball, or making something concrete, or looking at our surroundings. We get our blood flowing and we stimulate the production of chemicals that keep us feeling vital and alive. We remind our bodies that they were created to be active, and through our activities we allow them to be so.

"Re-creation" is not simply about entertainment. It's about taking care of ourselves and our minds, bodies, and spirits. It's about taking time away from our everyday pursuits and using that time to rejuvenate ourselves so that we can be more effective in what we do, and so that we can enjoy it more when we get back to our normal tasks. Too many businesses don't understand this, and they try to get people to stay focused only on work, hour after hour, day after day, week after week. They don't understand that the breaks that we take for recreation help us to do a much better job in the time we dedicate to our work.

Recreation's purpose is not to kill time, but to make

life, not to keep a person occupied, but to keep them
refreshed; not to offer an escape from life,
but to provide a discovery of life.

unattributed

What do you enjoy as a recreational activity? Do you do it often enough? If
not, how could you manage to work more recreational time into your
schedule? Remember, doing so isn't about trying to get out of work or to shirk
your responsibilities, but it is about trying to make sure that you're in an
optimal state for making sure that you meet those responsibilities. Be it a
game of frisbee or catch with a kid or a friend, or a nice walk at lunchtime, or a
pick-up basketball game somewhere, you can find opportunities for recreation
almost anywhere—and the benefits for doing so far outweigh any arguments
against taking the time to re-create yourself.

Questions to Ponder

1. Why do many people consider recreation something that we do only on
special occasions? Why would someone avoid doing something that can help
them to cope with the stresses of life and living?

2. What are your favorite forms of recreation? How often do you participate in
them?

3. What kinds of situations keep you from actively pursuing recreation? How
high is recreation on your list of priorities?

Thoughts on Recreation

Recreation is not a secondary concern for a democracy. It is a primary concern,
for the kind of recreation a people make for themselves determines the kind of
people they become and the kind of society they build.   -Harry Allen
Overstreet

We must be wise taskmasters and not require of ourselves what we cannot
possibly perform. Recreation we must have. Otherwise, the strings of our soul,
wound up to an unnatural tension, will break.   -Elizabeth Prentiss

Leave all the afternoon for exercise and recreation, which are as necessary as reading. I will rather say more necessary because health is worth more than learning.   -Thomas Jefferson

Have you known how to take rest? You have done more than he who hath taken empires and cities.   -Michel de Montaigne

Journal Entries

Day One: Is recreation a big part of your life? If so, why do you make it important? If not, why do you not make it important?

Day Two: Think of someone you know who doesn't get enough recreation in his or her life. Write that person a letter telling him or her why you think they should make recreation a higher priority.

Day Three: What are your favorite forms of recreation? How often do you practice them?

Day Four: Is sitting down and watching television really a form of recreation, or is it merely a pastime? In your eyes, what's the difference between the two?

Day Five: Is recreation more or less important in our world than it seemed to be when you were much younger? What are the effects of that shift?

Fifty-Seven

Competence

Many people feel that once they get a certain job, that's it—there's nothing more to learn that can't be learned while they're working. They might have taken two or four years of college courses to earn a certain degree, but now that they're earning a paycheck, the days of spending time studying the field are long gone. "If I don't learn it at work," they seem to think, "then I don't need to know it."

And perhaps they're right. It's possible that there are many things about their careers that they don't necessarily need to know. But why is it that we so often choose not to learn more about the very work that we're getting paid for, while we were so willing to study as much as was asked for us while we were hoping and praying to find work in the first place?

The truth is that most people don't push themselves very hard even when they're taking the courses necessary to get the jobs they want. Most people are satisfied with meeting the minimum requirements in order to get by, get their diploma or certificate, and move on with their lives. This is one of the reasons for which it's often so difficult to find well qualified people to promote into important leadership roles: very few people have distinguished themselves as leaders in their fields, preferring instead simply to get along with doing what's required of them, and little else.

I am, as I've said, merely competent. But in an age
of incompetence, that makes me extraordinary.

Billy Joel

There are a few very interesting truths, though, about striving to be more than just competent in our work. First of all, it seems that the more we learn about our work, the easier and the more interesting it becomes to us. Tasks that used to be tedious now make sense, and we see how they're related to other elements of our jobs. Plus, they're easier to take care of now, so they don't bother us nearly as much when we need to do them. When we know more about our work and its ramifications, we can see the connections between what we do and the effects that those things have on other people.

Secondly, as we become more competent, we accomplish more and we're able to branch out and include other things in our work. As a teacher, for example, I find that the more I know about the topic I'm teaching, the more I'm able to pull in material from other realms. As I become more competent at teaching Speech classes, I find it easier to relate material from other fields, such as Biology or History, to the material that we're studying in Speech. I no longer have to stick to the base material, for I'm able to bring more to my students.

Thirdly, when we take the time to learn more about what we're doing, we're putting ourselves in the position of being more qualified than others when it comes time for promotions or advancement. Very often, pay raises are based on job performance, and it's almost impossible to raise our knowledge level about our work without also raising the level of our performance.

Of course, there are some jobs that may not require competence above certain levels. When I worked at the front desk of two hotels, my job was clearly defined and I didn't need to know much more than what I did. However, there were other areas of the hotel that ran independently of the front desk, and I always had opportunities to learn about those. Also, there were always new things to learn about the area surrounding the hotel, so if someone were looking for things to do or places to visit, there was always more to learn, and I could be much more helpful to the guests when I took the time to learn about the area.

It's simple to seek substitutes for competence—such easy substitutes: love, charm, kindness, charity. But there is no substitute for competence.

Ayn Rand
The Fountainhead

Our culture doesn't seem to value competence as much as it used to. Now we seem to want to do and get everything as quickly as possible, which often leads to mediocre work and products. It seems to be the exception to find people at stores and businesses who are actually able to help us thoroughly with whatever problems we may have. We accept poor service and poor workmanship as if we deserve it—and when we decide to make a stand about something, it usually has to do with price or rudeness, but not about competence.

Nowhere have I seen this as strongly as I have in our schools. There are many, many wonderful teachers out there, but there are also a lot of people who are not at all competent in their jobs, yet they keep getting rehired and even rewarded for making it through a certain number of years, whether or not they've made any effort at all to address their own lack of competence. I've known quite a few teachers who do little teaching at all—they simply hand out packets to their students and have them work on their own while the teacher works at his or her desk, often searching the Internet for this or that, but certainly not engaged actively with the students.

If you can do a half-assed job of anything, you're
a one-eyed man in a kingdom of the blind.

Kurt Vonnegut

Competence is a choice, purely and simply. And it's a choice made over and over again—the choice to read another book this week about my career field, to register for a course related to my work, to spend some extra time researching a topic that will help me to be better at what I do. And it's a choice that may not show immediate dividends—it may take years to see the results of my efforts to be really good at what I do. Even after more than twenty years of teaching, I took two courses this past year and went to several seminars of three days each over the summer, simply because I need to add to my knowledge, even after all this time. I simply want to be good at what I do because I know that the people I work for—in my case, high school students—will be the ones who benefit from my abilities. And they deserve me to be the best I can be at what I do. I'll never be the best teacher ever, of course, but I can certainly try to be better this year than I was last year.

Questions to Ponder

1. Do you try to be as competent as possible in all that you do? Is it possible to be extremely competent in many different areas?

2. How does one go about developing competency? Is it easy, or does it take a lot of effort?

3. Does our society value competence as much as it used to? Are most employers concerned more with competence of their people or the amount of money they pay for them?

Thoughts about Competence

Competence takes work, which is why so few people care to develop it. It takes practice, and it takes time. It also takes faith that the work that we're doing is worth doing—and that the effort we put forth will end up making us competent in a chosen field. Any of us can develop a level of competence in almost anything we choose to do, though I certainly do not want to commit the time and effort necessary to develop competence in computer programming. I prefer to become competent in fields that I enjoy working in.

What are you competent in? Are there any fields in which you're "merely" competent? I know that I would rather have an insurance agent who has a high level of competence than one who has a basic level, and who is merely competent, not extremely competent. I've had the latter kind of insurance agent before, and it ended up costing my wife and me a significant amount of money.

We don't have to be really good at everything. We don't have to know how to do everything at basic levels. But the things that we love doing, and the things that we must do (parenting, for example) will be much more enjoyable and we'll do a much better job at them if we take the time and make the effort to become much more competent in them than we are. It's up to us.

Journal Entries

Day One: Name one area in which you feel you are completely competent. How often do you work or play in that area? Do you also enjoy doing it?

Day Two: What would it take for you to become "extremely competent" in another area or two?

Day Three: Is competence valued as widely in our society today? Discuss a couple of incidents that you've witnessed that support your answer.

Day Four: What does it mean to you to be "incompetent"? Why do you think incompetent people are often promoted or given even better jobs?

Day Five: If you were in a position to hire someone, why might it be difficult to be sure that the person you hire is competent in the field?

Fifty-Eight

Motivation: Intrinsic or Extrinsic?

One of the greatest challenges that I face when I'm working with high school students is trying to get them to understand the importance of developing their own intrinsic motivation. Simply stated, motivation that is intrinsic is that which comes from ourselves—we want to accomplish and achieve things because we want to do so. Extrinsic motivation, on the other hand, is the desire to achieve because someone else tells us to do so or because we want to please another person. If you're trying to do well on the job because you want to take pride in your work and you want to challenge yourself, then your motivation is intrinsic. If you're trying to do well at work because you're afraid of getting fired or because your boss is encouraging you to do so, then you're depending upon extrinsic forces to motivate you.

While extrinsic motivation in itself isn't necessarily a negative thing, it can become overwhelming when we don't develop our intrinsic motivation. My students, for example, tend to do their assignments because I assign them, not because they want to learn the material. They get things done because they want to get a certain grade—or because they want to avoid a zero on the assignment and the resulting lower grade. Rarely do they pay close attention to the assignments in an effort to internalize the process or information so that they can add something new to their knowledge base.

If you want to build a ship, don't drum up people
together to collect wood and don't assign them
tasks and work, but rather teach them to long
for the endless immensity of the sea.

Antoine de Saint-Exupéry

So I spend much of my time trying to encourage them by pointing out their strengths, and by letting them know the consequences of two separate approaches to life. The people who depend on extrinsic motivation rarely excel in anything, and they find it more difficult to be hired, promoted, or recognized for their achievements or even just their attitude towards life. Those who are intrinsically motivated find it easier to succeed at college and at work, and they find that life is a continual challenge. They almost never sit around waiting for someone else to come along to motivate them to do things—they can't wait to finish up their current project because they have something else they want to get started on.

What motivates you? What makes you want to do things? Is it the fear of criticism or punishment, such as getting fired? Or is it the desire to be really, really good at what you do and how you do it? The world is always in need of people who do very good jobs, no matter what the field, and you can make yourself an incredible asset to your organization or your family be deciding that you want to be very good at whatever it is that you want to do. Perhaps that will mean a few extra hours of reading every week, or a few extra hours of work so that you improve your skills. It may mean asking a lot of questions of people who do something better than you, and it may mean sacrificing a few episodes of some sitcom or television drama in order to spend time getting better at something rather than passively watching someone else's work.

You can motivate by fear [extrinsic], and you can
motivate by reward [extrinsic].
But both those methods are only temporary.
The only lasting thing is self-motivation.

Homer Rice

Sometimes when I'm about to do something, I have to stop and ask myself, do I really want to do this? Is this something that I truly want to do or feel called to do, or am I doing it because someone else expects it of me? And there are, of course, times when it's completely appropriate to do things to please others— people we work for and people we love, or in cases when we'd cause problems if we don't do something—but in general, once I'm clear on my motivation for doing something, it makes the task much easier. And I often see that even though my original motivation is extrinsic—I might win an award if I do this well—my intrinsic motivation kicks in and allows me to actually do the task very well because I want to feel satisfied with the job that I do.

On the other hand, if I'm doing something just because someone has convinced me to do it, I usually don't feel the passion and the desire to do it exceedingly well. I'm just fulfilling someone else's desires or expectations, and my motivation comes completely from outside of myself. And that rarely ends up with feelings of satisfaction and accomplishment.

The only lifelong, reliable motivations are those that come
from within, and one of the strongest of those is the joy
and pride that grow from knowing that you've just done
something as well as you can do it.

Lloyd Dobens

I wish that I could teach all of the young people with whom I work to do things well because they want to learn rather than because their grades depend on it. They would learn more, and they would enjoy themselves more. We don't want to reach an unhealthy point of pushing ourselves too hard, of course, but when our motivation originates from inside, we can be sure that we're taking steps to develop our authentic selves rather than simply fulfilling someone else's desires. When we do this, we can follow our hearts and learn and grow in authentic ways, becoming the people we're meant to be.

Questions to Ponder

1. Is most of your motivation for doing things in life intrinsic or extrinsic?

2. When people get used to following only extrinsic motivation, what can happen to them when the extrinsic motivation is no longer there?

3. Why do some people become dependent upon extrinsic motivation?

Thoughts on Motivation

Intrinsic: I'm going to do well on this paper because I want to be proud of it
Extrinsic: I'm going to do well on this paper because I want a good grade

Intrinsic: I'm going to volunteer my time because it's the right thing to do
Extrinsic: I'm going to volunteer my time because I'll impress people

Intrinsic: I'm going to take this class to improve my job skills
Extrinsic: I'm going to take this class to improve my chances of promotion

Intrinsic: I'm going to improve my play to help the team more
Extrinsic: I'm going to improve my play so that I can impress people more

Journal Entries

Day One: Think about something that has strong external motivation for you. How might you shift that motivation to internal?

Day Two: Why can it be important to try to find some intrinsic motivation when you're planning on doing things?

Day Three: Write a letter to a friend or family member encouraging them in ways that will spark intrinsic motivation, and not offering any external rewards.

Day Four: Why do so many people rely on extrinsic factors to motivate them to do the things they do?

Day Five: How have your motivations changed as you've grown older?

Fifty-nine

Now Again—Living in the Present Moment

Living in the present moment always has been a difficult task for me, as my mind tends to focus on things in the past or worries about things in the future. It's not something that I choose to do or choose to have happen, but it's something that does happen. I can be walking in an absolutely beautiful place on a lovely day, and because I'm worrying about some situation or another, I simply don't notice the beauty all around me. My presence in the present often is lacking, and I wish it weren't so.

I mostly wish it weren't so because I know that I'd be a happier person if I were able to focus on what's right here and right now—the gifts, the beauty, the trees and the birds and the people and the sky. I'm much better at being in the present moment now than I was twenty years ago, but my hope is that I'll be even better at it tomorrow and next year. Because one of the most important lessons that I've learned so far in my life is that life exists in the present moment only—we can live in the present moment only. Yes, we may be able to spend the present moment making plans for tomorrow, but then the time spent planning is time well spent.

To a large degree, the measure of our peace of mind is determined by how much we are able to live in the present moment. Irrespective of what happened yesterday or last year, and what may or may not happen tomorrow, the present moment is where you are—always!

Richard Carlson

Living in the present moment isn't about just enjoying life, either. It's about keeping ourselves sane and healthy, and as Richard says above, keeping our minds at peace. After all, it's only with peace of mind that we can really lower the stress that we feel, that we can maintain a sense of balance with ourselves. Without peace of mind it's difficult to maintain our calm and cool in many situations, and difficult things tend to build up on each other, bringing us down and keeping us in their grasp as we struggle to free ourselves from the frightening hold of worries and fears.

When I look around right here and right now, though, I gain a fresh sense of perspective on life and its challenges. Right here and right now, I have shelter, I have work, I have food, I have friends and family and relationships. There's an awful lot that may happen tomorrow, but right here and right now, I have all I need to be comfortable and to enjoy this moment. If I don't do so—if I lose my peace of mind because I'm afraid or worried of what's going to happen on Thursday, or I'm angry or frustrated about what happened two days ago—then I am keeping myself from living my life fully.

When you live in the present moment, time stands still.
Accept your circumstances and live them. If there is
an experience ahead of you, have it! But if worries stand
in your way, put them off until tomorrow. Give yourself
a day off from worry. You deserve it. Some people live
with a low-grade anxiety tugging at their spirit all day long.
They go to sleep with it, wake up with it, carry it around at
home, in town, to church, and with friends. Here's
a remedy: Take the present moment and find something
to laugh at. People who laugh, last.

Barbara Johnson

What I like most about what Barbara says is her focus on acceptance of things as they are right now. That acceptance is the key to getting the most out of any moment we're in. I may not like how things are, but they are as they are and I must accept that fact. Once I accept it, I can spend the present moment planning how to change it—or even starting the process of changing how things are so that they won't be the same next week. If I don't accept my circumstances, though, they will defeat me in the end, for we cannot beat enemies that we don't recognize as such. Am I facing financial problems? Then right now I need to do something to deal with them effectively. Worrying about them and putting off action will solve nothing.

Living in the moment is NOT about fulfilling every desire and practicing hedonism. Rather, it's about being aware of my world right now and doing those things that can make my world better or taking advantage of and recognizing the beauty and blessings and opportunity that already fill my life. If I'm trying to lose weight, it may mean passing on dessert at this moment, and feeling good about the decision I just made. It may mean not buying the new toy I really want, and realizing that I've made a very practical and responsible decision.

Are you present in this moment, right here, right now?
Or are you remembering what you didn't do yesterday,
thinking about what you have to do tomorrow,
regretting what you did last week. If you are in any of these places,
you are not here, right now in the fullness of this moment.

The richness of the present is here. The fullness of now is present.
If you are not here now, it means you could be missing the love,
joy, peace and brand-new ideas that are here right now.
Why not take a moment to gather yourself, to pull yourself together,
to collect all of your thoughts and feelings in this time and place?

Iyanla Vanzant

What's present in your life at this very moment that makes your life very special? Do you have to be with your friends to appreciate the fact that they are very special to you? Do you have to be at home to know and like the fact that your home is a very special place to you? And if things aren't going well for some reason, perhaps your present moment could best be spent writing down what's working and what isn't, and then coming up with a definite plan for improving things. Because at the very least, you have air to breathe, clothing to wear, electricity to light your home and run your computer, and many other blessings that are just waiting to be recognized as such, and that will brighten your life even more once you see how special and important they really are.

Questions on Living in the Present Moment

1. What is one simple benefit of being able to be fully present in the current moment?

2. Where are some of the places that your mind goes when you're doing things? What effect does this have on what you're doing? Are you able to give it your full attention?

3. How much time is your mind on the past? The future? Why? Are you able to actually change anything from either time?

Right Here, Right Now—Technology and Being Present

I know someone who is almost never present in the current moment in her current location. Her problem seems to be her cell phone—she's always talking to someone else about problems that the other people are experiencing. If she's in the supermarket, you can bet she's talking on the phone with her mother about some problem with the kids. If she's with the kids, she's talking with a friend about something that happened yesterday.

We all need someone to talk to sometimes. We all need to process things that have happened to us, and it's important to be able to talk to people about things that are going on in our lives. But there's a time and place for that. If we're constantly talking to other people who aren't even where we are, it's absolutely impossible for us to be *fully* aware of and involved with our surroundings. If our mind is on the past, yesterday or thirty years ago, it's impossible for us to be *fully* involved in the now.

The most common argument that you'll hear if you point this out to someone is that it's okay, that they know how to "multi-task." But I can guarantee you that someone who makes this claim is not aware of just how beneficial it can be to us to be *fully and completely* present in our right now.

I was with a friend once, and he was on vacation in a beautiful spot. Almost every hour, though, his wife called him to ask some other question that almost anyone could have answered. Every hour he was pulled away from thinking about his surroundings and the beauty of his location in order to think about problems at home—which was exactly what he was trying to get away from by going on vacation.

When I go on vacation, I do not carry a phone with me. When I'm at work, I do not have a phone that will pull me out of the present moment by making a noise when someone sends me a message or calls or posts something on Facebook. I never want to imply to someone I'm with that "I enjoy your company, but in this moment this message on my phone is more important to me than you. Sorry." If I'm with you right here and right now, then I'm with you, and I'll honor your presence by keeping present myself.

We fool ourselves if we think that our technology has improved our communication and observation skills. On the contrary, it has made us much less able to focus our attention for long periods of time in order to be fully present in each moment of our lives. We have to observe ourselves on our phones to know how much they affect us, and then make decisions— sometimes difficult ones—about limiting the influence that technology has over us. The very quality of our lives depends upon us doing so.

Journal Entries

Day One: What am I doing in the present moment that requires my attention? (I'm reading, and I don't understand the story as well if I split my attention; I'm working, and the quality of my work will go down if I'm not present in the moment.)

Day Two: How might I improve my ability to live in the moment? (Paying attention to what I'm thinking of versus what I'm doing, making decisions about how I spend my time.)

Day Three: What are some of the things that I love to do with my moments that aren't necessarily productive (in society's view), but are very valuable to me? (I like to read, I like to meditate or do yoga, I like to sit with a cup of coffee and look out the window and watch the world.) Why should I keep on doing them?

Day Four: What are some benefits of being fully present in all that I do? (I'll make fewer mistakes when I cook and the food will taste better, other people will appreciate that I'm paying close attention, I'll learn more when I pay better attention.)

Day Five: How might I help others to learn how to stay present in the moment, and to maintain that presence?

Sixty

Now, Take Three

This present moment—what an incredible gift it is! It has been rightly said that this moment truly is all that we have, for the only time that we truly act in our lives is in the right now—though we may spend now planning to act in the future, the actions themselves come only when what-will-be turns into what-is, and we're in a new present moment. And once we've acted, that moment becomes the past.

It took me many years to learn that we live exclusively in the present. I had grown up with my mind often in the future—especially on things that I hoped would happen—or in the past, being upset with something that had happened. Neither of these strategies did me any good, and I believe that both of them contributed a great deal to the debilitating depression that I used to go through. While I did a fairly decent job of getting out into the world and seeing and experiencing things, my mind very often kept me from enjoying the present moment because it would focus on what was missing from it. I could be on a mountain trail in a beautiful national park, yet my mind would be focused on the fact that I was there alone, and how "terrible" that was. I could be with someone I really liked having and enjoyable conversation, yet my mind would be focused on what was going to happen tomorrow, and how difficult it was going to be.

The only time that any of us have to grow or change or feel or learn anything is in the present moment. But we're continually missing our present moments, almost willfully, by not paying attention.

Jon Kabat-Zinn

In other words, I wasn't paying all that much attention to the here and now— my mind was on the future or the past, and it wasn't allowing me to fully experience all that was going on. I can't even begin to estimate just how many present moments I've squandered, just how many times I've missed the chance to get to know someone better—or even just to get to know someone— because my mind has been elsewhere. I'll never know just how many beautiful or hilarious or precious or rewarding moments I've missed because I have been fully present in the present.

I certainly don't say these things because I'm mad at myself or highly critical of myself—I'm just stating facts. But I do remind myself of all that I've missed because I don't want to miss any more present moments than I really have to, and by keeping myself reminded of the way that I've missed many of them, I can remind myself in each moment, "I don't want to miss what's going on now, because this moment is the most important moment of my life."

And each passing moment truly is the most important moment of our lives, because each is the only time when we can actually do something, when we can actually take actions that will change and improve our lives. Yes, we can plan to do something today at 3 p.m., but when the time gets here, that's when we have to act or lose the chance to do so. Planning is great, and planning is necessary, but it's the execution of the plan that makes the plan worthwhile.

What we are talking about is learning to live in the present moment, in the now. When you aren't distracted by your own negative thinking, when you don't allow yourself to get lost in moments that are gone or yet to come, you are left with this moment. This moment—now— truly is the only moment you have. It is beautiful and special. Life is simply a series of such moments to be experienced one right after another. If you attend to the moment you are in and stay connected to your soul and remain happy, you will find that your heart is filled with positive feelings.

Sydney Banks

I also want to notice more all of the opportunities that I have with each moment. I want to be aware of the beautiful things that fill my life as I pass through present moment after present moment. If I'm focused on anger for what someone did this morning, though, or fear of what's going to happen two hours from now, then I can be sure that I'm missing a great deal of what now has to offer. Sometimes, this takes a conscious effort on my part—I stop what I'm doing and I look around, seeing what's there that I'm not noticing. Very often this is a rather humbling exercise—it's amazing how many things I miss from day to day.

It's a shame that people don't teach us more about being present in the moment. We do tend to slip into denial about our particular responsibilities in the present if we don't remind ourselves constantly about what life means, and what it means to recognize the needs of the present moment instead of being bogged down by our own needs and wants. How many times have I not recognized it when someone needed a person to talk to, but I was too involved with my frustration about the past? How many times have I walked right by something that needed to be done because I was worried about what was going to happen tomorrow?

Enjoying the moment is easy if we're meeting a newborn for the first time, watching a puppy play, or eating our favorite dessert. But it's not as easy to do if we're not doing or seeing something out of the ordinary—we tend to take for granted the same kid that we see every day, the same foods that we eat often, the same scenery that we pass each morning and afternoon.

Not living in the present is a form of denial. It's easier to live in the past or future because then you don't have to be responsible for the present.

Jane Hendrix

It's easy enough to say "Open your eyes," "Be present," "Live in the now." But it's much more difficult to do. In many ways, most of the entire Buddhist philosophy towards life is a focus on being present in each moment that we live in, and being responsive to the needs and the gifts of the moment. When we do learn to live our lives this way, many of our cares and worries tend to fade away, for we start to see just how we fit into each present moment. And when we start to see how we fit in, we see our relevance and our importance to other people, to situations, and to life itself.

The present moment may be full of anticipation or fear, but we can change that when we realize that the future present moments will take care of themselves. Right now, our only responsibility is to live the moment that we're in, and to get all that we can out of that moment, and to give all that we can to it.

Questions to Consider

1. Jane Hendrix says that "not living in the present is a form of denial." What do you think that she means by that? Is she right?

2. Sydney Banks says that "this moment—now—truly is the only moment you have." What do you interpret that to mean? Do you agree with him?

3. Jon Kabat-Zinn says that "we're continually missing our present moments, almost willfully, by not paying atttention." Is this true? Why or why not?

Another Poem by Ella Wheeler Wilcox

The subtle beauty of this day
Hangs o'er me like a fairy spell,
And care and grief have flown away,

And every breeze sings, "all is well."
I ask, "Holds earth or sin, or woe?"
My heart replies, "I do not know."

Nay! all we know, or feel, my heart,
Today is joy undimmed, complete;
In tears or pain we have no part;
The act of breathing is so sweet,
We care no higher joy to name.
What reck we now of wealth or fame?

The past—what matters it to me?
The pain it gave has passed away.
The future—that I cannot see!
I care for nothing save today—
This is a respite from all care,
And trouble flies—I know not where.

Go on, oh noisy, restless life!
Pass by, oh, feet that seek for heights!
I have no part in aught of strife;
I do not want your vain delights.
The day wraps round me like a spell
And every breeze sings, "All is well."

Journal Entries

Day One: Look about yourself and find ten things that you're thankful for.
Write them down. Why do we not do this more often? (Lights, electricity,
heat, music, art, friends and family, etc.)

Day Two: Write a pledge to be present in the present moment as much as you
can in the future. What specific things will you do to help yourself meet this
goal? (I will remind myself that much around me deserves my attention, and I'll
look closely at it.)

Day Three: Write a letter to yourself of ten years from now, detailing the
blessings that you feel at this moment in your life.

Day Four: Think of something that pulls your thoughts from the present
moment, such as a worry about the future or a regret about the past. Does
thinking about those things change them or make them different? Do you lose
the worry, or does it grow? Do you overcome the regret, or is it stronger?

Day Five: List five benefits of being present in the moment. Are these benefits that you want in your life, or do you prefer to live without them?

And so that's that for this book. I sincerely hope that you've enjoyed it, but even more importantly, I hope that you've found something in here—even something small and seemingly trivial—to help you on your path to living life fully. After all, It's very often the small things that make the most difference.

If this were a perfect book, it would have more topics so that every possible topic would be covered for every possible person and every possible need. Of course, that's not going to happen, is it? So this book is what it is, and I'm trusting that it's what it needs to be, and please remember that it's supplemented constantly by the website at livinglifefully.com—it's always there for you to visit whenever you might need some encouragement or some uplifting words.

I thank you for your presence, both here reading this book and here on this planet that we're inhabiting for our rather short sojourn as human beings. It's an honor to share the planet with you, and I'm very glad that you're here with us—you do make a difference in your own ways, and the world would be less without you. You contribute to the common good and the positive energy of the world, and that's much appreciated!

(By the way, I was going to add a list of many of the books that I've been studying over the past several decades, but then I decided that was redundant. You can find all of those books on the website, so there's no need to list them here, too.)

Please take good care of yourself, and share all the good in you with others—if you help them to live their lives fully, you most certainly will live that way yourself! Here's to the rest of your life, filled with challenges and blessings, and filled with moments that will make you smile and love life ever, ever more!